Some Cambridge controversies
in the theory of capital

Some Cambridge controversies in the theory of capital

G. C. HARCOURT

Professor of Economics, University of Adelaide,
Sometime Fellow of Trinity Hall, Cambridge

CAMBRIDGE UNIVERSITY PRESS

Published by the Syndics of the Cambridge University Press
Bentley House, 200 Euston Road, London NW1 2DB
American Branch: 32 East 57th Street, New York, N.Y.10022

© Cambridge University Press 1972

Library of Congress Catalogue Card Number: 71–161294

ISBNS:
0 521 08294 3 hard covers
0 521 09672 3 paperback

First published 1972
Reprinted 1974

First printed in Great Britain
by C. Tinling & Co. Ltd, London and Prescot
Reprinted in Malta by St Paul's Press Ltd

Contents

Preface

In 1969 I published in the *Journal of Economic Literature* a survey of recent controversies in capital theory under the same title as this book. In writing the survey I was constrained by a word limit (which, nevertheless, I managed *ex post* to persuade the editor to allow me to exceed by a factor of $2\frac{1}{2}$) and so I often asserted rather than argued, leaving the reader to find the evidence for himself in the references that I provided. This clearly is an unsatisfactory procedure (though shortage of space is an excellent ploy with which to keep angry critics at bay); I therefore welcome the chance, which the Syndics of the Cambridge University Press have so kindly offered me, to extend the assertions into what I hope are persuasive or, at least, respectable arguments.

The plan of the book follows very closely the basic outlines of the survey. I have, however, added sections on some additional topics, most notably on the 'dual' to the wage-rate–rate-of-profits trade-off relationship, the maximum consumption per head–growth rate trade-off relationship in chapter 5, and have brought up to date the state of the debate in others. Of course, economics is no more immune from the knowledge explosion than any other modern discipline and anyone who attempts to write as well as to read, and who is as ill-equipped with modern techniques and memory as I am, must inevitably fall behind in the unequal race to be completely up to date. I can only comfort myself, and, I hope, the reader, by pointing out that lasting articles or books in this field shine like good deeds in a naughty world – and are as rare – so that simple expositions of the few gems and of their significance for the general contexts in which they are set, a poet's for poets account, should be of value. To support this contention let me cite as an excellent example that a thorough understanding of Champernowne's 1953–4 comment on Joan Robinson's famous article, 'The Production Function and the Theory of Capital', illuminates, as no other preparation could, the basic points of the subsequent controversies in the double-switching debate (see chapter 4).

The standard of mathematical analysis used in the book is at the level of the course of lectures that I used to give to first-year students in Adelaide and to undergraduates reading for Part I of the Economics Tripos at Cambridge. Pompously announced in the *Reporter* as 'Elementary Mathematics for Economists' they were known universally as Maths for Idiots (with me as Idiot, L.C.D.). I hope that this will not be a deterrent for the bulk of my readers; I know it will be a blessed relief for the few remaining poets in our trade. The book is addressed as much to third and fourth year undergraduates, and to graduate students, as to specialists in the area. I hope that the last group, and also economists who, though not especially interested in the advanced technical areas of this particular part of economic theory, nevertheless retain an interest in the general area as such, will find it worth at least the once-over-lightly treatment.

It is an irony of the book that while it is in the main critical of neo-classical and equilibrium analysis, yet much of the formal part is couched in these terms. This should be taken as reflecting the innate characteristics and vintage of the author rather than his inclinations. I hope that this will be counted a good-humoured book, the principal aim of which is to spread light rather than to generate heat. I should add that in this controversial area of economic theory as much as in the hurly-burly of the anti-war movement, a touch of humour should be taken as a sign of the need to maintain one's sanity rather than as a lack of seriousness of purpose. Finally, I have commented only marginally on C. E. Ferguson's *The Neoclassical Theory of Production and Distribution*, partly because it is obvious that we are 180° apart and partly because I have had my say in my review in the *Journal of Economic Literature*.

It remains for me to express gratitude and acknowledgements to a number of people and places, which I do most gladly. I shall not list again those friends who are thanked and absolved in the acknowledgement section of my survey article, but I know they will understand that their continued support and encouragement is more valued and appreciated than ever. To that list I should like to add Tom Asimakopulos, Krishna Bharadwaj, Paul Davidson, Christopher Dougherty, Walter Eltis, Basil Moore, David Newbery, Bill Nordhaus, Nobuo Okishio, Ajit Singh, Peter Wagstaff, Adrian Wood and my friends and charming and gracious hosts of Keio University, Masao Fukuoka, Denzo Kamiya, Tatsuro Ichiishi, and Tamotsu Matsuura and the members of the graduate seminar in Economics at Keio who allowed me to try out my ideas on them, pick their brains and display my woeful mathematical ignorance. I am greatly indebted to the University of Adelaide for giving me leave, to the Leverhulme Trust Fund for financing my stay in Japan, where the first draft of this book was written, and to Keio University and its Economics Faculty for allowing me the use of their wonderful library facilities and of room 738 (which has the delightful outlook of Tokyo Tower and the gardens of the Italian Embassy). I especially thank Professor Eiichi Kiyooka and his staff of the International Centre of Keio University for their kindness and help to my family and myself. I am greatly indebted to the three advisers of the Cambridge University Press – John Eatwell, Mario Nuti and Ian Steedman – who read the first draft of the manuscript. Their detailed comments allowed me to remove many slips and misunderstandings. (I, of course, accept responsibility for all errors and confusions that remain.) While reading the contents of the Eatwell file will ever be a traumatic experience, I appreciate – and reciprocate – the spirit of friendship and comradeship with which his trenchant criticisms were offered. Mario Nuti's comments serve as a morale booster in time of trouble and Ian Steedman's firmly keep feet on the ground. I am especially indebted to Neil Laing whose friendly – but sternly critical neoclassical – eyes read the entire manuscript. I have benefited greatly from his comments even when I have not always heeded them.

I thank again the University of Adelaide for generously financing a visit to Cambridge, England, in January and February 1971. This allowed me to read some papers that otherwise would not have reached me in time, to discuss a number of puzzles with many of the economists most directly concerned with the issues here discussed, and to have the third draft of the manuscript read and discussed by a much wider range of opinion than otherwise would have been possible. I appreciate greatly the kindness of members of the Faculty who, busy teachers all in the throes of Full Term, cheerfully answered my obsessive queries on particular points of capital-theoretic interest. I also thank those others who allowed me to bite more than marginally into the time allotted for their sabbaticals. The visit allowed me to renew old friendships, to enjoy the hospitality of the Sidgwick Avenue coffee room and of my old college, Trinity Hall, where the Master and Fellows, as well as providing a guest room for my visit, also most thoughtfully gave me the venerable status of Fellow Emeritus.

I should like to thank my friends and colleagues at Adelaide for letting me off for three months plus in the long vacation of 1969–70 and for seven weeks in that of 1970–1 so that I could write the book, tidying up my unfinished chores in the meantime (with Fred Bloch keeping the running going), and for their interest, generosity and friendship. I also thank my present and past students in the Fourth Year Honours option, 'Capital and Growth', for being the responsive audience on which this book was first tried out. I wish to thank Helen Wickens who not only drew the diagrams and prepared the references but also, good humouredly and without complaint, made the many trips needed to the Barr-Smith Library to obtain heavy volumes which, as an Australian rules footballer, I should have been ashamed to have asked her to carry. And I cannot praise too highly Laura Brock, Maureen Hunt, Christine Leckie, Gill Morgan, Laurica Tuckwell and Joan Wood for sticking womanfully to the task of making sense of a manuscript which, though a great improvement on what I usually produce, was by anyone else's standards, a disgrace. I am sure that none of the six will mind me singling out Laurica Tuckwell and Joan Wood for their efficient general overseeing of the arrangement and distribution of copies of the manuscript at its various stages. My friends on the Executive Committee of the Campaign for Peace in Vietnam were also suitably understanding when I shirked my role there in the interests of scholarship.

I am indebted to Mark Perlman, the editor of the *Journal of Economic Literature*, and to the secretary of the American Economic Association, for allowing me to use material from my survey article in this book, also to Alan Boxer and Dick Downing, the editors of the *Economic Record*, and to my co-author, Vincent Massaro, for permission to re-print, as part of the appendix to chapter 4, our review article of Sraffa's *Production of Commodities by Means of Commodities*.

Finally let me add the usual – but necessary if not sufficient – tribute to one's nearest and dearest: to my wife, Joan, and our four examples of planned, balanced growth – Wendy, Robert, Timothy and Rebecca – I dedicate this book, not least because, as uninvolved visitors in the strange (but most hospitable) environment of Japan, I was able to see more of them despite rather than because of the writing of it.

GCH

February 1971

Introduction

Capital theory is renowned for the controversies with which it is associated. In this book we survey the background to, and the issues of, the latest controversy, the debates between the two Cambridges – Cambridge, England and Cambridge, Mass. We designate the two sets of protagonists, for convenience but rather loosely, as the neo-neoclassicals and the neo-Keynesians. Geographically the borderlines get crossed; amongst the most prominent neo-neoclassicals are not only Samuelson and Solow of M.I.T. but also Meade of Cambridge, England. The most prominent neo-Keynesians include Joan Robinson, Kaldor and Pasinetti, all of Cambridge, England. The writings of another economist of Cambridge, England, Piero Sraffa, are also quite vital to the debates and issues though, in a sense, he has stood aloof from the recent exchanges.

The background to the 'Cambridge controversies in the theory of capital' is the renewed interest in the past quarter century in the causes and consequences of economic growth. Allied with this interest has been the examination of changes in the distribution of the growing social product between both the 'factors of production' and the different socioeconomic classes. This has involved analyses of expected and actual changes in distributive prices and shares. Capital theory is relevant at a number of points, for example, the course of capital accumulation over time, both in the absence and the presence of technical change; the attempts that have been made to estimate the relative contributions of technical progress and capital accumulation to the overall growth of productivity; and the choice which must be made amongst various alternative techniques when investment decisions are taken.

Lying behind the technical analysis, however, is a clash of views on the correctness and relevance of the marginal theory of value and distribution for these issues. There is a fundamental cleavage between the two groups, especially on whether distribution theory may be regarded as just an aspect of the marginal theory of value – the neoclassical[1] and neo-neoclassical view. By contrast, the neo-Keynesians consider that the elements of the theory of distribution do not necessarily coincide with those that are relevant to the theory of value. They are especially critical of the neoclassical links between equilibrium factor prices and the marginal products of 'factors'. In classical fashion, that is, in the tradition especially of Ricardo and Marx, they argue that the theory of distribution should be analysed in different terms from that of the neoclassical theory of value, with the theory of distribution preceding in context and priority, though not in time, the theory of value. As we shall see, once either the wage rate or the rate of profits is known, so, too, are prices in the neo-Keynesian schema.

Linked to this clash of views are ideological and political differences concerning the functioning of the capitalist system. One group, the neo-Keynesians, see capitalist institutions – private property, an entrepreneurial class, a wage-earning class – as giving rise to conflicts between the classes. It is argued that the distribution between the classes of the net product (which is itself viewed as the surplus of commodities over those used up in its production) cannot be understood independently of the institutional nature of capitalism.

The neo-neoclassicals, by contrast, regard the marginal principle as of overwhelming importance for the theory of value and distribution. They thus emphasize the role of the possibilities of technical substitution, both of 'factors' and of commodities, one for another. The principle of scarcity and the relevance of relative 'factor' supplies for 'factor' prices and 'factor' shares are the natural corollaries of their approach, as is the neglect of the institutional and sociological characteristics of societies. The quote from Samuelson [1966b], pp. 444–5, on the fly leaf of Ferguson's book, Ferguson [1969], illustrates well the present state of play.

Until the laws of thermodynamics are repealed, I shall continue to relate outputs to inputs – i.e. to believe in production functions. Until factors cease to have their rewards determined by bidding in quasi-competitive markets, I shall adhere to (generalized) neoclassical approximations in which relative factor supplies are important in explaining their market remunerations . . . a many-sectored neoclassical model with heterogeneous capital goods and

---

[1] By 'neoclassical' we mean the body of doctrine that derives from the writings of the first and second generations of marginalists, whose writings are critically reviewed in Stigler's *Production and Distribution Theories*, Stigler [1941]. The neoclassicals whose work is most relevant in the context of the issues discussed in this book are Marshall, Walras, Wicksell, J. B. Clark and Wicksteed.

somewhat limited factor substitutions can fail to have some of the simple properties of the idealized J. B. Clark neoclassical models. Recognizing these complications does not justify nihilism or refuge in theories that neglect short-term microeconomic pricing.

The footnote that Samuelson appended to this passage is not without significance also. Thus (pp. 444–5):

In my model below, although marginal productivity relations are not explicitly mentioned and although Chamberlinian imperfections are not ruled out, I do confine myself to well-behaved properties in which the capital–output ratio rises with increases in the ratio of capital to labour and in which the relative share of factors does depend on relative factor supplies.

Despite many explicit denials to the contrary by its proponents, the neoclassical approach both tends to highlight technical factors and to suggest harmony, if not justice, amongst the various groups in capitalist society. Joan Robinson, in particular, objects to this, albeit unintentional, support for the *status quo*. Indeed, she has called the approach, 'pre-Keynesian economics after Keynes', so emphasizing the use in much of the current debate of supply-determined models in which saving determines (*is*) investment, full employment is assumed, risk and uncertainty are absent, and money, by and large, is ignored.

The latest debate originated with Joan Robinson's 1953–4 article on the unit in which 'capital' is measured in the aggregate production function. We discuss her article and related comments in chapter 1. The construct of an aggregate production function is used in one version of the traditional neoclassical explanation of distributive shares and prices partly in terms of the technical conditions of production. It is indeed by far the most common version, if not intellectually the most serious or rigorous. (The latest and most full and explicit statement of it is by Ferguson [1969].)

Joan Robinson's article thus links the modern discussion on to an old puzzle: is there a unit in which aggregate or social capital may be measured, a unit which is itself independent of distribution and prices? The question reflects the historical development of marginal productivity theory whereby, in a perfectly competitive economy and in long-run equilibrium, the Ricardian and Malthusian theory of rent was extended to 'factors of production' other than land. The search for a unit in which to measure capital arose from the argument that both (homogeneous) labour and land could be measured in terms of their own technical units so that *their* marginal products could be defined independently of the equilibrium factor prices. This allowed their marginal products to be used in the explanation of their prices. Aggregate capital, though, could not be similarly defined in terms of its own technical unit. It could only be defined in value terms both because the rate of profits[1] or interest, a pure number, had to have a *value* to bite on in order to define the value of profits and because capital goods were specific, heterogeneous and *someone's private property*. (If capital goods were *not* someone's private property they would not need to be valued.) Was the extension of the theory of rent to 'capital' then 'arguing in a circle'?

Joan Robinson provided a measure of capital in terms of labour time which attempted to make sense of capital goods viewed as aids to production. It was *not*, however, and this was intended, independent of distribution and prices. Moreover, the use of 'real capital', as she called it, did not lead to traditional neoclassical answers whereby equilibrium factor prices and marginal products are either equated, or at least related in a relatively simple way. It *did* allow comparisons of the magnitudes of key variables – capital–output, capital–labour ratios – in different equilibrium situations to be made. The comparisons arose as either the wage rate or the rate of profits were assigned arbitrary values and the equilibrium values corresponding to them were calculated.

In constructing Joan Robinson's version of the production function, we introduce and define the major tool of these and the subsequent analyses, namely, the wage-rate–rate-of-profits trade-off relationship or factor-price frontier. It should be noted, though, that as the neo-Keynesian critics of the neo-neoclassicals do not regard 'capital' as a 'factor of production' on the same footing as labour (and land) they intentionally use the terms, 'wage-rate–rate-of-profits trade-off' or 'wage–interest frontier' rather than factor-price frontier. The neo-neoclassicals no doubt use the latter term because it expresses their belief that the wage rate and the rate of profits *are* factor prices on an equal footing. This relationship shows the *maximum* rate of profits which, under competitive conditions and given the value of the real-wage rate, a given technique allows to be paid. (Alternatively, from an analytical point of view, it shows the maximum real-wage rate which, given the same competitive conditions and the value of the rate of profits, a given technique

---

[1] Throughout this book we follow Sraffa [1960] in using the term, 'rate of profits', instead of the more usual 'rate of profit', in order to emphasize that we are interested principally in the macroeconomic concept of the overall ratio of total profits to total social capital. This magnitude is the yardstick to which, under competitive conditions, the individual activities of the economy must eventually conform.

allows to be paid.) Joan Robinson also discusses in her [1953–4] article the nature of the neoclassical concept of equilibrium and the limitations of the neoclassical approach for an analysis of accumulation over time.

Champernowne [1953–4] accepted the logic of Joan Robinson's measure of capital. However, he objected to some of its implications for the analysis of distribution and accumulation. He therefore provided, within the same analytical context, a chain index measure of capital. Under certain conditions his measure, when used in the production function, gave neoclassical results in the sense of equalities of equilibrium factor prices with suitably defined marginal products. Nevertheless, as we shall see in chapter 1, the chain index measure is not independent of distribution and prices; indeed, it may not be constructed unless either the wage rate or the rate of profits is known.

In 1956 Swan published one of the first of a spate of neoclassical models of economic growth in which the equality of factor rewards with marginal products plays a crucial role. In the appendix to his article he provided a rationale for his procedure. It contained two strands. The first was the device of using a primary unit, namely, a one all-purpose commodity – his famous meccano sets model – so that capital may be measured in terms of its own unit, i.e. itself. The commodity is, moreover, malleable so that both specificity and heterogeneity – two essential characteristics of capital goods – may be abstracted from, and the implications of disappointed expectations in the sense of actual quasirents differing from expected ones may be avoided. In effect it is 'as if' perfect foresight always prevailed. 'Capital' as an aid to production and as privately owned property, whether held or invested by its owners, become indistinguishable. A theory of production and of distribution may thus be invoked simultaneously. That is to say, the level of output and its distribution between labour and 'capital' are explained simultaneously by the same set of factors.

The second defence was to examine the neoclassical procedure of considering notional changes at equilibrium points in a stationary state. Swan argues that the Champernowne chain index measure of capital is peculiarly suited to cope with this procedure in the analysis of a process of accumulation over time. This viewpoint was – and is – vigorously disputed by Joan Robinson, who argues that comparisons of equilibrium positions one with another are *not* the appropriate tools for the analysis of out-of-equilibrium processes or changes, and that the neoclassical procedure is singularly ill-equipped to cope with the problem of 'time'.

One aspect of the puzzle that Joan Robinson raised concerns the revaluations of capital that are associated with the comparisons of situations characterized by one set of equilibrium prices with those characterized by another set. This aspect is discussed under the heading of *price* and *real* Wicksell effects. The revaluations occur under two sets of circumstances. The first is when we consider different values of the rate of profits and wage rate within the context of a *given* technique. The second relates to changes in the values of the rate of profits and the wage rate with which are associated changes in techniques as well. We close chapter 1 with Solow's first contribution to the debate, Solow [1956a], in which he sets out the very stringent conditions that allow heterogeneous capital goods rigorously to be aggregated into a single number. Solow's paper was intended, however, to bear more on econometric specification than on the pure theory of capital itself.

Aggregate production functions which invoke the concept of aggregate capital have been used not only in the pure theory of value, distribution and growth, but also in the early post-war econometric studies of productivity growth over time, and of the possibilities of capital–labour substitution in economies and individual industries. Two of the most influential of these studies are Solow [1957] and Arrow, Chenery, Minhas and Solow (ACMS) [1961]. We start chapter 2 with an exposition of them both. They represent two different ways of using the concept of disembodied technical change to make empirical estimates of changes in productivity over time, or comparisons between industries and economies of differences in the rate of growth of productivity. The concept of disembodied technical progress abstracts from the heterogeneity and specificity of capital goods and the related difficulty that capital is *either* funds waiting to be invested *or* specific capital goods (the results of past investments) but it is never *both* at one and the same time.

The response to these difficulties has been the emergence of *vintage* models. They have at least two applications; the first is in the pure theory of growth and the second is in empirical work on the explanation of productivity change over time. Common to both applications is the incorporation of the idea that while capital–labour substitution possibilities are *ex ante* possibilities *before* investment decisions are made, they are, to a very considerable extent, closed, no longer possible in the *ex post* situation where production and pricing decisions are made, in the context of a given existing capital stock. The pioneering works of Salter [1960] and Johansen [1959, 1961] are discussed as the natural representatives of this point of view.

The remainder of chapter 2 is concerned with refinements and criticisms that have been made of these approaches, both in theoretical models and in econometric specification, together with a digression in which some of the concepts developed beforehand are used to analyse the choice of techniques *at a micro level*. The refinements include the discussion in recent years (principally by Jorgenson and Griliches [1966, 1967]) of the concept of 'total factor productivity'. This involves an hypothesis which is an attempt to remove 'technical progress' as such from the explanation of productivity growth, so enabling an explanation entirely in terms of traditional neoclassical 'factors of production', now more 'suitably' and 'correctly' measured.

Concurrent with these developments has been the up-dating of Irving Fisher's work on the rate of return on investment, in particular by Solow [1963a, 1966, 1967, 1970]. Solow's purpose was, in part, to get away from the obstacles of the measurement of capital and its related problems by developing instead the concept of the rate of return on investment. His own contributions were to graft technical progress on to Fisher's analysis and to apply the resulting concepts empirically, in order to obtain estimates of the orders of magnitude of the rates of return on investment in post-war U.S.A. and West Germany. In chapter 3 we discuss his contributions and Joan Robinson's criticisms of them. Her criticisms highlight, in a simple manner, some of the major differences between the two groups. It is argued that neither in theory nor in empirical work has Solow been able completely to escape from the need to define and measure aggregate capital and to work within the confines of a one-commodity model. Consequently, the criticisms that were levelled against the work of earlier neoclassicals who invoked the concept of malleable capital may fairly be levelled against his analysis as well.

The final and possibly most damaging criticisms of marginal analysis discussed in the book are those associated with the 'double-switching' and 'capital-reversing' debates. These debates, which reached their climax in the 1966 symposium in the *Quarterly Journal of Economics*, had their origins in earlier work by Sraffa [1926, 1951, 1960], and by Champernowne [1953–4] and Joan Robinson [1953–4, 1956]. Sraffa's book, *Production of Commodities by Means of Commodities*, was published in 1960. However, the author tells us that the main propositions of the book date from the 1920s. It is subtitled *Prelude to a Critique of Economic Theory*; the economic theory that is to be appraised is the neoclassical marginal theory of value and distribution. The propositions in the book were 'designed to serve as a basis for a critique of that theòry' and if the foundation held the critique was to be attempted later, not necessarily by Sraffa himself, see Sraffa [1960], p. vi. The recent contributions by the neo-Keynesian writers may, perhaps, best be seen as the actual critique that is being built on the foundation so laid.[1] They are discussed in chapter 4 and a review of the major propositions of Sraffa's book and of some related topics is given in the appendix to chapter 4.

'Double-switching' is the possibility that the same technique may be the most profitable of all possible techniques at two or more *separated* values of the rate of profits even though other techniques have been the most profitable at rates of profits in between. 'Capital-reversing' is the possibility of a positive relationship between the value of capital and the rate of profits. It is argued in chapter 4 that capital-reversing as much as double-switching itself strikes at the foundations of *all* versions of the neoclassical theory of distribution, whether they be in an aggregate production form or in terms of a supply and demand approach at either a macro- or a micro-level.

In chapter 4, we define double-switching and capital-reversing and give some simple examples of them both. We then review Samuelson's 1962 paper on the surrogate production function, the object of which was to provide *some* theoretical justification for the use, under certain conditions, of a one all-purpose commodity model both in pure theory and econometric work. We also discuss the papers in the 1966 symposium in the *Quarterly Journal of Economics*, and their important successors, especially those of Joan Robinson and Naqvi [1967], Bhaduri [1969], Garegnani [1970a, 1970b] and Pasinetti [1969, 1970].

Bhaduri's paper spells out a Marxist interpretation of the controversies. In particular he shows that the assumption in Samuelson's 1962 paper is akin to that of Marx in volumes I and II of *Das Kapital*, namely, a uniform organic composition of capital for the processes (or activities) of each technique. Garegnani and Pasinetti examine the logical foundations of the neoclassical theories in terms of modern analytical methods that involve the use of model economies in which, typically, commodities are produced by themselves, other commodities and labour. Garegnani's articles are especially concerned with critiques of Samuelson's 1962 paper, and of the demand and supply theories that

---

[1] Thus Dobb· [1970], p. 347, writes: 'It may be remembered that the sub-title of Sraffa's book is "Prelude to a Critique of Economic Theory". It is to such a critique that this work has so largely contributed (if not originating it) over the last decade.'

derive from Wicksell, Marshall, and Hicks [1932]. He shows that Samuelson's assumptions amount to confining the analysis to a world in which there is a pseudo-neoclassical production function, that is to say, a set of comparisons of stationary states which allow us to spell out associations and relationships which are *seemingly* akin to the processes that would occur in an all-purpose, malleable one-commodity world.

Pasinetti concentrates on Irving Fisher's contributions to the theory of the rate of interest, but the discussion is suitably translated into aggregate terms and modern dress. Pasinetti argues that the major neoclassical results depend upon the introduction into the analysis of 'an unobtrusive postulate' which excludes capital-reversing. We close chapter 4 with discussions of the reactions of the neo-neoclassicals to these arguments and of their counter arguments.

Dissatisfaction with or outright rejection of the marginal productivity theory of distribution has been associated with a plea for a return to classical modes of analysis in which, if you like, pricing is an aspect of distribution rather than, as in neoclassical thought, distribution being but an aspect of pricing. One response to the plea has been the development of macro-theories of distribution, especially of the share and of the rate of profits. These theories derive from the pioneering works of von Neumann [1945–6] and Kalecki [1939]. In the modern literature, they are especially associated with the writings of Kaldor [1955–6, 1957, 1959a, 1959b], Pasinetti [1962, 1964, 1965, 1966b, 1966c] and Joan Robinson [1956, 1965a, 1966a, 1970a, 1971].

It is now argued that the share of profits in the national income is the outcome of the Keynesian saving–investment relationship and the differing values of the saving propensities of wage-earners and profit-receivers. The equilibrium rate of profits (r) in a capitalist economy is associated with the underlying rate of growth of the economy (g) (which may be either demand- or supply-determined, potential or actual, depending upon which author's work is consulted) and the saving propensity of the capitalist class (s_c). In its simplest and most general form, $r = g/s_c$, Pasinetti's result.

In chapter 5 we review the contributions of Kaldor and Joan Robinson concerning the share and the rate of profits, and Pasinetti's result, together with the criticisms of it by Meade, and Samuelson and Modigliani. The last three writers provide a 'dual' to Pasinetti's result whereby the output–capital ratio is given by $Y/K = g/s_w$, where s_w is the saving propensity of the wage-earning class. It is argued that the 'dual' is not relevant to an explanation of the rate of profits in *capitalist* society.

The chapter – and the book – close with discussions of, first, the Golden Rule of Accumulation or neo-neoclassical theorem and, secondly, of another 'dual' – that between the wage-rate–rate-of-profits trade-off relationship and the relationship between maximum consumption per head and the rate of growth. We derive the Golden Rule both for a neoclassical model and for a heterogeneous capital-goods one in which there are no direct substitution possibilities. We show that the wage-rate–rate-of-profits trade-off relationships of both models are identical with the relationships between the rate of growth and maximum consumption per head that may be derived from the two models. Nuti [1970b] analyses the application of this 'dual' in a competitive capitalist economy and in two types of socialist economies, one decentralized, the other centralized. We discuss Nuti's paper and his conclusion that the concept of aggregate capital is the fifth wheel of a coach in a socialist economy.

1 Search for a will-o'-the-wisp: capital as a unit independent of distribution and prices

Square one

To begin at the beginning. In 1953 Joan Robinson wrote 'The Production Function and the Theory of Capital' (Robinson [1953-4]) in which she made a number of specific complaints about the state of economic theory and the state of some economic theorists, who soon were to become identified as the latter-day neoclassicals whose H.Q. is now Cambridge, Mass. Her complaints related to the ambiguity concerning the unit in which capital was measured in the neoclassical aggregate production function, the concentration on factor proportions and the neglect of factor supplies and technical progress in the explanation of distributive prices and shares, and what she saw as the deficiencies of the neoclassical definition of equilibrium. In her article, though, Joan Robinson did not specifically name the economists that she had in mind and some of those who subsequently stood up to be counted, including Samuelson and Solow, had not yet published papers on these particular topics. Stigler had, though (see Stigler [1941], especially chapter XII), and the implicit standard against which he measures the performances of the great neoclassical economists whom he discusses is a case-book example of the neoclassical economist of Joan Robinson's article.

The response to her article was many articles (some sympathetic, some critical), a number of books, including four of her own, Robinson [1956, 1960, 1962a, 1971], and several new strands of economic analysis and econometric investigation. The controversies still rage and judging from one of the more recent exchanges, that between Pasinetti, Kaldor and Joan Robinson in one corner, and Samuelson and Modigliani in the other (see Pasinetti [1962], Meade [1963], Pasinetti [1964], Meade and Hahn [1965], Meade [1966], Pasinetti [1966b], Samuelson and Modigliani [1966a], Pasinetti [1966c], Kaldor [1966], Robinson [1966], Samuelson and Modigliani [1966b]), the contestants are as cross as ever with one another. They are, moreover, still far away from agreement, even to the extent that one side (interchangeably) can argue that the other docs not know what is being discussed – and this, not for the first time. Thus, Solow [1962a], in a rare display of bad temper, opened his 1962 paper with: 'I have long since abandoned the illusion that participants in this debate actually communicate with one another, so I omit the standard polemical introduction and get down to business at once.' (p. 207.)

Consider also the rather pained response of Samuelson and Modigliani [1966b] to Pasinetti's comment [1966c], that their paper, Samuelson and Modigliani [1966a], which was 'excellent in many respects', has '... one unfortunate drawback; it has been written with the aim of defending a specific theory [the neoclassical theory of marginal productivity]'. 'We must begin,' starts their rejoinder, 'by recording our dismay that our long paper should end up appearing to Dr. Pasinetti as primarily apologetics for a specific theory ... we trust other readers will conclude otherwise.' And readers as opposed to participants are appealed to again when they add [1966b], p. 321: 'Readers who have followed these discussions – read the 1962 Pasinetti article, the 1963 Meade paper and the 1964 Pasinetti reply, the 1965 Meade-Hahn paper and the resulting 1966 interchange between Meade and Pasinetti, and our present paper – will, we think, sense which way the wind is blowing.' Solow and Pasinetti are at it again in the June 1970 *Economic Journal*: see Solow [1970], Pasinetti [1970] and chapter 4, pp. 157–8 and pp. 172–3 below.

Part of the trouble is that many of the participants started their working lives on this side of the recent revolution in analytical techniques that has occurred in the teaching and writing of economics, especially in the United States of America, so that the possibility of communicating to practitioners outside the charmed circle of those whose staple diet is the *Review of Economic Studies*, the *International Economic Review*, or those purple mimeographs that wing their way ceaselessly around the leading universities of the States and occasionally reach the more primitive outposts of the trade, is steadily diminishing. The extent of this communication gap may perhaps be gauged by the reader if he compares the number of articles that he feels he can understand in the 1953–4 issue of 'The Green Horror' (the issue that contains Joan Robinson's paper) with the number of which he can say the same in a representative sample of the latest vintage. The reader who claims a ratio other than one approaching infinity (or zero) is an intuitive genius, a liar or a graduate of M.I.T.

One must add that there are ideological reasons as well. These are harder to document, indeed, by their very nature, can only reflect impressions obtained from reading the literature and talking to the participants in the present debate. Nor do I mean that ideologies necessarily affect either logic or theorems. Rather they affect the topics discussed, the manner of discussion, the assumptions chosen, the factors included or left out or inadequately stressed in arguments, comments and models, and the attitudes shown, sympathetic or hostile, to past and contemporary economists' works and views. It is my strong impression that if one were to be told whether an economist was fundamentally sympathetic or hostile to basic capitalist institutions, especially private property and the related rights to income streams, or whether he were a hawk or a dove in his views on the Vietnam War, one could predict with a considerable degree of accuracy both his general approach in economic theory and which side he would be on in the present controversies. And vice versa: a knowledge of the latter predicts excellently the former, or at least it did in those years in which an American victory in Vietnam was still thought to be on. (That is to say, over time the relationship has changed from a linear one, with two or three notable extreme points way off the regression line, to a curved one, as the 'middles' changed their position in one dimension while holding fast in the other.)

No doubt this would be denied by many, vehemently by some. Sceptics may like to read the views of the late-sixties' angry young men on the role of ideology in bourgeois social science. (They are set out in Cockburn and Blackburn [1969], especially, and most challengingly and forcefully, in the two long essays by Blackburn and Anderson.) They might also like to ponder the following quotes from E. H. Carr [1961] concerning historians which, with suitable amendments, seem to me admirably applicable to economists:

> Progress in history is achieved through the interdependence and interaction of facts and values. The objective historian is the historian who penetrates most deeply into this reciprocal process. (p. 131.)

[For 'history' read 'economics'; for 'historian' read 'economist'; beside 'facts' insert 'theories'.]

> Somewhere between these two poles – the north pole of valueless facts and the south pole of value judgements still struggling to transform themselves into facts – lies the realm of historical truth. (p. 132.)

[Again insert 'theories' after 'facts'; for 'historical' read 'economic'.]

And, most of all, his comments on Freud and historians, though many economists still seem to need to be persuaded of the soundness of Freud's advice!

Freud, reinforcing the work of Marx, has encouraged the historian to examine himself and his own position in history, the motives – perhaps hidden motives –which have guided his choice of theme or period and his selection and interpretation of the facts, the national and social background which has determined his angle of vision, the conception of the future which shapes his conception of the past. Since Marx and Freud wrote, the historian has no excuse to think of himself as a detached individual standing outside society and outside history. This is the age of self-consciousness: the historian can and should know what he is doing. (p. 139.)

[For 'historian' definitely read 'economist'.]

Yet, as I said in my 1969 survey article, there is a real need for a poet's-eye-view of what is going on because important issues – growth, distribution, accumulation, in fact, all the classical, if not classic, puzzles of our trade – are being discussed. The aim of the book, as of the survey, is, therefore, to review the puzzles that were thrown up by Joan Robinson's article and related work, especially that by Sraffa in his introduction to the Ricardo volumes (Sraffa with Dobb [1951–5]) and his *Production of Commodities by Means of Commodities* (Sraffa [1960]).

Sraffa's book had an incredibly long gestation period (in the preface we read of the author showing 'a draft of the opening propositions' to Keynes in 1928 and that 'the central propositions had taken shape in the late 1920s') and Joan Robinson in particular acknowledges her indebtedness, for the development of her own analysis and views, to the hints of what was to come contained in Sraffa's introduction to the Ricardo volumes. The magnitude of the impact which Sraffa's analysis, as spelt out in Sraffa [1960], subsequently was to make on her views may be found by reading her warmly written and perceptive review article, Robinson [1961b], also Robinson [1965b], pp. 7–14, of Sraffa's book (see also, Robinson [1970a], pp. 309–10).

The following is another by-product of the book's long gestation period. In the preface of *The Economics of Imperfect Competition* [1933] Joan Robinson tells us that the analysis of the book grew out of the 'pregnant suggestion' contained in Sraffa's well-known 1926 article, 'The Laws of Returns under Competitive Conditions' (Sraffa [1926]), whereby monopoly once let out of 'its uncomfortable pen in . . . the middle of the book' swallowed up the rest 'without the smallest effort' (Robinson [1933], p. 4). Subsequently she repudiated the method of analysis in Robinson [1933], see the new preface to the recent reprint, Robinson [1969a], viewing it as wrong-headed and on the wrong track.

The irony of this development may the more fully be perceived when the Italian version of Sraffa [1925] is compared with the English [1926].[1] The passages on monopoly, which gave rise to the 'imperfect competition' saga, evidently were added to placate an English audience accustomed to pragmatic judgements about the real world. The article itself can now with hindsight be seen as the start of a logical trail which leads through the Ricardo introduction to reach its fullest expression in the 1960 book, expressing, as it does, a plea for economists to leave marginalist modes of analysis and return to classical ones – a plea to which Joan Robinson and others have responded with enthusiasm and industry: see, for example, Pasinetti [1965], Bhaduri [1969], Nuti [1970b], Garegnani [1970a], Spaventa [1968, 1970].

Joan Robinson's article was written near the start of the post-war revival of interest in the problems of economic growth and the pattern of income distribution over time. This interest was partly a response to the real problems of the post-war era in both developing and developed countries. It was also, in a Blaugian sense (see Blaug [1968]), a response to the stimulus provided by the solution of the employment-creating aspects of investment which was provided in *The General Theory* (Keynes [1936]), and the vistas opened up by Harrod's work on the capacity-creating effects of investment, see Harrod [1939, 1948]. The great bulk of the modern work in the theory of capital is placed in a context of an analysis of advanced industrial societies, usually capitalist but sometimes treated as socialist, M.I.T. rather than real-world brand.

Joan Robinson's complaints

Joan Robinson's first complaint related to the fuzzy nature of the capital variable in the aggregate production function, the concept of which, she argued, was used by the neoclassicals to explain the distribution of income between profit-receivers and wage-earners in capitalist economies, taking as given the stocks of labour and capital and the knowledge of how one may be substituted for the other, so that their

---

[1] An English translation of the Italian version of Sraffa [1925] is being prepared by Mario Nuti and will be published in *Australian Economic Papers*.

respective marginal productivities were known.[1] It is worthwhile quoting in full the well-known opening paragraphs on p. 81 of her article, especially as this work is intended for students (and is written by a professor).

The dominance in neoclassical economic teaching of the concept of a production function, in which the relative prices of the factors of production are exhibited as a function of the ratio in which they are employed in a given state of technical knowledge, has had an enervating effect upon the development of the subject, for by concentrating upon the question of the proportions of factors it has distracted attention from the more difficult but more rewarding questions of the influences governing the supplies of the factors and of the causes and consequences of changes in technical knowledge.

Moreover, the production function has been a powerful instrument of miseducation. The student of economic theory is taught to write $Q = f(L,K)$ where L is a quantity of labour, K a quantity of capital and Q a rate of output of commodities. He is instructed to assume all workers alike, and to measure L in mán-hours of labour; he is told something about the index-number problem involved in choosing a unit of output; and then he is hurried on to the next question, in the hope that he will forget to ask in what units K is measured. Before ever he does ask, he has become a professor, and so sloppy habits of thought are handed on from one generation to the next.

[I have changed the notation of the original article in order to make it consistent with the notation of this book.]

[1] There are passages in Wicksell's *Lectures* [1934] which serve as early, if not typical examples of what Joan Robinson had in mind, see pp. 111–16 and 147–84, especially pp. 150–4 and 172–84. Wicksell was, of course, well aware of the puzzles that Joan Robinson discusses; he tried, though, to get around them, only to give up in despair at the end of his life. For example, in a letter to Marshall (6 Jan. 1905), he wrote: '. . . the theory of capital and interest cannot be regarded as complete yet . . . so long as capital is defined as a *sum of commodities* (or of value) the doctrine of the marginal productivity of capital as determining the rate of interest is never quite true and often not true at all – it is true individually but not in respect of the whole capital of society', quoted in Gårlund [1958], p. 345. The account of Marshall's and Wicksteed's views given by Stigler [1941], chapter xii, together with his own views on the marginal productivity theory of distribution at an *aggregate* as well as at an industry level, provide further evidence for Joan Robinson's complaint. See also J. B. Clark [1891], especially pp. 300–1, 304–7, 312–13, 316–18 and Hicks [1932], chapter 1. Nevertheless it must be said that it was her article itself which brought forth in their most pure form, the sorts of statements to which she objected. Lerner must be exempted from these charges as he independently expressed at the same time many of the criticisms voiced by Joan Robinson (see Lerner [1953]).

Her third paragraph opens with the classic understatement: 'The question is certainly not an easy one to answer.'

The neoclassical way of looking at the problem, Joan Robinson argues, directed interest away from the forces that determine the growth of capital and labour, and how technical advances affect growth, accumulation and income shares. By contrast, her own interest in capital theory was in order to analyse what she regarded as a secondary factor in the list of factors which explain growth and distribution over time, namely, the role of the choice of techniques of production in the investment decision.

Her article appears to have been written as a result of visits to traditional theory in order to search for the orthodox answer to this puzzle. The main propositions of *The Accumulation of Capital*, Robinson [1956], are established in a model in which there is only one technique of production available at any moment of time; see also Worswick [1959], Johnson [1962], Harcourt [1963a]. (As an example of the old adage that there is nothing new under the sun we may note a recent paper, Atkinson and Stiglitz [1969], in which essentially the same view is taken of the nature of innovations at any moment of time.) Removing the cross-section choice of technique from an analysis of investment and accumulation does not preclude her model from bringing out the simple but profound role of the real wage in the growth process. Indeed it allows to be highlighted the vital significance of the real wage for the potential surplus available at any moment of time, the saving aspect whereby consumption is forgone, and the investment aspect whereby the real wage determines the command of a given amount of saving over labour power to be used in the investment-goods sector. The productivity of that labour is, of course, the place where (past) choices of technique are relevant, and past real-wage levels, and expectations formed because of them, bear vitally on this aspect of the processes of production and accumulation.

The emphasis by Joan Robinson on the priority of forces other than the ability to choose from a number of available techniques at any moment of time does not necessarily place her in the group of economists whom Hicks [1960] (in his reflections on the Corfu conference on capital theory) has, loosely and dangerously, labelled 'the accelerationists', but it certainly puts her apart from the aggregate production function boys, who, Hicks argues, armed with M.I.T.-type techniques, are providing a strong backlash for a key role for the rate of interest in an explanation of long-run accumulation and distribution. For convenience, but just as loosely and dangerously, I shall refer to the two groups in what follows as the neo-Keynesians and the neo-neoclassicals. The leaders of each group are so well known that a Who's Who is unnecessary. As Nell [1970] has pointed out, neo-Marxists would in certain respects be as apt a description of the first group as neo-Keynesians, for their roots are as much embedded in the Ricardian–Marxian 'vision' of the capitalist process as in the Keynesian one and many of their theoretical and policy implications would have been more congenial to Marx than to Keynes.

The first puzzle is to find a unit in which capital, social or aggregate value capital, that is, may be measured as a number, i.e. a unit, which is independent of distribution and relative prices, so that it may be inserted in a production function where along with labour, also suitably measured,[1] it may explain the level of aggregate output. Furthermore, in a perfectly competitive economy in which there is perfect foresight (either in fact or for convenience of measurement, see Champernowne [1953–4]) and, as we shall see subsequently, static expectations that are always realized, this unit must be such that the partial derivative of output with respect to 'capital' equals the reward to 'capital' and the corresponding one with respect to labour equals the real (product) wage of labour. The unit would then provide the ingredients of a marginal productivity theory of distribution as well.[2] *If* such a unit can be found, two birds may be killed with the one stone; for we may then analyse a system of production in which capital goods – produced means of production – are an aid to labour, a feature of *any* advanced industrial

---

[1] Several commentators have remarked on the aggregation puzzles and index number problems associated with the existence of different qualities and kinds of *labour* – and *output* – and some have suggested that they in no way differ, *in principle*, from those associated with the measurement of 'capital'. In recent years, really heavy artillery has been brought to bear on the rigorous aspects of the problems of aggregation of labour – and 'capital': see, for example, F. M. Fisher [1965, 1969, 1970], and Whitaker [1966].

[2] In the analysis of this chapter we ignore the distinction between the composition of the real wage as seen by the recipients – the command in real terms (but provided by the *money* wage) over the sorts of goods which make up wage-earners' budgets – and as seen by the businessmen who employ labour and establish cost-minimizing ratios under a regime of perfect competition, i.e. the value of the money wage in terms of *their* product. The Keynesian emphasis on the significance of this vital distinction is stressed by Joan Robinson on pp. 96–8 of Robinson [1953–4], and, more recently, has been given renewed prominence in Leijonhufvud's definitive study of Keynesian economics (or, rather, the economics of Keynes), Leijonhufvud [1968]. See also Joan Robinson's review [1969d] of Leijonhufvud's book, the new preface to her *Introduction to the Theory of Employment* [1969b], and Solow and Stiglitz [1968].

society and, simultaneously, we may analyse distribution in a *capitalist* economy in which the institutions are such that property in *value* capital means that its owners share in the distribution of the national income by receiving profits on their invested capital, *where both the amount of these profits and the rate of profits itself are related to the technical characteristics of the system of production.* Moreover, by making the pricing of the factors of production but one aspect of the general pricing-process of commodities, itself regarded as a reflection of the principles of rational choice under conditions of scarcity and so thought to be independent of sociological and institutional features, both the original neoclassicals and now their successors hoped to escape from uncomfortable questions thrown up by the Ricardian–Marxian scheme, for example, whether relative bargaining strengths or differing market structures could affect the distribution of income, see Dobb [1970].

The discovery of such a unit would also overcome a puzzle which Joan Robinson describes in the following passage, a passage that highlights the institutional and production aspects of capital in a capitalist economy.

> We are accustomed to talk of the rate of profits on capital earned by a business as though profits and capital were both sums of money. Capital when it consists of as yet uninvested finance is a sum of money, and the net receipts of a business are sums of money. But the two never co-exist in time. While the capital is a sum of money, the profits are not yet being earned. When the profits (quasi-rents) are being earned, the capital has ceased to be money and become a plant. All sorts of things may happen which cause the value of the plant to diverge from its original cost. When an event has occurred, say, a fall in prices, which was not foreseen when investment in the plant was made, how do we regard the capital represented by the plant? (Robinson [1953–4], p. 84.)

That capital is meant to be measured in a unit that would serve these two purposes is made explicit, for example, in Champernowne's comment [1953–4] on Robinson [1953–4] (which we discuss below, pp. 29–34) and in the appendix to Swan's 1956 article (which is also discussed below, pp. 34–9). Consider also the following passage from J. B. Clark [1891], pp. 312–13:

> It [the principle of differential gain] ... identifies production with distribution, and shows that what a social class gets is, under natural law, what it contributes to the general output of industry. Com-

pletely stated, the principle of differential gain affords a theory of Economic Statics.

Solow, though, denies this view – for him, capital as a unit only has significance in empirical work, not in rigorous theory. Samuelson [1962], too, puts a similar view in the introduction to his 1962 paper on the surrogate production function, albeit with some reluctance, because, as he says somewhat ruefully, easy papers drive out hard as far as readers are concerned.

Joan Robinson had been concerned to deny that such a unit could be found even in the conditions of a stationary state. She has, as Swan [1956], p. 344, puts it, 'spoilt this game for us by insisting that social capital, considered as a factor of production accumulated by saving, cannot be given *any* operative meaning – not even in the abstract conditions of a stationary state'. That she has been successful in spoiling the game which Swan among many others was playing at the time, there can be little doubt. But to claim that she denied that 'capital' could be given an operative meaning in a stationary state is a bit hard, especially as she proceeds in her article to give it some (limited) meaning, a meaning which does not, however, encompass *both* requirements of the neoclassicals and their Austrian forbears.

The basic reason is that it is impossible to conceive of a quantity of 'capital in general', the *value* of which is independent of the rates of interest (or interchangeably, profits, given the present assumptions) and wages. Yet such independence is necessary if we are to construct an iso-product curve showing the different quantities of 'capital' and labour which produce a given level of national output, or, as is more usual in the theory of economic growth, if we are to construct a unique relationship between national output per man employed and 'capital' per man employed for any level of *total* national output. That is to say, if we are to construct the neoclassical production function, as set out, for example, in Solow's 1957 article on the aggregate production function and in the 1964 Hahn–Matthews survey of growth theory. The slope of this curve plays a key role in the determination of relative factor prices and, therefore, of factor rewards and shares. However, the curve cannot be constructed and its slope measured *unless* the prices which it is intended to determine are known beforehand; moreover, the value of the same physical capital and the slope of the iso-product curve vary with the rates chosen, which makes the construction unacceptable.

Kaldor advanced independently the same arguments for rejecting the concepts of an aggregate production function and an independent unit in which to measure capital, with their accompanying roles in the determination of factor rewards: see, for example, Kaldor [1955–6, 1959a]. Some critics have suggested that this particular set of arguments shows a failure to understand both the nature of the solution to a set of simultaneous equations, such as is, for example, the essential nature of the Walrasian general equilibrium system, and the lack of any necessary link between the variables in which the equilibrium values of key magnitudes are expressed, on the one hand, and causation, or determination, or explanation, or what you will, on the other. See, for example, Swan [1956], p. 348 n14; Samuelson and Modigliani [1966a], pp. 290–1 n1.

This criticism is, however, unfair. Thus, for example, to argue that, in equilibrium, the wage rate equals the marginal product of labour is *not* to argue that one is the cause of the other, or that one determines the other. Moreover, it is abundantly clear from the manner in which Joan Robinson's version of the production function is derived (see below, pp. 23–9), and the constructions which are used, that these are not the points at issue. The neo-Keynesian critics really cannot be sloughed off as neo-Böhm-Bawerkians, spurning, as Stigler [1941], p. 18, puts it, 'mutual determination . . . for the older concept of cause and effect'. An argument that the destruction of the concept of an aggregate production function is *not* the same thing as destroying the marginal productivity theory of distribution is on safer ground (see chapter 4, pp. 155–8 below), but even then the neoclassicals are not yet safe on Jordan's shore (see Garegnani [1970a, 1970b], Pasinetti [1969, 1970], and chapter 4, pp. 158–69 below).

Joan Robinson's response was to measure capital in terms of labour time. Sets of equipment with known productive capacities (when combined with given amounts of labour) were to be valued in terms of the labour time required to produce them, compounded over their gestation periods at various given rates of interest. The same sets of equipment would thus have different values for different rates of profits and different sets would have different values at the same rate of interest. Which set of equipment would actually be in use in *given equilibrium* situations may be found by supposing the wage rate to be given and finding the highest rate of profits and therefore set (or sets) of equipment consistent with this wage rate. Competitive forces will, moreover, ensure that these *are* the equipments chosen and that the associated rate of profits is in fact the one paid.

For several reasons this measure has an intuitive appeal as a measure of capital in its role of productive agent in capitalist society. Thus,

Robinson [1953–4], p. 82: 'when we consider what addition to productive resources a given amount of accumulation makes, we must measure capital in labour units, for the addition to the stock of productive equipment made by adding an increment of capital depends upon how much work is done in [and time is spent on] constructing it, not upon the cost, in terms of final product, of an hour's labour'. (The latter is the 'saving' or 'consumption-forgone' aspect of the decision to accumulate whereby current production is continuously put aside to pay the wages of labour in the investment goods trades: see chapter 5, p. 235 below. In the investment-goods trades themselves, of course, labour is employed now 'in a way which will yield its fruits in the future', Robinson [1953–4], p. 82.) Coupling labour amounts applied indirectly to the production of final output with the rate of interest over gestation periods puts an order of magnitude on the *private* costs to businessmen in a competitive capitalist society of using labour in the investment-goods trades, so neatly reflecting the influence of the basic mechanism in capitalist economies whereby Sammy is made to run. Of course, some such ploy must also be used in socialist economies in order to introduce elements of efficiency and rationality into investment decisions. But the socialist approach is (or, ideally, should be) a conscious plan rather than an unconscious reflection of the basic institutions of society. (Which is preferred is a matter of individual taste – and political conviction.)

Equilibrium is italicized above in order to highlight its importance and also to draw attention to the concept as defined by Joan Robinson, a concept which she contrasts strongly with that of 'the neoclassical economist' whose concept she regards as containing 'a profound methodological error . . . which makes the major part of [the] neoclassical doctrine spurious' (Robinson [1953–4], p. 84). Joan Robinson defines equilibrium as a situation in which expectations are fulfilled so that a given rate of profits has long been ruling and is confidently expected to continue to do so in the future. This definition overcomes the 'puzzles which arise because there is a gap in time between investing money capital and receiving money profits [and] in that gap events may occur which alter [*in an unforeseen way*] the value of money'.

Implicit in the definition are assumptions of perfect foresight and lack of uncertainty, the removal of which, Solow considers, has far more serious consequences for the neoclassical theory of capital than any puzzles associated with measuring 'it' or 'its' marginal product (see Solow [1963a], pp. 12–14). Thus,

To abstract from uncertainty means to postulate that no such [un-foreseen] events occur, so that the *ex ante* expectations which govern the actions of the man of deeds are never out of gear with the *ex post* experience which governs the pronouncements of the man of words [unless he is an accountant],[1] and to say that equili-brium obtains is to say that no such events have occurred for some time, or are thought liable to occur in the future. (Robinson [1953–4], p. 84.)

Equilibrium to the neoclassical economist, though, is a position to-wards which an economy is tending to move as time goes by, possibly a reference to Marshall's description of the nature of equilibrium prices in his analysis of supply and demand but now applied to the motion of the system as a whole. It reflects the attempt by neoclassical economists to handle 'time' within their analytical framework. Joan Robinson says the approach is fundamentally wrong-headed; an economy cannot *get into* a position of equilibrium – either it is in one and has been for a long time, or it is not.[2] If it is in equilibrium, a given item of capital equipment has the same value whether it be valued at its expected future earnings discounted back to the present at the ruling rate of profits, or as work done in order to produce it, cumulated forward to the present at the ruling rate of profits (supposing, for the moment, that equipment is made by labour alone). Moreover, as we have seen, the rate of profits on *capital* has a definite meaning and is equal to the expected rate of profits on investment. With more sophisticated techniques whereby durable capital goods help to make capital goods (and/or circulating ones also help), we have to use a more complicated model in which there are balanced stocks of durable capital goods. Used capital goods are treated as one-year-older goods (*jointly produced* with consumption goods), in order to avoid the puzzle of tracing productive inputs back to the Garden of Eden.

With this background, we now derive Joan Robinson's version of the production function as presented in Robinson [1953–4, 1956], using, in order to illustrate it, a simple arithmetic example of Champernowne's from Champernowne [1953–4]. We shall be doing aggregative analysis and must be thought of as comparing, one with another, different

[1] See Harcourt [1965a] where it is shown that an accountant could be a nuisance even in a Golden Age.

[2] This definition of equilibrium includes the analysis in the theory of economic growth which is associated with the concept of Golden Ages – steady-state, long-run equili-brium growth paths. For a thorough account of this branch of the modern theory of economic growth, see Hahn and Matthews [1964], part 1.

possible stationary states – Solow's isolated islands of stationary equilibrium, each a point on the pseudo-production function, see Solow [1962a, 1963b]. The net products of these islands consist of quantities of an all-purpose consumption good; capital goods are already created and last forever, the rates of profits and real wages have long been ruling and are expected confidently to continue to do so in the future, and one uniform technique (or two equi-profitable ones) rule. We also assume – quite vitally – constant returns to scale in the sense of the possibility of complete divisibility (though often no substitutability) so that labour–equipment ratios may be repeated at *any* scale of operation. Competition rules supreme – and pure.

It follows from our definition of equilibrium that

$$K = wL_g(1+r)^t = \frac{Q-wL_c}{r} \qquad (1.1)$$

where K = capital measured in terms of the consumption commodity
    w = wage rate in terms of the consumption commodity
    r = rate of profits (and interest)
    L_g = input, t periods ago, of labour required to produce a unit of equipment, where t is the gestation period of investment[1]
and Q = output of consumption good when L_c men work with a unit of equipment (which is assumed to last forever)

Capital in terms of labour time (K_L) therefore is

$$K_L = K/w = L_g(1+r)^t \qquad (1.2)$$

Given L_g, K_L is seen to be a simple increasing function of r.

All known techniques – sets of equipment producing final outputs of the consumption good – now may be ordered according to the sizes of their outputs per head of a constant, consumption-good-trade labour force.[2] If each is 'costed up' at various rates of interest and expressed as amounts of K_L per head, we may derive the *real-factor ratio* – the set of equilibrium relationships between output per head, capital in terms of labour time (or *real capital*, as Joan Robinson dubs it) and all conceivable wage rates. Corresponding to each equipment will be the relationship

$$Q = wL_c + rwL_g(1+r)^t \qquad (1.3)$$

---

[1] The simplest possible gestation period and pattern of input of labour to construct equipment has been chosen for illustrative purposes only.
[2] The list is known in the trade as the 'book of blue-prints'.

so that

$$w = \frac{Q}{L_c + rL_g(1+r)^t} \qquad (1.4)$$

(Notice that expression (1.4) is also implied by the two sides of the equality of expression (1.1).) For any given value of $w (\leqslant Q/L_c = w_{max}$, which prevails when $r = 0$ *and is the consumption good output per head of each technique*), we may find the *highest* value of r associated with this value of w and this equipment. This reflects the view that if the equipment were viable at a given wage rate, so that it was in fact in use on the relevant island, the forces of competition would ensure that the rate of profits which exhausted the product would in fact be paid. (Whether the implied distribution of income would be such as to ensure that the product was in fact consumed is a Keynesian effective demand puzzle banished completely from our analysis, but see below, chapter 3, pp. 99–105.)

The costing and valuation process is repeated for all equipments, ws and rs and then the relationship between output per head and real capital is plotted to give Joan Robinson's version of the aggregate production function – her pseudo-production function – which has, as we see below in fig. 1.1, a rather bizarre appearance relative to the smooth curves of the textbooks. Points on it should be regarded as positions of long-period *stationary* equilibrium which may be compared one with another since capital and output are all measured in units which allow corresponding comparisons. However, movements up and along it may *not* be regarded as processes occurring in historical time, the results of *actual* accumulation, rises in wage rates and falls in rates of profits.

It is an absurd, though unfortunately common, error to suppose that substitution between labour and capital is exhibited by a movement from one point to another along a pseudo-production function (see, for example, Solow [1970]). Each point represents a situation in which prices and wages have been expected, over a long past, to be what they are today, so that all investments have been made in the form that promises to yield the maximum net return to the investor. The effect of a change in factor prices cannot be discussed in these terms. Time, so to say, runs at right angles to the page at each point on the curve. To move from one point to another we would have either to rewrite past history or to embark upon a long future. (Robinson [1971], pp. 103–4.)

Moreover, as we shall see, neither the wage rate nor the reward to capital can be obtained by suitable partial differentiation of the factor-ratio relationship.

Table 1.1 contains the engineering data associated with four possible equipments, numbered 1 to 4, and an indefinite number of islands, each of which contains four men, all of whom are the current labour force of the consumption-good trade. It may be seen that the productivity of men working with equipment 1 is lowest – two and a half units of consumption good per head per period – as are the input of labour needed to make it – 20 units – and the length of its gestation period (it is in fact an instant machine). Men working with equipment 4, which requires the greatest input of labour (40.216 units) and has the longest gestation period (four periods), are the most productive (four units of consumption good per head).

Table 1.1   *Engineering data on four equipments with a consumption good trade labour force of four men*

Equipment	L_c	Q	Q/L_c	L_g	t
1	4	10	$2\frac{1}{2}$	20	0
2	4	12	3	22.924	1
3	4	14	$3\frac{1}{2}$	29.840	2
4	4	16	4	40.216	4

SOURCE: Adapted from Champernowne [1953–4], p. 126.

In table 1.2, the values of the rates of profits and real capital (in total and per head) associated with arbitrarily given wage rates in the range of one to four units of consumption good per head per period are shown. (The figures are approximate only, having been obtained from fig. A1 on p. 126 of Champernowne [1953–4].)

Table 1.2   *Wage rate, rate of profits, real capital in total and per head, equipments 1–4*

Equipment:	1			2			3			4		
w	r	K_L	K_L/L_c	r	K_L	K_L/L_c	r	K_L	K_L/L_c	r	K_L	K_L/L_c
1.000	[30]	20	5	27	29.1	7.3	22	44.4	11.1	16	72.8	18.2
1.250	[20]	20	5	[20]	27.5	6.9	17	40.8	10.2	13	65.6	16.4
1.500	12	20	5	[15]	26.4	6.6	13	38.1	9.5	10	58.9	14.7
1.837	7	20	5	[10]	25.2	6.3	[10]	36.1	9.0	8	54.7	13.7
2.000	5	20	5	8	24.8	6.2	[9]	35.5	8.9	7	52.7	13.2
2.481	0+	20	5	4	23.8	6.0	[5]	32.9	8.4	[5]	48.9	12.2
3.000	n.a.	—	—	0	22.9	5.7	2	31.0	7.8	[3]	45.3	11.3
4.000	n.a.	—	—	n.a.	—	—	n.a.	—	—	0	40.2	10.1

NOTE: Square brackets indicate most or equi-most profitable equipments and corresponding values of r at given values of w.
SOURCE: Champernowne [1953–4], p. 126.

It may be seen that at the wage rates of 1.25, 1.837 and 2.481, equipments 1 and 2, 2 and 3, and 3 and 4, respectively, are the equi-most profitable, at rates of profits of 20, 10 and 5 per cent, respectively. In between, only one type of equipment is the most profitable; for example, at a wage rate of 1.5 it is equipment 2 at a rate of profits of 15 per cent. If, therefore, we were to land on an island in which an equi-most-profitable wage rate rules, we could find the four men equipped either with all of one type of equipment, or all of the other, or with any possible combination of the two types in between (because of the assumption of complete divisibility allied with constant returns to scale). Thus when we draw the real factor ratio 'curve' (or pseudo-production function) (see fig. 1.1), we get a continuous relationship between Q/L_c and K_L/L_c – albeit with zig zags at the points where we cross from one island to another – even though the productivities of the men working with the different equipments differ by discrete amounts. (As Solow [1956a], p. 106, quipped, 'Everyone who invents linear programming these days seems charmed by it.') As well as showing, in unbroken lines, the possible positions of long-period stationary equilibrium – what we might hope to discover from an expedition to the islands – we also show, as dotted lines, the relationships between the outputs per head of the various equipments and the values of real capital per head *when r is kept constant* – what Joan Robinson calls productivity curves. We show three, those for rates of profits of 5, 10 and 20 per cent respectively.[1] Along the upward-sloping sections of the pseudo-production function, for example, from 2 to 3 along the relevant segment of the 10 per cent rate of profits productivity curve in fig. 1.1, we gradually move from islands completely equipped with 2 to islands completely equipped with 3, passing on the way those equipped with all possible combinations in between. It is *we* who are moving, though, not the islands. A horizontal movement (again by us), for example, from 2 to 2 along the unbroken line in fig. 1.1, reflects travelling from an island which is completely equipped with 2 at a rate of profits of 20 per cent to one which is completely equipped with 2 at a rate of profits of 10 per cent, passing on the way islands completely equipped with 2 at all possible values of rates of profits in between 10 and 20 per cent (one rate of profits only, of course, on each).

[1] One puzzle that should be pointed out (I am indebted to Masao Fukuoka for doing so to me) is that the maximum rate of profits payable on islands where $w = 0$ is not defined in our present example. The interested reader may examine the diagram in Champernowne [1953-4], p. 126, in which the curves fade out before $w = 0$.

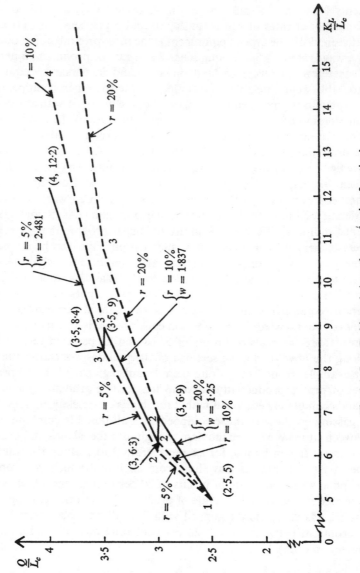

Fig. 1.1. Joan Robinson's 'pseudo-production function'

It has been stressed that an implication of Joan Robinson's definition of equilibrium is that points on the pseudo-production function are equilibrium positions and that comparisons between points are just that, comparisons of one equilibrium position with another. The comparisons are certainly *not* a description of a process – a change – whereby accumulation occurs and new, or, rather, different techniques (technical progress is ruled out by assumption) replace old ones as a result, for example, of changes in relative factor prices. Moreover, a point which has been reiterated again and again in the literature by neo-Keynesians, especially by Joan Robinson, is that the application of results obtained from such equilibrium comparisons to long-period analyses of actual changes can be, at the least, most seriously misleading and, usually, just plain wrong. This fact vitiates many analyses of the past and, to be fair, has been countered in recent years by an enormous growth of models in which out-of-equilibrium processes are explicitly analysed, often (but not exclusively) by neo-neoclassical economists equipped with the appropriate techniques to do so.[1]

The missing link, Champernowne-style

Champernowne [1953–4] accepted the logic of Joan Robinson's approach and measure but objected to the possibility that the same physical capital could have a different value as between two situations 'merely' because it was associated with a different set of equilibrium rates of wages and profits. He felt it offended against the Gertrude Stein dictum (also Solow's) that a spade is a spade is a spade . . .

> It doesn't seem to bother her much that on [her] definition two physically identical outfits of capital equipment can represent different amounts of 'capital'. It wouldn't bother me either except that from the point of view of *production* two identical plants represent two identical plants. (Solow [1956a], p. 101.)

[1] The act of faith which applies equilibrium comparisons to actual changes certainly underlies the multiplier analyses of most textbooks on 'Keynesian Economics' (including *Economic Activity*) and should be recognized as such by all true believers. Recently Leijonhufvud [1968] has argued that this approach is a distortion of what Keynes was attempting to do in *The General Theory*, namely, to analyse out-of-equilibrium processes in the short run, a view the existence of which Joan Robinson as an early Keynesian (without quotes) was well aware. Leijonhufvud argues that Keynes was hampered, formally, by his Marshallian background which could tempt the unwary – but not Keynes – into committing just those sins that are criticized in the text. For a different view of Keynes' objects in *The General Theory*, see Davidson [1968b] and for an attempted compromise for teaching purposes, see Harcourt [1969b].

This objection is valid from the point of view of the theory of production, i.e. the ability to predict the rate of flow of output from a knowledge of factor supplies, but it is neither valid nor relevant for 'capital' viewed as value property, i.e. as reflecting the institutions of capitalist society. There *is* a real difference between the two situations and value capital ought to reflect it. The *economic* significance of a given plant may vary from one economic environment to another.

Nevertheless Champernowne appears to have been searching for a unit which could do both tricks at the same time. Thus he further felt it would be convenient – and more in keeping with the orthodox neoclassical tradition – to have a measure of capital such that the rewards to the factors of production could be obtained by partial differentiation of the relationship between output and capital (so measured), on the one hand, and labour, on the other. Furthermore, despite the strictures on using comparisons to analyse processes, he was keen to analyse the process of accumulation and deepening, tracing the development of capitalism over time, approaching its 'crisis' as real wages rose and rates of profits fell. Even if, in fact, equilibrium were ruptured repeatedly, Champernowne hoped to make the process slow enough to proceed *as if* this had not occurred, to measure capital each step on the way and to provide a means of comparing capital stocks over time as well as between different situations of stationary equilibrium.

Such an all-purpose measure is provided in a chain index whereby the 'normal' concave relationship between output per head of a constant labour force and capital per head would be established, *provided that any one technique, having been the most profitable or equi-so at a given rate or range of interest rates, could never reappear again at another rate or range of rates, and that, of two techniques which are equi-profitable at a given rate of interest, it is the one with the higher output per head and higher value of capital per head that is the more profitable at a lower rate of interest.* (The significance of these provisos will emerge in the discussion of the double-switching and capital-reversing debate in chapter 4 below. Champernowne [1953–4] examined the case where the provisos do not hold in the appendix to his article, see pp. 128–30.)

We return to the islands of stationary equilibrium involving the possible uses of techniques (= equipments) 1 to 4. In fig. 1.2 we plot the various wage-rate–rate-of-profits trade-offs corresponding to each technique (their respective equations (1.4), see p. 25 above.)[1] The *w–r*

---

[1] See chapter 4 below where they are also described as *w–r* relationships and factor-price frontiers. Champernowne [1953–4] and Sraffa [1960], p. 22, must be credited

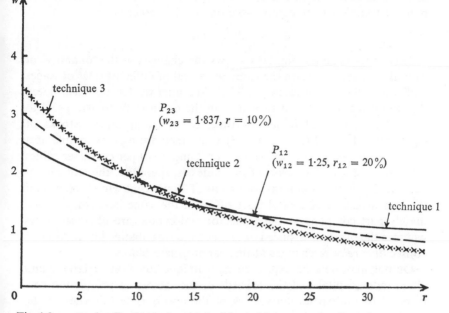

Fig. 1.2. *w–r* trade-offs of techniques 1–3 with resulting *w–r* trade-off envelope

trade-off of technique 1 intersects that of technique 2 at P_{12} and that of technique 2 intersects that of technique 3 at P_{23}. At P_{12}, where techniques 1 and 2 are equi-profitable (at a wage rate, w_{12}, of 1.25 and a rate of profits, r_{12}, of 20 per cent), the ratio of their (total)[2] capital values in terms of *either the consumption commodity or in labour time (it makes no difference)*, as given by their respective equations (1.1) (see p. 24 above), is 20:28. (The ratio obtained from measuring capital in terms of the consumption good is

$$\frac{w_{12}L_{g2}(1+r_{12})^{t_2}}{w_{12}L_{g1}(1+r_{12})^{t_1}} = \frac{L_{g2}(1+r_{12})^{t_2}}{L_{g1}(1+r_{12})^{t_1}}$$

which is the ratio of their real-capital values.) At P_{23} (where $w_{23} = 1.837$, $r_{23} = 10$ per cent), the corresponding ratio for the capital values

---

as the parents of this construction though it was Samuelson who subsequently christened it: see below, chapter 4, pp. 137–8 and appendix to chapter 4. Technique 4 has been omitted in order to simplify the figure. Notice that the curves do not intersect the *r* axis.

[2] Four men on each island have to be equipped with four items of equipment.

of 2 to 3 is 25:36. Then the chain index of capital whereby consecutive pairs of techniques are comparable one with another is

$$20:28:28\tfrac{36}{25}(\approx40):\ldots$$

This series of index numbers shows the changes in the 'quantity' of capital after the effects on the value of capital of different rates of wages and profits have been removed. The discerning reader will have noted that the values of the first two links in the chain in fact correspond to the values, measured in labour time, of the total capital stocks of equipments 1 and 2 (then 2 and 3) when they are equi-profitable at a rate of profits of 20 per cent (then, for 2 and 3, 10 per cent), see tables 1.1 and 1.2 above. The base of our index is, therefore, the real-capital value of equipment 1 at a rate of profits of 20 per cent. However, even if the two measures of capital start off from the same base, they immediately part company as the values of real capital are *absolute* values whereas the others are spliced or chained indexes obtained by linking on consecutive *relative* changes at their appropriate places.

Output may now be expressed as a unique function of labour and chain index capital and the rewards of the factors of production correspond to the partial derivatives of the appropriate branches of the function. (If we are dealing with discrete technologies this is only true of the 'mixed' stationary states in which two sets of equipment are equi-most profitable. In the 'pure' cases, the coefficients of the production function set the upper or lower limits to the factor prices: see Champernowne [1953–4], p. 127.) The partial derivative of output with respect to labour equals the equilibrium wage rate and the partial derivative of output with respect to capital equals the equilibrium rate of profits multiplied by the 'price' of 'capital'. The price itself is a chain index price since the chain index removes, as it were, the 'quantity' of capital from the coefficient of the capital term. In effect Champernowne has removed the 'zigs' – the horizontal stretches – from Joan Robinson's real-factor-ratio curve in fig. 1.1, and changed the slopes of the 'zags' – the upward-sloping stretches – so that they now equal the relevant equilibrium values of the 'price' of 'capital'.

The chain index method is not, however, confined to the case of discrete technologies. Champernowne gives an example containing a *continuous* spectrum of techniques and shows that we may always value consecutive techniques at common rates of profits and real-wage rates, even if each is the *only* technique most profitable at *its* r and w. When he examines accumulation he uses current factor prices for valuation purposes *at any moment of time* and he argues that we may make the errors as small as we like by decreasing the size of the links in the chain. When he compares stationary states, in the continuous case he uses lower rs and higher ws for linking purposes: see Champernowne [1953–4], p. 115. Finally, it should be noted – and noted well – that the chain index method depends upon knowing from elsewhere and already, the rate of profits or wage rate and calculating a price of output which corresponds to the unit cost of producing it. Capital is therefore not measured in a unit which is independent of distribution and prices.

A verbal explanation of the properties of the chain index capital production function is as follows: consider, say, equipments 1 and 2 which we know are equi-most profitable at the rate of profits of r_{12} (= 20 per cent). Equipment 2 allows a higher output per head (3 units) than equipment 1 ($2\frac{1}{2}$ units). Let island A employ quantities 5 of 1 and 7 of 2, measured in terms of the chain index; island B uses $5+1$ (= 6) of 1 and $7 - 1$ (= 6) of 2 (constant returns to scale allow divisibility of this nature). Then the costs at wage rate w_{12} (= 1.25), and rate of profits r_{12} (= 20 per cent), of the total sets of equipment are the *same* on *both* islands, namely, 12 chain index units each, so that the interest bills (or normal profits payments) are the same on both islands also. Therefore the difference between the total product flows of the two islands ($\frac{1}{14}$ units of the consumption good) must equal the difference between their total wage bills ($1.25 \times \frac{2}{35}$ men $= \frac{1}{14}$). Thus the extra product of the island with the greater amount of labour, B in this case,[1] is just sufficient to pay the wages of the extra labour *at the competitive wage rate*. That is to say, the wage of labour (1.25) equals the marginal product of labour ($\Delta Q/\Delta L_c = \frac{1}{14}/\frac{2}{35} = 1.25$), the 'quantity' of capital being held constant. (But see pp. 44–5 below, where it is shown that $\Delta Q/\Delta L_c$ does not correspond to the traditional definition of a marginal product.)

We now show that the partial derivatives of the appropriate branches of the production function, when we consider mixed stationary states, do indeed equal the equilibrium factor prices. Consider the two branches that correspond to the islands with mixed amounts of equipments 1 and 2, and 2 and 3 respectively. Following Champernowne [1953–4], pp. 126–8, they may be written (in total form) as:

1, 2

$$f(L_c, K_{ci}) = 1.25L_c + 0.25K_{ci}$$
$$5L_c \leqslant K_{ci} \leqslant 7L_c$$

[1] The islands we visited before had equal amounts of labour but different capital endowments.

2, 3   (1.5)

$$f\ (L_c,\ K_{ci}) = 1.837L_c + 0.1661K_{ci}$$
$$7L_c \leqslant K_{ci} \leqslant 10.08L_c$$

where K_{ci} = capital, chain index measure, and the inequalities show the ranges of the values of capital within which the expressions apply, e.g. the range 20–28 corresponds to the 1, 2 branch.

The values of the coefficients of the L_c and K_{ci} terms were derived as follows: consider, for example, the 2, 3 branch,

2, 3

$$f\ (L_c,\ K_{ci}) = 1.837L_c + 0.1661K_{ci}$$
$$7L_c \leqslant K_{ci} \leqslant 10.08L_c$$

We know that:

$$12 = a4 + b28$$
$$14 = a4 + b40$$ (1.6)

where a and b are the unknown coefficients and the values of output, labour and capital (chain index measure) corresponding to equipments 2 and 3, and at the rates of wages and profits where the two equipments co-exist (see pp. 30–2 above) have been inserted. Solving expression (1.6) for a and b gives the values of the coefficients of the 2, 3 branch.

Partially differentiating the branches with respect to labour, for example, does indeed give marginal products of labour equal to the appropriate equilibrium wage rates. The values of the coefficients of the capital terms are, of course, affected by the base from which the chain index starts. The interested reader may check for himself that the choice of a base, either one of capital valued in terms of the consumption good or for real does not affect the coefficients of the labour terms. If, however, *real capital* were used in all branches, it would *not* be true in general that the respective capital and labour coefficients equalled the equilibrium factor prices. In fig. 1.3 we show the three branches of the production-function where output per man is measured in terms of the consumption good and capital per man is measured as a chain index.

Swan's way

In Swan's model of economic growth, Swan [1956], capital–labour ratios need to change considerably as accumulation occurs over time, in order that both stable equilibrium capital–output and capital–labour ratios may be re-established following a change in a parameter, for example, the saving ratio. In this manner, considerable processes occur,

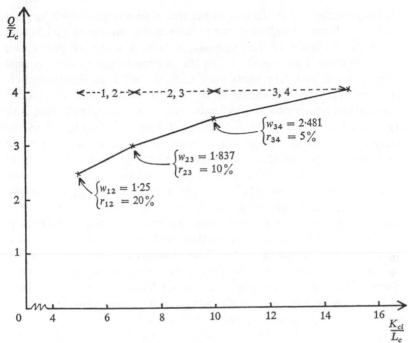

Fig. 1.3. Champernowne's production function

or, rather, are analysed. Moreover, he uses a Cobb–Douglas production function, and assumes that saving determines investment, and that there are constant returns to scale, full employment, static expectations and perfect competition, so that the wage of labour equals its *full-employment* marginal product and the rate of profits on capital equals its marginal product. (Also, of course, the shares of labour and capital in the national product equal the ratios of their respective *full-employment* marginal to average products, which, in turn, equal the respective exponents (also output elasticities) of the production function.)[1]

---

[1] Swan writes

$$Q = L^{\alpha}K^{\beta} \qquad (1.ia)$$

where $\alpha + \beta = 1$, and Q = output, L = labour and K = capital, unit undefined, so

$$Q = L^{1-\beta}K^{\beta} \qquad (1.ib)$$

$$\frac{\partial Q}{\partial K} = \beta L^{1-\beta}K^{\beta-1} \qquad (1.ii)$$

But
so that
$$Q/K = L^{1-\beta}K^{\beta-1}$$

Having carried out in the text of his article an analysis which 'takes a neoclassical form' so enjoying 'the neoclassical as well as the Ricardian vice', Swan spells out in the appendix, in 'a back foremost' procedure, the assumptions that would justify the approach, the scarecrow that would keep off both 'the index number birds and Joan Robinson herself'. His first line of defence is to suppose that capital consists of meccano sets which can be costlessly and timelessly transformed into any desired form, as given by the latest booklet of instructions (so incorporating technical progress), in order to co-operate with labour in response to the pull of changes in relative factor prices and to technical advances. The relative prices of products (including meccano sets) *never* change, no matter how rates of wages and profits (and, sometimes, rents, when land, which we ignore, is considered) do.

In this way the aggregation of heterogeneous items of capital, both as cross-sections and over time, where they are both 'infinitely durable and instantaneously adaptable', is possible in terms of their own technical unit and 'the basic model of [his] text could be rigorously established in a form which deceived nobody' – an answer which proceeds by abolishing the question. For, with malleability, disappointed expectations and imperfect foresight can be avoided since the capital stock can be made into any form that is wanted and adapted to any labour supply that is forthcoming.

Thus it is hoped that the long-run implications of capital–labour substitution may be analysed independently of any troublesome short-run Keynesian and other puzzles. As Ferguson [1969] puts it, the *tendencies* inherent in the Marshallian long run may be analysed free of interference from other, *for this purpose, he believes*, irrelevant factors. His argument has been severely criticized in, for example, Robinson

$$\frac{\partial Q}{\partial K} = \beta \frac{Q}{K} \qquad (1.\text{iii})$$

and the share of capital in output, w_k, is

$$w_k = \frac{rK}{Q} = \frac{\partial Q/\partial K \cdot K}{Q}$$

(remembering that $r = \partial Q/\partial K$ by assumption) so that

$$w_k = \beta \qquad (1.\text{iv})$$

Because β is the ratio of the marginal to the average product of capital it is the *elasticity* of output with respect to capital. Similarly, it may be shown that

$$\frac{\partial Q}{\partial L} = (1-\beta)\frac{Q}{L} = \alpha\frac{Q}{L} \qquad (1.\text{v})$$

and
$$w_l = (1-\beta) = \alpha \qquad (1.\text{vi})$$

[1970a], Harcourt [1970b] and chapter 2, pp. 65–6, below. The main point of the criticism is that all economic decisions are of necessity made in the short run, where all actions are of necessity also, even though some decisions, e.g. those relating to investment, relate to longer horizons than do others, e.g. those relating to output. We find in Swan's appendix perhaps the first and certainly the clearest statement of the notorious malleability assumption which underlies many neoclassical growth models and econometric exercises, for example, Swan [1956], Solow [1956b, 1957], Meade [1961].

By measuring capital in terms of its own technical unit (and by assuming that the quantity of capital in terms of this unit is uniquely associated with, say, the annual flow of services from it, measured in machine years), it is in the appropriate form for inclusion in a production function viewed as an *engineering* description of the flow of output which may be expected from the inputs of certain flows of man and machine years: on this, see Bruno, Burmeister and Sheshinski [1968]. The marginal product of capital, so measured, is equal to the rate of profits multiplied by the price of the technical unit of capital in terms of product (p). But if this price does not change when accumulation occurs, as Swan assumes, capital may also be measured in *value* units, in which case its marginal product equals the rate of profits. Thus, *in equilibrium*,

$$\frac{\partial Q}{\partial \overline{K}} = rp, \quad \text{while } \frac{\partial Q}{p\partial \overline{K}} = r \tag{1.7}$$

where Q = product and $\overline{K}$ = capital measured in terms of its technical unit. As Q and $p\partial\overline{K}$ are measured in the same units, the units cancel, leaving a pure number which is the dimension of the rate of profits.

As Hicks [1965] has pointed out (also Swan [1956]), outside a one-commodity world the price of capital services – its rental – is the rate of profits multiplied by the price per unit of capital goods. In a one-commodity world the rate of profits and the marginal product of capital, one a pure number, the other an instantaneous rate of change, can be equal and the valuation problem can be dodged. Malleability cannot, however, because we must suppose that capital can change its form (or be viewed 'as if' it could) in order to identify its marginal product: see Samuelson [1962], and chapter 4 below, also the appendix to Pasinetti's [1969] article where this point is admirably explained. In a world of heterogeneous capital goods, valuation is needed so that we have a sum to which to apply the rate of profits. As we shall see below in chapter 4, this rate of profits is not in general equal to the maiginal product of 'capital'.

The neoclassical procedure can be regarded as an examination of virtual displacements around an equilibrium point, so that any relative price changes may be ignored and capital may be measured in terms of 'an equilibrium dollar's worth'. With this procedure it is legitimate – and essential – for individual economic actors to take all prices as *given* (they are, after all, price-*takers*) and it is market forces – the overall outcome of their individual but, consciously anyway, unco-ordinated actions – which are responsible for *actual* price changes, changes which cease, by definition, at equilibrium. Moreover, any accumulation which is *conceived* to have taken place is marginal so that any change in the value of meccano sets in terms of product is *confined to this marginal addition, and so may be ignored.*

The trouble is that when either comparisons are made between different economies with different equilibrium wages, rates of profits and factor endowments – what Swan calls 'structural comparisons in the large' – or, far worse, when accumulation is analysed, these equilibrium points with all their accompanying (instantaneous) rates of change cannot be extended into visible curves associated with the *same* equilibrium values. An enormous revaluation of existing capital stocks occurs whenever an *actual* change (as opposed to a *virtual* one), no matter how small, is contemplated. Hence the need either for meccano sets (and the accompanying unacceptable assumption of perfectly timeless and cost-less malleability) or for resort to Champernowne's chain index which both he and Swan argue also allows an analysis of *slow* accumulation, in Champernowne's case, without technical progress.[1] The operative word is *slow*, so that it takes a long time to pass between points which are far apart, and the conditions necessary for equilibrium at each point have a 'reasonable chance' of being established as the economy passes from one point to another. This particular act of faith has been a feature of many subsequent growth models constructed by true neo-classical believers, see, for example, Meade [1961].

In Champernowne's example, where the function is assumed to be single-valued and well-behaved, the progress is from a high rate of profits, low wage rate, low-productivity technique to a low rate of

---

[1] In a series of papers, Robinson [1958, 1959, 1970a, 1970b], Joan Robinson attributes to Wicksell this process of constructing through accumulation the techniques shown on successive pages of the book of blue-prints (which itself is given for all time) under the pull of changing factor prices – 'moving down the production function' – and provides some cogent analysis and criticism of it.

profits, high wage rate, high-productivity method: see Champernowne [1953–4], pp. 118–19. The Champernowne method is to use a series of snap-shots of stationary states that are reasonably close together. He supposes that enough accumulation has occurred to move the economy from one state to another, the amount of accumulation being analysed by the chain index method, so that the *differences* between the consecutive islands are treated *as if* they were equivalent to the changes *occurring* over time: '. . . the interest of a comparison of a sequence of stationary states is due to the presumption that this will give a first approximation to a comparison of successive positions in a slow process of steady accumulation'. (p. 119.) Champernowne adds that the presumption is more likely to be realized in the case of continuous technologies than in the case of discrete ones. During his discussion of this viewpoint, Champernowne cites an example whereby measuring capital *in terms of labour time* (what he calls *JR* units), associates a situation requiring *positive* net investment with one of apparent *negative* net investment, i.e. a reduction in real capital per head. This puzzle occurs because of a negative bias in the measurement of net investment due to the fall in the rate of interest; it disappears when the chain index method is used.

Wicksell effects, price and real, exposed

In the last two sections of the appendix of Swan [1956], Swan discusses the nature of the Wicksell effect, which Joan Robinson had commented on in her article, Robinson [1953–4], and returned to in more detail in her book, Robinson [1956], and later articles, Robinson [1958], and Robinson and Naqvi [1967]. In particular, Swan is concerned to show in terms of Wicksell's own examples (the point-input–point-output case and the analysis of Åckerman's problem, see Swan [1956], pp. 352–61) that '*the Wicksell Effect is nothing but an inventory revaluation*' (p. 355). In establishing this point, he accused Joan Robinson of confusing the change in the value of a stock of capital with the value of the change, a charge which she understandably took rather amiss, see Robinson [1957], p. 107 n6. Wicksell demonstrated that an increase in social capital is partly 'absorbed by increased wages . . ., so that only the residue . . . is really effective as far as a rise in production is concerned'. As Swan shows (see pp. 352–3) this implies that the marginal product of capital (in Wicksell's point-input–point-output case) is *less* than the rate of interest, an obstacle in the way of the acceptance of 'von Thünen's thesis' (which was its main interest to Wicksell).

In the modern literature the 'real' and 'financial' aspects of an increase in social capital have come to be discussed under the heading of *real* and *price* Wicksell effects, respectively. The wage-rate–rate-of-profits trade-off analysis developed earlier in the chapter allows a simple discussion of this distinction and allows us to show in a simple way what Swan had in mind when he described the (price) Wicksell effect as an inventory revaluation.

The *price* Wicksell effect relates to changes in the value of capital as w and r change their values but techniques do not change, i.e. it is associated with the w–r relationship that corresponds to *one* technique. *Real* Wicksell effects relate to changes in the value of capital associated with changes in techniques as w and r take on different values, i.e. they are differences in the values of capital at (or, rather, very near) switch points on the envelope of the w–r relationships. Switch points are the intersection points where two techniques are equi-most profitable. Both effects reflect the influence, through w and r, of the 'time' pattern of inputs of production, but real effects reflect in addition changes in production methods, i.e. changes which reflect real production potentials, not just their market values.

Consider an economy-wide technique which has a net output per head of a consumption good, q. Assume that we are in a stationary state (which is formally equivalent to what Garegnani [1970a] calls an integrated consumption-good industry) and that capital goods last forever. Then

$$q = rk + w \tag{1.8}$$

where all values are measured in consumption-good units per head, so that

$$k = \frac{q - w}{r} \tag{1.9}$$

When $r = 0$, $q = w_{\max}$, the maximum wage which is also output per head.

Because of our assumptions, $q = w_{\max}$ for *all* values of r. If we had more than one consumption good, or were considering a growing economy in which net investment formed part of the national product, $q = w_{\max}$ would hold *only* when $r = 0$ and net investment were either zero or the *same* good, because the value of q is affected by the relative prices of capital goods in terms of consumption goods which are themselves affected by the value of r.[1]

---

[1] I am indebted to Masao Fukuoka, Neil Laing and Edward Nell for making me see this point. It is discussed further in chapter 4, p. 149 below. The model discussed here is originally due to Bhaduri [1966].

We write the w–r relationship as

$$w = w_{max} - f(r) \qquad (1.10)$$

where, for $r = 0$, $f(0) = 0$, and $f'(r) > 0$, i.e. the w–r 'curve' slopes downward. Then

$$k = \frac{q - w}{r} = \frac{w_{max} - (w_{max} - f(r))}{r} = \frac{f(r)}{r} \qquad (1.11)$$

$$\frac{dk}{dr} = \frac{1}{r^2}(f'(r)r - f(r)) \qquad (1.12)$$

with

$$\frac{dk}{dr} \gtrless 0 \text{ according to whether} \frac{f'(r)r}{f(r)} \gtrless 1 \qquad (1.13)$$

Expression (1.13) provides a very simple method by which we may determine the relationship between the shapes (and slopes) of w–r curves and dk/dr. Consider a w–r curve which is concave to the origin, and for which, $w_{max} = OS$ (see fig. 1.4). Consider any value of r, say r_1; draw a tangent at P (which is the point on the w–r curve corresponding to r_1) and extend it to meet the w axis at Q. Draw a horizontal line from P to join the w axis at R. Then $RQ = f'(r_1)r_1$ and $RS = f(r_1)$. It may be seen that $RQ/RS > 1$, which by expression (1.13) implies that $dk/dr > 0$. That is to say, a w–r curve which is concave to the origin implies a *negative* price Wicksell effect – the value of capital is *lower*, the *lower* is the value of r, the inventory revaluation is negative. By exactly analogous reasoning we may show that a w–r relationship which is convex to the origin implies a *positive* price Wicksell effect and that a straight-line one implies a zero or *neutral* price Wicksell effect, a crucial result which we shall meet again in chapter 4.[1]

The following simple diagrams, in which the relationship, $k = (q-w)/r$, is used, are an alternative means of making the same points. Consider a w–r curve that is concave to the origin and the values of k associated with r_1 and r_2 in fig. 1.5a. Clearly $k_1 < k_2$, i.e. the value of k is *lower*, the *lower* is the value of r – a *negative* price Wicksell effect. The other two possibilities are shown in figs. 1.5b and 1.5c.[2]

---

[1] Economic interpretations which relate the slopes and shapes of the w–r curves to the technical coefficients of production in each sector of the economy may be found in Bhaduri [1969], Garegnani [1970a], Hicks [1965], Robinson and Naqvi [1967], Samuelson [1962], Spaventa [1968, 1970], Nuti [1970b]. See, also, chapter 4 below, pp. 133–6.

[2] I am indebted to Ian Steedman for suggesting these diagrams to me.

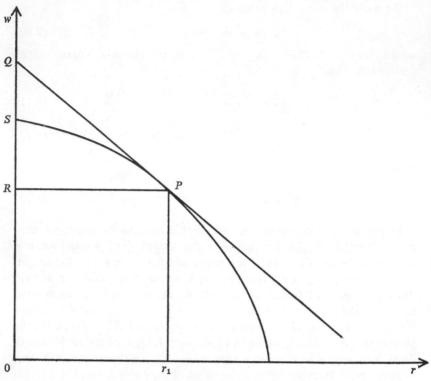

Fig. 1.4. Negative price Wicksell effect

We may identify a *positive real* Wicksell effect as one in which a technique with a higher output per head and higher value of capital per head at a switch point is chosen at a rate of profits just below the switch-point rate of profits. Thus, in fig. 1.6, technique *b*, having been equi-profitable with *a* at r_{ab}, becomes the more profitable at rates of interest $<r_{ab}$. The value of capital associated with *b* at $r_{ab}, k_b\{= (w_{b\,max} - w_{ab})/r_{ab}\}$, exceeds the corresponding value of capital associated with *a*, $k_a\{= (w_{a\,max} - w_{ab})/r_{ab}\}$. (Both allow the same wage rate and the same rate of profits to be paid but as labour equipped with *b* is more productive than that equipped with *a* ($w_{b\,max} > w_{a\,max}$), *a* must have a lower value of *k* in order that its smaller amount of profit, when expressed as a proportion of k_a, equals r_{ab}.) As the price Wicksell effect is negative for *a* and neutral for *b*, the value of capital for *b* for rates of profits $<r_{ab}$ will also continue to exceed those for *a*, indeed, by greater and greater amounts. At r_{ba} a *negative* real Wicksell effect occurs.

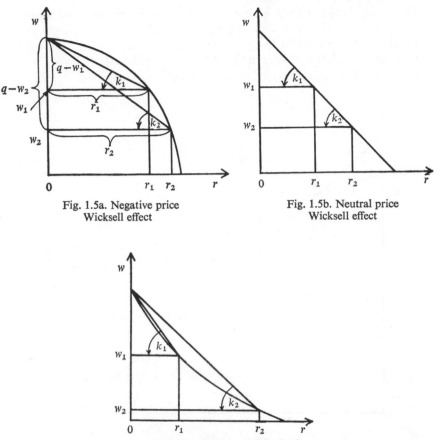

Fig. 1.5a. Negative price
Wicksell effect

Fig. 1.5b. Neutral price
Wicksell effect

Fig. 1.5c. Positive price Wicksell effect

The differences just below the switch points reflect both differences in productivity as between the two methods *and* valuation or price effects. It is only at *switch points* that the differences can be said, in general, to be entirely 'real'. For it is *only at switch points* that the wage and profits rates are the same for *both* methods so that any difference between the values of their ks must be attributable to the differences in the productivities of the methods. Anywhere else, though one factor price will be common to both, the other one will not, it being greater for the technique which is in use, i.e. is on the w–r envelope. (Moving horizontally across the diagram, it is w which is common; moving vertically it is r.) If both relationships are straight lines, though, the differences between their *k*s are nevertheless 'real' away from switch points because the price effects of both are neutral. Finally, if one *w–r* relationship is a straight line and the other curved, as in fig. 1.6, or if both are curved, the *changes* in the differences between the *k*s away from the switch points are entirely price Wicksell effects.

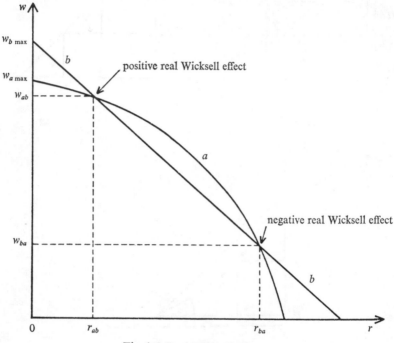

Fig. 1.6. Real Wicksell effects

At switch points such as r_{ab} and r_{ba}, the careful reader will notice that as the wage rates and the rates of profits are the *same* for both techniques, the additional amount of product associated with the more productive technique, when expressed as a proportion of the differences in capital values as between the two techniques, *is equal to the equilibrium rate of profits*.

Thus

$$\frac{w_{b\max} - w_{ab}}{k_b} = \frac{w_{a\max} - w_{ab}}{k_a} = r_{ab} \qquad (1.14)$$

i.e.

$$w_{b\max} - w_{a\max} = r_{ab}(k_b - k_a)$$

i.e.

$$\frac{w_{b\,max} - w_{a\,max}}{k_b - k_a} = r_{ab} \quad \left(= \frac{q_b - q_a}{k_b - k_a} \right) \tag{1.15}$$

It would be tempting to call the ratio, $(q_b - q_a)/(k_b - k_a)$ $(= \Delta q/\Delta k)$, the *marginal product of capital* and so deduce that it equals the – externally given – rate of profits. It would also be wrong to do so as Pasinetti [1969], pp. 529–31, shows with great insight and clarity. The marginal product of capital, as defined in the traditional literature, is *not*, he argues, the (limiting) ratio of the increment of output to the increment of capital when two techniques are equi-profitable, i.e. the rate of profits is unchanged, and the proportions in which the techniques are used are changed. It is, rather, the (limiting) ratio of the corresponding increments when we compare two techniques which are the most profitable at *different* rates of profits, *not at one and the same one.*

That is to say, in the traditional case, we consider the implications of a change in the rate of profits (which in the limit becomes infinitesimally small) for the ratio of the change in output to the change in the 'quantity of capital'. In the case above, though, we consider the implications, for the (limiting) ratio of the increments, of a change in the *proportions* in which two equi-profitable techniques are combined, the rate of profits remaining *unchanged* – as does, of course, the amount of labour *in both cases.* The differences between the two concepts highlight the crucial point that *if* the marginal product of capital is to be part of an explanation of the rate of profits itself, the changes in the 'quantities' as we go from one technique to another *must* themselves be *independent* of changes in the rate of profits. 'Capital', like labour, has to be measured in a unit which is independent of distribution and prices. Clearly in the *definition* above, whereby $\Delta q/\Delta k = r$, the seeming independence is only superficially so because r, *by assumption*, does not change.

The above considerations may appear to raise doubts about the verbal explanation, see pp. 33–4 above, that when we use the chain index method of measuring capital, the marginal product of labour equals the equilibrium wage rate. The answer is that it *should* raise doubts, very considerable ones, even though the chain index method is specifically designed to deal with this point, especially in the case of a continuous spectrum of techniques whereby we obtain values of capital of techniques which are the most profitable at *different* rates of profits from one another.[1]

---

[1] See also Swan's excellent discussion of this point in Swan [1956], pp. 352–7.

Solow's opening skirmish

It would be unfair – also foolhardy – to end the chapter without reference to Solow's comment in Solow [1956a] on Joan Robinson's [1953–4] article. Solow investigated the conditions under which it would be legitimate to aggregate heterogeneous capital items into a single figure, no doubt having in mind his subsequent econometric studies. He found that the conditions were very stringent – the rate at which one capital good could be substituted for another had to be independent of the amounts of labour which subsequently would be used with each. (He discusses in this context a neoclassical model in which continuous substitution is possible, not the discrete case of Joan Robinson's article, but he also looks at the latter towards the end of his article.) His conclusion is quoted in full below because it is an extremely clear statement of the stand that he takes in the debates that followed:

I conclude that discreteness is unlikely to help matters. Only in very special cases will it be possible to define a consistent measure of capital-in-general. Some comfort may be gleaned from the reflection that when capital–labour ratios differ widely we hardly need a subtle index to tell us so, and when differences are slight we are unlikely to believe what any particular index says. (p. 108.)[1]

For Solow, 'Capital as a number is *not* an issue of principle. All rigorously valid results come from n-capital-good models. In particular there is no justification ever for supposing that output can be made a function of labour and the VALUE of capital whose partial derivatives do the right thing.' Capital as a number is purely an aid to empirical work 'and you want to get away with the smallest dimensionality possible' (Solow [1969]). Had the contestants been content to leave the discussion here, the literature of the following years might have served to generate far more light – and certainly a lot less heat.

---

[1] Solow's latest statement of these views is in Solow [1970], pp. 424 and 427–8 (but see, also, Pasinetti [1970], pp. 428–9).

2 Treacle, fossils and technical progress

Cobb–Douglas's last fling?

The use of the malleability assumption and a simple marginal productivity theory of distribution underlies the early post-war work on aggregate production functions: the attempts to sort out from actual statistics the increases in output per man that are due to technical progress, i.e. shifts *of* an aggregate production function, from those which are due to capital deepening, i.e. movements *along* a given production function.[1] In this chapter we use Solow's famous 1957 article to illustrate the approach.

Solow assumed a constant-returns-to-scale aggregate production function, static expectations and competitive conditions. It followed that paying factors their marginal products exhausted the total product, which consisted of a Clark–Ramsey one all-purpose commodity, see J. B. Clark [1889], Ramsey [1928]. (Capital may then be measured in the same units as output, remembering that one is a *stock*, the other a *flow*, see Solow [1956a], p. 101.) Solow did not specify the form of the production function until after he made the empirical fittings when Cobb–Douglas gave the best fit.

Technical progress was assumed to be neutral and completely disembodied, i.e. left all factors unaffected, so that marginal rates of substitution between factors at given factor ratios were unchanged, though, at each ratio, there was a mystical rise of the same proportion in the total output associated with each ratio. All capital goods were treated alike, whether they were newly created and incorporated the latest advances in technical knowledge (and the effects of the pull of

[1] This is not, of course, an exhaustive list of factors. Economies of scale are also an important source of productivity growth but they are usually (especially is this true of the early days) excluded by assumption. Solow [1961] argues that the economist who provides an econometric method which allows the contributions to productivity growth of returns to scale to be distinguished from those due to technical progress and deepening should receive the George Cross and Bar. It is my impression that Katz [1968b] for one is due to be decorated.

expected factor prices) or whether they were fossils inherited from the past, previous years' investments which *in fact* could be expected to reflect the *then* prevailing technical conditions, expectations and relative factor prices. It was *as if* we were in Swan's world where, at any moment of time, all existing capital goods could be costlessly and timelessly taken to pieces and, using the latest booklet of instructions as our guide, changed into the latest cost-minimizing form as indicated by expectations of future product and relative factor prices. (Indeed, the expectations themselves must be a mirror image of present happenings.) Thus disembodied neutral technical progress may be likened to a mysterious manifestation of grace – when two or more, in this case, capital and labour, are gathered together in this life, there immediately occurs a rise (of considerable dimensions) in *total* factor productivity.

With a production function and technical progress of these natures, it is almost inevitable that 'technical progress' will explain most of the growth in output per man (except, unhappily, in Australia.)[1] We write the production function as

$$Q = A(t)f(K, L) \tag{2.1}$$

where Q, K and L are measured in appropriate technical units and $A(t)$ is a shift factor, a function of time, which reflects the pull of all the forces of technical change.

We differentiate expression (2.1) with respect to time to obtain

$$\dot{Q} = \dot{A}(t)f(K, L) + A(t)\frac{\partial f}{\partial K}\dot{K} + A(t)\frac{\partial f}{\partial L}\dot{L} \tag{2.2}$$

where dots over variables indicate derivatives with respect to time. Dividing by Q

$$\frac{\dot{Q}}{Q} = \frac{\dot{A}(t)}{A(t)} + A(t)\frac{\partial f}{\partial K}\frac{\dot{K}}{Q} + A(t)\frac{\partial f}{\partial L}\frac{\dot{L}}{Q} \tag{2.3}$$

Now

$$A(t)\frac{\partial f}{\partial K} = \frac{\partial Q}{\partial K} \quad \left(\text{and } A(t)\frac{\partial f}{\partial L} = \frac{\partial Q}{\partial L}\right)$$

---

[1] See Sampson [1969], chapter 3, where an application of Solow's method to Australian data shows that capital deepening gets considerably more credit than technical progress for the rise in productivity in the post-war period. Indeed, fitting a CES production function (see below, pp. 51–4) reduces the latter's contribution to – nothing.

so that, *if* factors are paid their marginal products, the share of capital in Q, w_k (and of labour in Q, w_l) is

$$\frac{\partial Q}{\partial K}\frac{K}{Q} \quad \left(\text{and } \frac{\partial Q}{\partial L}\frac{L}{Q}\right)$$

Therefore, we may write expression (2.3) as

$$\frac{\dot{Q}}{Q} = \frac{\dot{A}(t)}{A(t)} + w_k\frac{\dot{K}}{K} + w_l\frac{\dot{L}}{L}$$

which, if $w_k + w_l = 1$, becomes

$$\frac{\dot{Q}}{Q} - \frac{\dot{L}}{L} = \frac{\dot{A}(t)}{A(t)} + w_k\left\{\frac{\dot{K}}{K} - \frac{\dot{L}}{L}\right\} \tag{2.4a}$$

or

$$q^* = a + w_k k^* \tag{2.4b}$$

where

$$q^* = \frac{\dot{Q}}{Q} - \frac{\dot{L}}{L}, \quad a = \frac{\dot{A}(t)}{A(t)} \quad \text{and} \quad k^* = \frac{\dot{K}}{K} - \frac{\dot{L}}{L}$$

If we start with Cobb–Douglas (Swan's model) then, with technical progress added, we may write expression (2.4b) as

$$q^* = a + \beta k^* \tag{2.4c}$$

Thus the growth in output per head equals the rate of growth of the shift factor ('technical progress') plus the rate of growth of capital per man ('deepening'), the latter being weighted by capital's share in the national product. It follows from expression (2.4b) – and the assumptions – that

$$a = q^* - w_k k^* \tag{2.5}$$

To estimate a we only have to obtain statistics on q^*, w_k and k^*, all of which exist or may be constructed. As q grows at an order of 2–4 per cent per annum (except in Japan) and as w_k is of the order of one quarter to one third, there must be an enormous rate of growth of k^*, i.e. of $\dot{K}/K$ relative to $\dot{L}/L$, in order that capital accumulation (and deepening) explain much of the observed growth in output per head. It is therefore no surprise that Solow found (with Hogan's arithmetic help, see Hogan [1958]) that 90 per cent of the rise in output per head in the U.S.A. over the period 1909–49 was due to a.

In order to find the contribution of k^* to the growth of q^*, Solow deflated the annual observations on Q/L by his annual estimates of $A(t)$ (where $A(t) = A(t-1)\ \{1+\Delta A(t)/A(t-1)\}$, where $\Delta A(t)/A(t-1) = a$) in order to remove, as it were, the 'effects' of technical progress from the annual series of output per head. The resulting values of Q/L were plotted against the corresponding values of K/L. An aggregate production function was estimated by fitting econometrically a number o f possible statistical functions to the resulting points and selecting from them the 'best' fit, which was – surprise, surprise – Cobb–Douglas.

Solow's method is a most ingenious means whereby annual observations which are viewed *as if* they came from underlying production functions which drift up neutrally over time (see fig. 2.1) are boiled down into observations on one function which itself is an appropriately scaled down image of all the others. Thus, we only observe points such as P_1 and P_2; we deflate the value of Q/L at P_2 by A_2 to give the point, P_2'. Then $P_2'P_1'/P_1k_1$ is the growth in Q/L attributable to deepening of the order of k_1k_2/Ok_1. Solow's method gives many points such as P_2'

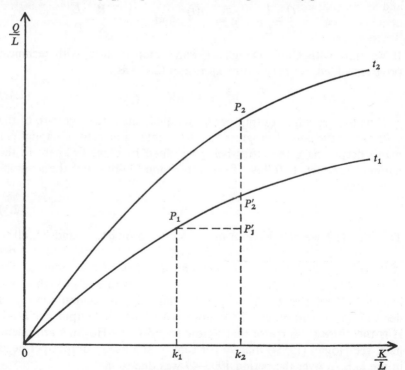

Fig. 2.1. Solow's production function

to which the statistical functions are fitted – we ignore statistical errors in fig. 2.1. Solow regarded the analysis as an exercise in empirical aggregation, claimed *no* rigorous justification for his procedures (though Samuelson later attempted to provide one, see Samuelson [1962], and chapter 4 below) and regarded any errors as specification errors, the nature and sizes of which ought to be investigated, rather than as sins against the Holy Grail.

At last, the ACMS *show: enter the lovely homohypallagic production function*

The CES[1] production function is another famous example where malleability, perfect competition, disembodied technical progress, static expectations and constant returns to scale were, initially at any rate, crucial assumptions. This particular function made its debut to a wide audience in an article published in 1961 by Arrow, Chenery, Minhas and Solow (ACMS) (see also, Minhas [1963]).[2] The particular empirical findings which led to its debut were the close associations, as confirmed by the appropriate regressions, between the logarithms of labour productivity and money-wage rates in the *same* industries in *different* countries. The regressions had the following equation

$$\log \frac{Q}{L} = \log A + b \log w + \varepsilon$$

i.e. $$\log q = \log A + b \log w + \varepsilon \tag{2.6}$$

where $q = Q/L$ and ε = error term, see ACMS [1961], p. 228.

The observations on labour productivity were treated *as if* they came from a constant-returns-to-scale production function which spanned national frontiers. The function was characterized by disembodied technical progress and *ex post* variability of factors; so that, at any moment of time, the machines in the capital stock of each country could be treated *as if* they had been moulded into the form of the most up-to-date machines, namely, those which would be chosen from the various possibilities currently existing and known in each country by cost-minimizing, profit-maximizing businessmen who had static expectations. To suppose that the observations, some facts in search of

[1] Constant elasticity of substitution, now referred to as the homohypallagic production function, see Minhas [1963].
[2] The first person to use the function was Champernowne in the mid-forties. Solow [1956b] used it in 1956 and Pitchford [1960] exhaustively examined its role in growth models in 1960.

a theory, should be so treated was, to ACMS, just the natural thing to do – or, at least, 'a natural first step', see ACMS [1961], p. 228. With these assumptions, the regression coefficients of the relationships (the values of b in expression (2.6)) were shown to be estimates of the elasticity of substitution between capital and labour, were usually less than one and greater than zero, and varied considerably as between industries. These findings were in turn brought to bear on such diverse topics as the factor-price equalization theorem, see, for example, Minhas [1963], and the measurement of technical progress, see, for example, Sampson [1969]. Indeed a considerable new literature was born as a result, so that the coming out of the CES in 1961 was quite a fecund debut.

The essential methodology of ACMS is as follows: if the form of the production function is known, and provided that there are constant returns to scale and perfect competition in the factor and product markets, it is always possible to derive the implied form of the relationship between productivity and the wage rate. Thus, consider the production function

$$Q = F(K, L) \tag{2.7a}$$

which, because of constant returns to scale, may be written as

$$\frac{Q}{L} = f\left(\frac{K}{L}, 1\right) \tag{2.7b}$$

i.e.

$$q = f(k) \tag{2.8}$$

where $q = Q/L$, $k = K/L$
Now

$$\frac{\partial Q}{\partial K} = f'(k)$$
$$\frac{\partial Q}{\partial L} = f(k) - f'(k)k \tag{2.9}$$

and, assuming perfect competition and static expectations

$$w = f(k) - f'(k)k \tag{2.10}$$

Equation (2.10) has an inverse function that relates k to w and, because $q = f(k)$, it also allows q to relate to w, say

$$q = g^*(w) \tag{2.11}$$

ACMS then turn this procedure around and suppose that the *form* of the relationship between productivity and the wage rate is known (as it was to them). Let it be

$$q = g^*(w) \qquad (2.12)$$

(i.e. expression (2.12) is the general form of the regression equation (2.6) above.) Then, with their assumptions

$$q = g^*(q - f'(k)k) \qquad (2.13)$$

which is a differential equation for $f(k)$ with a solution

$$q = f(k; \bar{A}) \qquad (2.14)$$

where $\bar{A}$ is a constant of integration. (Equation (2.14) is constrained to make $f'(k) > 0$ and $f''(k) < 0$.)

We next show that *if* there is this link from the productivity–wage rate relationship (expression (2.6) above) to the production function, the regression coefficient, b, is not only the elasticity of productivity with respect to the wage rate, $(dq/dw)(w/q)$, but also the elasticity of substitution of capital for labour, σ.[1] σ measures the responsiveness of the capital–labour ratio to changes in the ratios of the marginal products of capital and labour, and, therefore, *with perfect competition and static expectations*, to changes in relative factor prices. With constant returns to scale, σ may be defined as follows, see Allen [1938], p. 343:

$$\sigma = \frac{(\partial Q/\partial K)(\partial Q/\partial L)}{Q(\partial^2 Q/\partial K \partial L)} \qquad (2.15)$$

We already have expressions for $\partial Q/\partial K$ and $\partial Q/\partial L$, see expression (2.9) above. $\partial^2 Q/\partial K \partial L$ may be shown to be: $(1/L)(-kf''(k))^2$ and we know that $Q = Lf(k)$.

Substituting these expressions in expression (2.15) gives

$$\sigma = -\frac{f'(k)(f(k) - f'(k)k)}{kf(k)f''(k)} \qquad (2.16)$$

---

[1] I am indebted to Denzo Kamiya for explaining this derivation to me; it is based on ACMS's procedures.

[2]
$$\frac{\partial^2 Q}{\partial K \partial L} = \frac{\partial}{\partial K}\left(\frac{\partial Q}{\partial L}\right)$$

$$= \frac{\partial}{\partial K}\left(f(k) - f'(k)k\right)$$

$$= \frac{\partial k}{\partial K}\left(\frac{d}{dk}(f(k) - f'(k)k)\right)$$

$$= \frac{1}{L}\left(-kf''(k)\right)$$

Now, by our key assumption, the wage rate equals the marginal product of labour, i.e.

$$w = f(k) - f'(k)k \tag{2.10}$$

so that

$$
\begin{aligned}
dw &= f'(k)dk - f'(k)dk - kf''(k)dk \\
&= -kf''(k)dk
\end{aligned}
\tag{2.17}
$$

From $q = f(k)$ we obtain

$$dq = f'(k)dk$$

and, thus

$$dk = \frac{1}{f'(k)}dq \tag{2.18}$$

Substituting expression (2.18) in expression (2.17), we obtain

$$dw = -kf''(k)\frac{dq}{f'(k)}$$

and, so

$$\frac{dq}{dw} = -\frac{f'(k)}{kf''(k)} \tag{2.19}$$

Therefore

$$\frac{dq}{dw}\frac{w}{q} = -\frac{f'(k)(f(k) - f'(k)k)}{kf(k)f''(k)} = \sigma \tag{2.20}$$

But (dq/dw) (w/q) is, by definition, b in equation (2.6), so that b is an estimate of σ. ACMS then derive the exact form of the CES production function associated with expression (2.12), knowing now that it must have a constant σ because b in the original regression equation is a constant, see ACMS [1961], pp. 229–31. This need not concern us here.

Enter fossils

The malleability assumption has been removed from the analysis of neoclassical growth models (and, partially, from econometric studies of productivity change) as the embodiment hypothesis with regard to technical progress has replaced the disembodied view. Both patriotism and judgement lead me to select the late W. E. G. Salter's work (Salter

[1959, 1960, 1962, 1965]) which was originally developed in Cambridge, England, over the years 1953–5, as one of the finest – and earliest[1] – examples of the embodiment hypothesis and the attempt to get away from the puzzles associated with the measurement of capital, while, at the same time, recognizing the importance of distinguishing between *ex ante* and *ex post* substitutability, the heterogeneity of capital goods and the distinction between comparisons and processes.[2]

Salter accepted Joan Robinson's view that the production function is relevant only in an *ex ante* sense when investment decisions – what to scrap, what to add, how much to add (and how to pay for it) – are being made, so that only the margins of the capital stock are affected, both by scrapping and by additions. The neoclassical assumptions of substitutability and cost-minimization (*with static expectations*) now relate to the choice from the set of 'best-practice' techniques available – the book of blue-prints or *ex ante* production function, new-style – of that technique which will minimize costs and maximize profits in the sense of maximizing the present value of expected net receipts (quasirents) with given (expected) rates of wages and prices. The choice is analysed at the micro level – we deal principally with the firm – so that wage rates, product prices and investment-good prices, as well as the expected rate of profits which is used as the discount factor in present-value calculations, may be taken as given. It comes as no surprise that, in this aspect of the investment decision, the technique which is chosen is that for which the marginal rate of substitution of labour for investment, i.e. the ratio of the respective marginal products (and the slope of the *ex ante* production function) equals the ratio of the factor prices.

We should note that though Salter accepted Joan Robinson's view about the *ex ante* production function, her own views have since altered. She would now confine the *ex ante* production function at any moment of a time to a *point*, a point which, moreover, is often designed by the

---

[1] Though *Productivity and Technical Change* (Salter [1960]) was published in 1960, his basic ideas were worked out in Cambridge in the early 1950s and were contained in his Ph.D. dissertation which was submitted in 1955. The consequent lag has tended until recently to rob Salter of proper recognition in the literature.

[2] This is not the appropriate place to pay a full tribute to Wilfred Salter. Suffice it to say here that Salter's work is a model which all aspiring (and established) economists profitably could have before them. Its characteristics are a flair for formulating relevant *theory* which, clearly, neatly and excitingly expressed, is carried no further than the requirements of the problem in hand – and is immediately tested against the facts. Readers may also like to read Swan's obituary note (Swan [1963]), where he fittingly describes Salter's work as 'unfulfilled renown' and Reddaway's tribute in the preface to the second edition of *Productivity and Technical Change*, Salter [1966].

investor himself in such a way as to reflect his expectations about future movements in relative factor prices: see Robinson [1971], ch. 8. Some 'casual empiricism' that suggests that ACMS's *ex ante* production function, *which spans national borders*, may not exist at any moment of time is the complaint by Indian businessmen that foreigners seldom design machines which are appropriate for *Indian* needs and conditions. There is also their practice of buying second-hand machines at reduced values, even though the productivity levels of the machines are considerably below those of the latest vintage.[1] But, at a *national* industry level, surely Salter could be allowed a small arc of 'best-practice' possibilities, techniques that are the *near* neighbours of the 'best-practice' technique actually chosen? We proceed under this dispensation.

To illustrate, consider the simple case in which all investment goods associated with the *ex ante* production function are expected to last for the same length of time, and wages, product prices and the rate of interest (equals the rate of profits) are expected to be constant over their lifetimes. The *ex ante* production function, if we assume constant returns to scale and continuity,[2] may be written as

$$l = f(i) \qquad (2.21)$$

where $f'(i) < 0$, $f''(i) > 0$, $l = $ labour input per unit of output and $i = $ investment input per unit of output. (Expression (2.21) applies only at one point of time. Salter analyses technical progress by moving the iso-quant, of which expression (2.21) is the equation, inwards toward the origin as time goes by, changes in the form of f reflecting any biases that are associated with technical improvements.)

The expected present value per unit of output of the investment expenditure associated with each 'best-practice' technique (V) is

$$V = (p - w_m l)B - i$$
$$= (p - w_m f(i))B - i \qquad (2.22)$$

where p is price per unit of output, w_m money wage rate, r rate of interest used as the discount factor, and $B = \{(1+r)^{\bar{n}} - 1\}/r(1+r)^{\bar{n}}$, i.e. B is the present value of the stream of one dollar a year for $\bar{n}$ years, where $\bar{n}$ is the (constant and equal) expected lifetimes of the techniques.

---

[1] I am indebted to E. A. Russell for this point.

[2] A feature of Joan Robinson's analysis of the choice of technique is, as we have seen, discontinuities – gaps between output per head of one technique and another. This does not imply, though, gaps in the relationship between output per head and real capital per head, as two techniques may be equi-profitable at a given rate of profits and one may be the most profitable over a range of rates of profits: see fig. 1.1, chapter 1 above.

To choose the technique which has the highest present value, we find the condition for which

$$\frac{\partial V}{\partial i}\left(= -w_m Bf'(i) - 1 \right) = 0 \qquad (2.23)$$

It is

$$f'(i) = -\frac{B'}{w_m} \qquad (2.24)$$

where $B' = 1/B$. But B'/w_m is the ratio of the factor prices (for the expected payment on investment each year – the rental on capital – will be $B'i$) and $f'(i)$ is the slope of the *ex ante* production function, i.e. businessmen (and the economy) are instructed to go, in the old-fashioned way, to the points where the iso-quants are tangential to the appropriate iso-cost lines.

To show that cost-minimization – a more general hypothesis (in the sense that it need not be confined to either perfect competition or profit-maximization) – gives the same result (and to satisfy all except Kaldor, see Kaldor and Mirrlees [1962], and pp. 80–1 below) we write

$$c = w_m f(i) + B'i \qquad (2.25)$$

where c is total annual cost per unit. Then

$$\frac{\partial c}{\partial i}\left(= w_m f'(i) + B' \right) = 0$$

when

$$f'(i) = -\frac{B'}{w_m} \qquad (2.24)$$

If capital goods are assumed to last for ever, we write

$$c = w_m f(i) + ri \qquad (2.26)$$

so that

$$\frac{\partial c}{\partial i} = 0 \quad \text{when } f'(i) = -\frac{r}{w_m} \qquad (2.27)$$

It should be remembered that in this analysis we are considering price-taking perfect competitors. In long-run competitive equilibrium in which uncertainty and risk are absent and expectations are realized, the technique chosen will have a (maximum) present value of zero. (Those of all other techniques will be negative.) However, in a disequilibrium situation, or where risk and uncertainty enter, or in an imperfectly competitive situation, the maximum *expected* present value of the technique in fact chosen may well be positive. In these situations, if we suppose that risk and uncertainty are allowed for in a very simple way, the rate of profits used as the discount factor will also exceed the rate of interest.

Once we depart from the simple assumptions that all machines are expected to have the same life and that wages and prices are expected to remain constant – and equal to current levels – over these lives, i.e. static expectations, these simple results no longer hold. We may illustrate the point with the following model (see Harcourt [1968a, 1968b]). Assume that businessmen, when they are making investment decisions, expect the prices of their products and the wage rates of their labour to rise at constant rates which reflect recent past experiences. Wage rates are expected to rise *faster* than prices because wages are expected to reflect increases in prices *and* overall productivity, the most simple plausible assumption about expectations that we could make. That is to say, businessmen expect real wages in terms of *their* product to rise over time.

If these expectations are combined with the *ex ante* production function, $l = f(i)$, and if we suppose further that businessmen will expect to keep their machines running as long as they 'earn' positive quasi-rents (which, alas, is only true of perfect competitors, see Nuti [1969], Robinson [1969c]), the expected life of each machine is given at the point where its expected quasi-rent falls to zero, i.e. where the expected product price equals the expected wage cost per unit of output. Moreover, with our present assumptions, there is a negative association between the labour-intensity of the techniques and their expected lifetimes, see fig. 2.2, where expected quasi-rents (QR) are plotted on the vertical axis and expected lifetimes (n) on the horizontal axis and $QR_1 < QR_2 < QR_3$ and $n_1 < n_2 < n_3$. (Also, for any given value of n, the more labour-intensive technique will have the lower QR.)

Let g be the expected rate of growth of the product price (the current level of which is p_0) and h be the expected rate of growth of the money wage (which is w_{m0} at the moment). Then the present values per unit of output of the investment expenditures associated with each 'best-practice' technique may be written as

$$V = p_0 G - w_{m0} f(i) H - i \tag{2.28}$$

where
$$G = \frac{(1+g)[\{(1+g)/(1+r)\}^n - 1]}{g - r}$$

$$H = \frac{(1+h)[\{(1+h)/(1+r)\}^n - 1]}{h - r}$$

.i.e. the discounted values of a unit of expected receipts and wage payments, respectively, over the expected lifetimes of each technique. We suppose that $r > h > g$; this is not an unreasonable assumption for moderate rates of increase of prices and money wages.

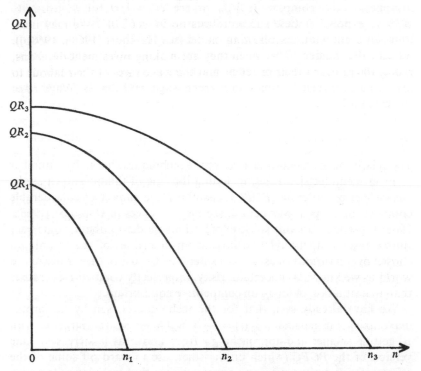

Fig. 2.2. Labour-intensity, expected quasi-rents and expected lifetimes of techniques

In order to maximize the expected present value of his investment the businessman will choose that technique for which $\partial V/\partial i = 0$, i.e. for which

$$f'(i) = -\frac{1}{w_{m0}H - (\partial n/\partial l)\{p_0(\partial G/\partial n) - w_{m0}l(\partial H/\partial n)\}} \qquad (2.29)$$

Although expression (2.29) is ghastly, it does, happily, reduce to $-(1/w_{m0}B)\{= -(B'/w_{m0})\}$ for $h = 0$ (static expectations) and $n = \bar{n}$, i.e. to the result that we met before as expression (2.24) above.

It is difficult to generalize on the basis of expression (2.29) because conflicting factors are at work, i.e. the sign of the second expression in the denominator cannot be determined *a priori*. Nevertheless it does appear from expression (2.29) that non-static expectations will result in the choice of less labour-intensive, more investment-intensive techniques than do static expectations. For example, consider the case where $n = \bar{n}$, so that the second expression in the denominator of expression (2.29) disappears, and compare H'/w_{m0}, where $H' = 1/H$ for $n = \bar{n}$, with B'/w_{m0}, expression (2.24). Then, because $H' < B'$, it is obvious that non-static expectations result in the choice of the more investment-intensive technique. This is hardly surprising as an expectation of rising wages over the lifetimes of machines is, of course, equivalent to expecting over their lifetimes an *average* wage level that is greater than the current level.

Slight digression

The relative investment-intensities of the techniques chosen by a number of investment-decision rules, including the rule of thumb known as the pay-off period criterion (*POPC*), have been the subject of considerable comment in the post-war period, see the references in Harcourt [1968a, 1968b]. We may use our static expectations model to obtain some very simple results on the relative investment-intensities of the techniques chosen by the various rules. We consider here the use of these rules in the world as we know it – uncertain, risky, imperfectly competitive – rather than in a situation of long-run competitive equilibrium.

We have already seen that for the technique chosen by the profit-maximizing businessman, $f'(i) = -B'/w_m (\approx -r/w_m$ for large n, with B' getting smaller and approaching r from above as n increases). One version of the *POPC* (which businessmen use to ward off some of the effects of risk and uncertainty) states: choose that technique for which the sum of the expected quasi-rents over the pay-off period (*POP*) (said to be b = five years) is largest, subject to the constraint that this sum will at least 'pay for' the investment by the end of the *POP*, i.e. choose that technique which maximizes

$$b(p - w_m l)$$

subject to
$$b(p - w_m l) \geqslant i \qquad (2.30)$$

The equality form of the constraint may be written as

$$l = \frac{p}{w_m} - \frac{1}{b w_m} i \qquad (2.31)$$

which is a straight line with a slope of $1/b w_m$.

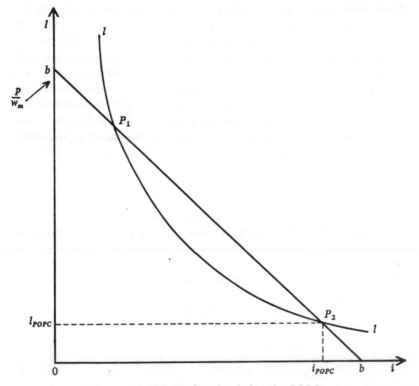

Fig. 2.3. Choice of technique by *POPC*

In fig. 2.3, we show $l = f(i)$ as the curve, *ll*, and expression (2.31) as the straight line, *bb*, which cuts the vertical axis at the value p/w_m. The technique chosen by the *POPC* is that associated with the second intersection of *bb* with *ll* (P_2). (P_1 satisfies the constraint – it lies on both *ll* and *bb* – but does not maximize the sum of the expected net receipts over the *POP*.) Thus, at P_2

$$f'(i) \leqslant \frac{1}{bw_m} \qquad (2.32)$$

(the equality occurring when *bb* is tangential to *ll*). Now, if $b = 5$ years, $1/b = \frac{1}{5}$, so that we know that the slope of *ll* at P_2 is $\leqslant 1/5w_m$. If expected rates of profits of the order of 20 per cent or more are required by businessmen, a not unreasonable order of magnitude in a risky and uncertain world (whether they in fact earn them *ex post* is an entirely different story), the slope of *ll* at the technique chosen by the application of the present value rule will be $\geqslant 1/5w_m$ ($= 20$ per cent$/w_m$). That is to say, in this case the *POPC* results in the choice of a *more* investment-intensive technique than would be chosen by a cost-minimizing, profit-maximizing businessman acting in best textbook tradition (and also dutifully doing what academic economists, civil servants – and some businessmen – have enjoined him to do in recent years by their enthusiastic advocacy of *DCF* procedures). That is *not* to say that any have acted wrongly, only that what businessmen are predicted by economic theory to have done and are enjoined by policy-makers to do, may not in fact coincide with what they actually do.

On the other hand, if he were (wrongly) to choose the technique with the highest expected internal rate of return (ρ), he would put in the least investment-intensive technique of all. Thus, if, for simplicity, we suppose that capital lasts for ever, then, as ρ is that rate of discount which makes

$$\frac{p - w_m f(i)}{\rho} = i$$

i.e.

$$\rho = \frac{p - w_m f(i)}{i} \tag{2.33}$$

This is a maximum when $\partial\rho/\partial i [= 1/i^2 \{ -iw_m f'(i) - (p - w_m f(i)) \}] = 0$

i.e. when

$$f'(i) \left[= -\left\{ \frac{p - w_m f(i)}{w_m i} \right\} \right] = -\frac{\rho}{w_m} \tag{2.34}$$

As

$$\frac{\rho_{\max}}{w_m} \geqslant \frac{r}{w_m} \geqslant \frac{1}{bw_m}$$

the result follows. ($\rho = r$ when the (maximum) present value of one technique is zero and those of the rest are negative – which applies in the riskless, certain world of long-run competitive equilibrium but not necessarily in the one that we are considering at the moment.) We may also note that, with the present simple assumptions, choosing that technique which maximizes ρ is equivalent to choosing the technique with the highest expected accounting rate of profit (π) (another popular 'real world' decision rule), whether capital lasts for ever or not and supposing that straight-line depreciation is used in the second instance. This result follows from the definition of π as either:

$$\pi = \frac{p - w_m f(i)}{i} \quad \text{or} \quad \pi = \frac{p - w_m f(i) - (i/\bar{n})}{i}$$

The major results of our digression are summarized in fig. 2.4. On the vertical axis we measure the sum of the undiscounted expected net receipts over the *POP* associated with each technique, *U*, their present values (where *r* is the rate of interest used as the discount factor), *PV*, and the investment expenditure per unit of output itself, *i*. On the horizontal axis we also measure investment expenditure per unit of output; *ii* is therefore a 45° line – *i* plotted against itself. *UU* relates each value of *U* to its corresponding value of *i* and is concave to the origin because, though $w_m f(i)$ gets smaller as *i* increases, it does so at a decreasing rate. *VV* relates the values of *PV* to their corresponding values of *i*. Initially, suppose that $\bar{n} = b$. With $\bar{n} = b =$ constant, *VV* is below *UU* at each point by a *given* proportion. i_{POPC} is the investment expenditure associated with the technique chosen by the *POPC*. *UU* cuts *ii* at this level of *i*, so satisfying the constraint that the technique chosen at least 'pay for itself' by the end of the *POP*. i_{PV} corresponds to the choice of technique by the present value rule – notice that *VV* is parallel to *ii* at this point and therefore has a slope of unity. (This is implied by expression (2.23), see p. 57 above, whereby $(-w_m Bf'(i))$, the slope of *VV*, equals unity at the point of cost-minimization and profit-maximization.)

Finally, if we raise the rate of interest used as the discount factor until *VV* is lowered (*proportionately*) to tangency with *ii*, see *V'V'* in fig. 2.4, we obtain the choice of technique by the internal rate of return rule, i_ρ. It is obvious that i_ρ must be to the left of i_{PV}. If, now, we relax the assumption that $\bar{n} = b$, clearly there must be some value of $\bar{n}$ that allows *VV* to be so far above *UU* that it is parallel to *ii* *to the right* of the *UU*, *ii* intersection. Our analysis suggests, though, that the orders of magnitude met in the real world make this an unlikely possibility.[1]

Onwards and upwards – with vintages

With the embodied view of technical progress, whereby gross investment is the medium for transmitting both technical change and capital–labour substitution to the capital stock, so bringing about productivity growth, the capital stock consists at any moment of time of layers of fossils, or

---

[1] A more detailed analysis of the choice of technique, coupled with investment-incentive schemes, may be found in Harcourt [1968a, 1968b].

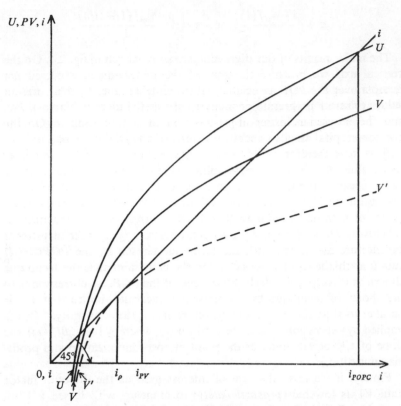

Fig. 2.4. Choice of technique by *POPC*, *PV* and ρ rules, with $\bar{n} = b$

vintages. Each layer represents the amount of gross investment in the technique that was chosen under the pull of expected relative factor prices, technical advances and demand conditions at the time when the investments were made. There are, on this view, *ex ante* substitution possibilities – when making investment decisions businessmen have to decide *where* on the $f(i)$ function they wish to be – but not necessarily *ex post* possibilities. Even if the initial substitution possibilities remain open *ex post*, one variant of the vintage approach assumes that nevertheless these possibilities are unaffected by later technical advances.

The amount of new investment which is done and the total amount and number of vintages that are in use, at any moment of time, are determined, at the industry level, by demand and supply conditions, and by the condition that only vintages with positive to zero quasi-rents are to be kept working. Output expands until the price of the product is such that only the normal rate of profits is expected to be earned on new vintages. Labour requirements per unit of output rise as the age of the vintage increases. The real-wage level (which is rising over time) therefore determines the scrapping margin in each industry and in the economy as a whole: see Salter [1960, 1965], Sargent [1968]. In this way, technical progress, productivity changes and distributive shares may be analysed as historical processes without there being any need to measure capital stocks as such: see, for example, Salter [1965].

This procedure is an extremely neat solution of the conundrum associated with the application of Marshallian long-period analysis to actual historical processes. Clearly, it is impossible to suppose that other things will be equal, i.e. stand still long enough to allow the economy (or even an industry) to establish, overall, the optimum capital–labour and capital–output ratios implied by expectations concerning prices, costs and levels of sales at any moment of time, i.e. we cannot expect *ex ante* and *ex post* production functions ever fully to coincide one with another. Therefore the notion that both *actual* prices and outputs could be at levels which offer only the normal rate of profits on the *entire* capital stock seems to be a non-starter; indeed, it is difficult, if not impossible to conceive of any uniform or stable link between conceptual normal values and the values of the movements of actual economic series over time, with the exception of prices and provided that we take the not implausible view that expectations almost always turn out to be falsified, often by large margins.

However, if we assume that 'other things' have to stand still only long enough to allow suitable adjustments to be made at the *margins* of the capital stocks, while the bulk of production is done by existing vintages which must take whatever quasi-rents they can get (even if they are disappointing in relation to the high hopes that were held when the machines concerned were first installed), we may salvage Marshall's insight and add a new dimension of realism – and relevance – to his brand of period analysis. The time-period involved has shrunk greatly and provided that innovations do not roll over us in great waves, crowding in on one another, we may generate values of key theoretical variables – gross investment, output, productivity, wages, profits, as well as prices – which reasonably may be said to have as their empirical counterparts the *trend* values of the statistics available on them.

Moreover, we may do this without the need to measure the capital stock; we only need to know the labour requirements per unit of output of the vintages in existence and the current prices at which the latest vintages are selling, so that businessmen may be thought of as estimating the expected rates of profits on them. Competitive industrial market forces will establish prices of products and rates of output which at equilibrium will allow the expected payment of the normal rate of profits on new vintages (though we have not yet a theory of what determines *its* level, but see below, chapter 5). Simultaneously, the same forces will determine what proportion of the accompanying rates of output must be catered for by new investment expenditures and what proportion may be undertaken by the existing vintages. (There is a lag puzzle here which static analysis of competitive situations always dodges.) The distribution of the product between wages and profits will then be related to the historical natures of the vintages in operation and to current levels of factor prices.

This being neoclassical analysis at its very best why, then, we may all be neoclassicals now – well, nearly all. It is also the essence and the measure of Salter's achievement, one which, on any reckoning, is worthy to be called a major break-through.[1] It is true that Salter himself was uncomfortable once he left the confines of perfect competition and that his handling of economies of scale was sketchy. Sampson [1969] has also questioned the econometric specification of his model when applied to the actual statistics. But, in contrast to his positive contributions, these are details, work for boys to do now that the men have been sorted out.

As an interesting half-way house between the malleable capital world in which technical progress is disembodied and the vintage world where it is embodied, we may cite a paper by Johansen [1961]. (Johansen, in a justly famous article, Johansen [1959], and independently of Salter, also pioneered the introduction of vintages and of the distinction between *ex ante*, plenty, and *ex post*, none, substitution possibilities into growth models.) The present paper, Johansen tells us, was stimulated by 'the reading of Dr Salter's study' and a desire to answer Kaldor's contention (in Kaldor [1957]) '. . . that it is not meaningful or useful to try to separate the influences of technical progress and capital accumulation' (p. 782). Johansen attempts to do just this by starting with Solow's model, adding some plausible empirical assumptions, for example, the stability over time of relative wage structures, and the likely constancy

---

[1] A good index of this may be obtained by reading the account in Stigler [1941], chapter xi, of J. B. Clark's attempt to grapple with the same puzzle. See also J B. Clark [1891], Hicks [1932].

over time (secularly if not cyclically) of *relative* (and absolute) desired returns on investment, and by devising a statistical method which does *not* require the measurement of capital stocks.

Johansen's method allows the contribution of capital deepening to productivity growth to be distinguished from that of technical advance in a cross-section study of several industries, provided that there are statistics available on capital's share in the values added of the different industries and the rates of increase of productivity in the same industries. The drawbacks of the method, as he candidly admits, are the dependence on a traditional (Cobb–Douglas) production function and the vital importance of assuming neutral technical progress, perfect competition and – he should have added – static expectations in factor markets.

Johansen assumes a Cobb–Douglas production function that is characterized by neutral technical progress and constant returns to scale in each industry $i(i = 1, \ldots, n)$, i.e.

$$Q_{it} = A(t)_i L_{it}^{\alpha_i} K_{it}^{\beta_i} \qquad (2.35)$$

where t is the time-period and $\alpha_i + \beta_i = 1$.

He is concerned with comparisons between two years (in his empirical work, 1924 and 1950, using United Kingdom data from the first edition of Salter [1960]).

Productivity in industry i in year t is

$$\frac{Q_{it}}{L_{it}} = q^*_{it} = A(t)_i \left(\frac{K_{it}}{L_{it}}\right)^{\beta_i} \qquad (2.36)$$

and the increase in productivity between year 1 and year 2 is

$$\frac{q^*_{i2}}{q^*_{i1}} = \frac{A(2)_i}{A(1)_i}\left(\frac{K_{i2}/K_{i1}}{L_{i2}/L_{i1}}\right)^{\beta_i} \qquad (2.37)$$

a combination, it may be seen, of the 'shift of' and the deepening or 'movement along' factors. (Equation (2.37) is formally equivalent to Solow's equation (2.4b), see p. 49 above, with $w_k = \beta$, but is applied at the *industry* level.)

We now introduce the crucial cost-minimizing, price-taking procedures, supposing the wage rates in industry i to be w_{it} and the cost of one unit of capital to be r_{it}. With businessmen taking these prices as given, cost-minimization implies that the ratios of the prices of factors to their respective marginal products be equal, i.e. that

$$\frac{w_{it}}{\alpha_i(Q_{it}/L_{it})} = \frac{r_{it}}{\beta_i(Q_{it}/K_{it})} \quad \text{or} \quad \frac{w_{it}L_{it}}{\alpha_i} = \frac{r_{it}K_{it}}{\beta_i} \qquad (2.38)$$

From expression (2.38)

$$\frac{w_{it}L_{it}}{r_{it}K_{it}} = \frac{\alpha_i}{\beta_i} \qquad (2.38a)$$

Therefore

$$\frac{w_{i1}L_{i1}}{r_{i1}K_{i1}} = \frac{w_{i2}L_{i2}}{r_{i2}K_{i2}} \quad \text{and} \quad \frac{K_{i2}/L_{i2}}{K_{i1}/L_{i1}} = \frac{w_{i2}/w_{i1}}{r_{i2}/r_{i1}} = \bar{w}_i \qquad (2.39)$$

Johansen [1961], p. 776, calls $\bar{w}_i$ 'the relative increase in wages'. (But note that we have met $\bar{w}_i$ before in the guise of the extent of capital deepening that has occurred as between two periods, see above, pp. 48–9.) Now suppose that the relative wage structure in the economy is stable over time, as is the pattern of relative capital costs (which are also constant), so that

$$\bar{w}_1 = \bar{w}_2 = \ldots = \bar{w}_n = \bar{w} \qquad (2.40)$$

Substituting $\bar{w} = \dfrac{K_{i2}/L_{i2}}{K_{i1}/L_{i1}}$ in expression (2.37), we obtain

$$\frac{q_{i2}^*}{q_{i1}^*} = \frac{A(2)_i}{A(1)_i} \bar{w}^{\beta_i} \qquad (2.41)$$

which, written in log form is[1]

$$\log\left(\frac{q_{i2}^*}{q_{i1}^*}\right) = a_i + (\log \bar{w})\beta_i \qquad (2.42)$$

where

$$a_i = \frac{\log A(2)_i}{\log A(1)_i}$$

Provided that the values of a_i are not correlated with those of β_i (see Johansen [1961], pp. 777–8), fitting a regression line to industry observations on $\log q_{i2}^*/q_{i1}^*$ – the increases in productivity – and β_i – the shares of capital in value added, which, with the present assumptions, equal β_i – allows $\log \bar{w}_i$ and a_i to be estimated. When applied to Salter's figures for United Kingdom industries over the period 1924–50, capital deepen-

---

[1] If 1 and 2 are consecutive years, expression (2.42) is Swan's model,

$$q^* = a + \beta k^* \qquad (2.4c)$$

which, however, is now applied to cross-section as well as to time series data, and k^* and a are estimated from our (assumed) knowledge of q^* and β, rather than using, as Solow did, q^*, w_k ($= \beta$), and k^* to estimate a.

ing is shown to play a more significant role than in Solow's study, though shifts in the (implied) production function are still estimated to be substantial, see Johansen [1961], pp. 779–82.

In one paper, Solow [1960] accepted the embodiment hypothesis – technical advance enters only via gross investment – but maintained *ex-post* the *ex ante* substitution possibilities on existing vintages. Thus the *average* productivities of labour on vintages when they are manned at their 'optimum ratios', as determined by expectations concerning factor prices when they were installed, are lower, the older (i.e. earlier) are the vintages, but technical variations in the amounts of labour manning each vintage allow these levels of productivity to be departed from and *any* of the investment–labour ratios of the (then) *ex ante* production functions to be reproduced *ex post*. Adopting the neoclassical view that full employment of labour is either automatically·assured in the short run, *à la* Wicksell [1934], pp. 111–16, or is contrived by an all-wise government, see Meade [1961], Robinson [1961a], also Robinson [1965b], pp. 15–29, Swan [1956] (advised now and then and at the highest levels, by such well-known neoclassical Keynesians as Samuelson and Tobin), the available labour supply is allocated at each point of time over the existing vintages such that the *marginal* product of labour on each vintage is the same, equals the overall wage rate and total output is maximized. (The older is the vintage, the *less* labour-intensively will it be worked.) This viewpoint allows technical progress to affect the growth of labour productivity only when it is embodied via gross investment expenditure.

In order to illustrate the process, we show in fig. 2.5a the average and marginal productivity curves of three vintages – the latest (v_1), a medium-early (or -late) one (v_n), and one on the margin of scrapping (v_s) – together with the (product) wage rate (w_m/p). We in fact use a more complex production function than Cobb–Douglas which Solow used. The more complex function allows us to obtain a maximum average product and a minimum average cost for each vintage, and so, plants that can be scrapped. With Cobb–Douglas, scrapping of this nature *never* occurs because the *AP*s and *MP*s of *all* vintages go all the way from just above zero to just below infinity. Moreover, when the total labour force is distributed over the existing vintages so that the marginal product of labour is the *same* on each vintage, it is a further property of the Cobb–Douglas function that, *provided that the exponents are the same for each vintage*, the average product of labour will be the same on each also. In fig. 2.5b we show the corresponding cost curves

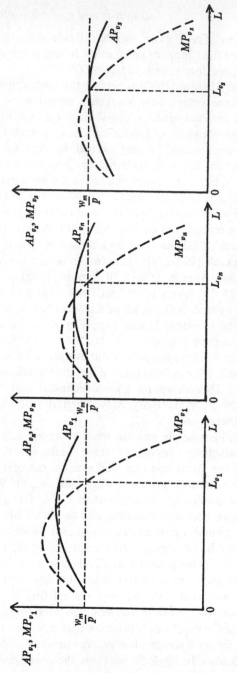

Fig. 2.5a. Solow's embodied, malleable model, productivity view

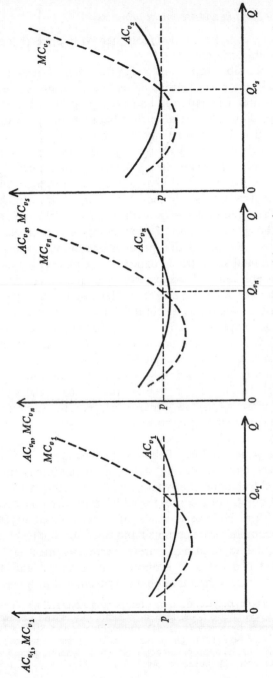

Fig. 2.5b. Solow's embodied, malleable model, cost view

(for our more complex model), together with price (equals marginal cost of all vintages in use).

Selecting plausible orders of magnitude Solow uses the model to perform again his measurement of technical progress exercise and to show that capital accumulation and deepening have a more significant part to play, though the relationship between the pace of investment and the rate at which productivity rises is not a simple one. Solow also provides a timely warning against being bedazzled by constant exponential rates of growth when doing 'back-of-an-envelope' calculations. Once we adopt the embodied view of technical progress, sudden spurts upwards (or downwards) in the *rate* of gross investment are more significant than trend rates of growth of the capital stock, as far as the impact on the rate of growth of productivity is concerned.

Solow also examines in this paper a one-number value measure of the vintage capital stock which depends crucially on the assumption of perfect foresight and realised expectations and which, given this, may take the place of K in his earlier model discussed above, pp. 47–51. 'Thus, if asset valuations faithfully reflected perfect foresight, the "homogeneous capital" model ... would be accurate, provided the capital stock were measured not by a count of machines but by the real market value of the stock of capital.' (Solow [1960], p. 100.)

But it would be unfair to imply that Solow takes much notice of this result, though he does call it 'remarkable'. This is the view of Solow, vintage '59. However, Solow, vintage '63, uses the same result in both his theoretical *and* empirical work on the rate of return on investment (see chapter 3, pp. 114–17 below).

In a later paper, Solow, Tobin, von Weizsäcker and Yaari [1966] analysed the case of 'quickening' – that in which there is only one viable 'best-practice' technique at any moment of time (the *ex ante* production function is a point, not a curve) for which there are no *ex post* substitution possibilities. No use is made of a generalized capital concept, competitive conditions are assumed and three sorts of technical progress – purely capital-augmenting, purely labour-augmenting and Hicks neutral[1] – and two types of economy – neoclassical and Keynesian – are examined. Purely capital-augmenting technical progress means that

---

[1] As the authors point out, technical progress is exogenous and autonomous. Making technical progress endogenous, related to factor prices and endowments, is the subject of papers by Kennedy [1964] and Atkinson and Stiglitz [1969], among others. Joan Robinson [1971], ch. 8, discusses the choice of technique in terms of the construction of the appropriate equipment in a dynamic setting with technical advances often occurring in the process.

only capital productivity rises over time; purely labour-augmenting means exactly the opposite – that labour alone gets the treatment. Hicks neutral means that factor productivities grow at the same rate so that marginal rates of substitution remain unchanged at given factor ratios. (In the case of 'quickening', however, where only one ratio of factors is relevant at any one time, Hicks neutral technical progress means that the ratio remains the same because the absolute amounts of the factor inputs per unit of output both decline by the same proportion.) The neoclassical economy is one in which the full employment of labour is automatically assumed; the Keynesian economy is one in which effective demand determines the level of output. In both economies, neoclassical modes of analysis are used, quasi-rents on vintages are shown to equal their marginal products, and the wage rate is shown to equal the marginal product (equals the average product) of the vintage on the margin of scrapping (the Salter process).

We may note in passing a basic disagreement between the two sides of the present debate which relates to whether or not it is legitimate, when analysing particular problems, to abstract from results established either earlier on or in other parts of the discipline. Thus neo-neoclassicals are very keen to sweep short-run effective demand puzzles under the carpet in their hurry to get on with the analysis of the long-run development of the economy and the part played by the price mechanism and competitive markets in this process. They tend to take it for granted that the Keynesian puzzles are being looked after either by the government (and not, one must say, without Keynes' own blessing, see Keynes [1936], pp. 378–9) or by the automatic working of an economic system *from which the effects of money have been removed*, and so are irrelevant.

Wicksell's work, see Wicksell [1934], provides an example of a neoclassical economist with the same tendencies. In his monetary theory he has a *short-run*, dynamic analysis of booms and slumps, of changes in prices, in which investment is a function of expected rates of profits, and divergences between the latter and money rates of interest determine whether investment levels are or are not sufficient to absorb planned savings. On the other hand, his interest in stationary states arose as much from his life-long concern with the *long-run* problems of overpopulation as from his *long-run* analysis of distribution through the workings of competition and the principle of marginal substitution. Finally, his passionate desire for greater equality in the distribution of income and property and for greater equity in the tax system, coupled with a fundamental belief in liberal principles and the importance of them for the flourishing of both enterprise and political freedoms, irresistibly calls to mind the basic interest and approach of the leading neoclassical Keynesian of our times, James Meade: see Samuelson [1965], p. 804.

Kaldor has flirted at various times with this approach, too: see Kaldor [1955–6, 1957, 1959a, 1959b], Kaldor and Mirrlees [1962], Harcourt [1963b] (but his reasons for either assuming or trying to demonstrate that full employment is established are different). Indeed his flirtation is so notorious that he has been teased by Samuelson [1964], p. 345, as Jean-Baptiste Kaldor. It has been the insistence by Joan Robinson in particular that this is *not* a legitimate procedure, that, *instead*, one must *always* view systems of thought and systems of analysis as integrated wholes, that has led to analyses such as the present one and to the two papers by Solow discussed on pp. 76–8 below.[1]

There are two key features of the 'quickening' model, the significance of which will become clear in our discussion of the double-switching debate in chapter 4 below. First, it is a one, all-purpose commodity model (though capital goods are described as heterogeneous). Secondly, the capital-augmenting case is dismissed as relatively uninteresting even though capital-augmenting technical progress has been shown to be the necessary and sufficient condition for the rigorous aggregation of hetero-geneous capital goods into one figure to be used in a neoclassical pro-duction function in which there are vintages and embodied technical progress: see Diamond [1965], F. M. Fisher [1965, 1969], Whitaker [1966].

As we have seen already in chapter 1, p. 46, Solow [1956a] had, earlier on, spelt out the conditions for aggregation in a simple world of two malleable capital goods and no technical progress, conditions which are akin to the present ones in that the rate of substitution of one capital good for another has to be independent of the amounts of labour used with each. In the 'quickening' case, when capital-augmenting technical progress occurs, the *average* productivity of labour never changes, *by definition*, from vintage to vintage. It follows that total 'capital' is just a head count of machines and knowledge of total employment and the average productivity of labour *on any vintage* is sufficient to determine the level of output – the distribution of labour amongst the machines need not be known *in this special case*. As we saw on pp. 69–72 above, when the total labour force is distributed amongst vintage Cobb–Douglas functions that have identical exponents so as to maximize their

[1] For a very clear statement of Solow's views on this point, see Solow [1962b], p. 76.

potential output, the average products of the vintages are equalized. This result is the basis of the empirical work that uses an 'effective' stock of capital in an aggregate production function, see chapter 3, pp. 116–17 below.

Neoclassical vintage models appeared to have reached their finest hour in Bliss's recent paper, 'On Putty Clay' (Bliss [1968a]), only for Bliss to be capped by Bardhan [1969] who claims to be able to do all that Bliss can do – and more (if not better). Bliss's paper is a rigorous examination of the earlier models of Salter [1960, 1965] and Johansen [1959]. It starts by emphasizing that there may *not* be a unique choice of technique under profit-maximizing assumptions, once very simple factor price expectations are departed from and the expected *economic* lives of the 'best-practice' techniques differ.

Bliss's point may perhaps be most simply put as follows. Suppose that the elasticity of substitution of the *ll* curve in fig. 2.3 above is very great and suppose further that businessmen have the simple but plausible expectations concerning the future course of their product wages set out on p. 58 above. Then, as we have seen, we get a positive association between expected longevity and investment-intensity. If the possibilities of substitution of investment for labour are very great, small (proportionate) increases in investment expenditure will lead to large savings in labour and so to considerable (proportionate) increases in expected economic lives. It follows that if we were to plot the discounted values of the expected quasi-rents of each technique (PV) against the investment expenditure per unit of output with which they are associated (i), we might not get a smoothly rising, concave-to-the-origin curve such as VV in fig. 2.6a, but, rather, one with bumps in it, such as $V''V''$ in fig. 2.6b.

If, now, we draw the 45° line, *ii*, in both figures, in fig. 2.6a there is a unique choice of technique – the maximum present value of investment expenditure is associated with i_1, the investment expenditure corresponding to the point where VV is parallel to *ii*. In fig. 2.6b, however, there may be more than one point, for example, those associated with i_2 and i_3. (Bliss is concerned to find points of zero as opposed to negative present values of investment expenditure – competition assures this in his model – so, strictly, we should show points of tangency of the VV and $V''V''$ curves with *ii*; the outcome, however, is essentially the same.)

Bardhan [1969] shows that Bliss's result holds *only* if the elasticity of substitution of the *ex ante* production function is greater than unity.

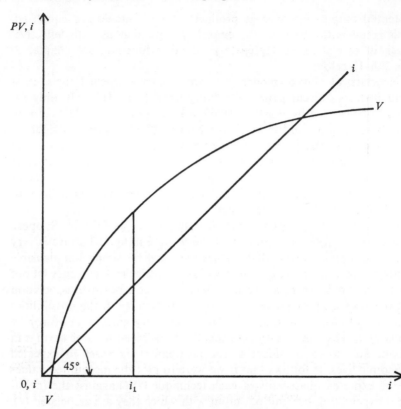

Fig. 2.6a. Unique choice of technique by *PV* rule

This cheers up Bardhan, though we may certainly ask why, since, as we show below, partly by drawing on his own work, see Bardhan [1967], we have as yet no reliable evidence as to what *are* the reasonable orders of magnitude that we should expect for this statistic.

The embodiment hypothesis has also been used, especially by Solow, to discuss the process of 'deepening' in a world of non-malleable capital goods, where there is therefore no possibility of *ex post* substitution, see Solow [1962a, 1963b], Robinson [1958, 1959, 1960]. The model is essentially Salter's but applied at the economy level. The purpose of the exercises was twofold: first, to show that neoclassical methods of analysis could be used and neoclassical results obtained in such a world, especially those that relate to factor productivities and factor rewards; secondly, to argue that observations taken from *short-run* production

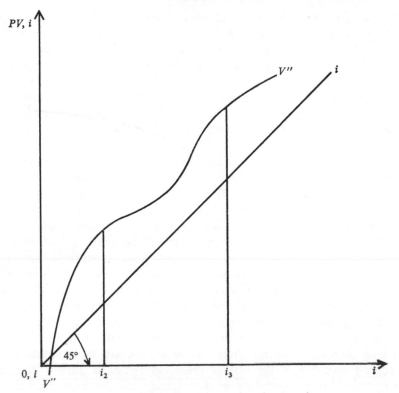

Fig. 2.6b. Multi-choice of technique by PV rule

functions in which the possibilities of substitution are limited or nil can
nevertheless provide data for good estimates of long-run substitution
possibilities as the types of machines installed change in response to
changes in factor prices over 'time', i.e. in the long period.

The pseudo-production function which is estimated is a series of
isolated islands of long-period equilibrium. This point is made very
clearly in Solow's discussion of a hoary old puzzle, the effect of changes
in the wage rate on the use of machinery, see Solow [1962a], pp. 215–16.
He shows that 'an increase in the wage rate leads to the construction of
new machinery of lower (i.e. more mechanized) type' *after* account has
been taken of the need for the higher (equilibrium) wage rate to be
associated with a lower (equilibrium) rate of profits. It is also an excellent example of, in this context, a legitimate application of the results of
a comparison to an analysis of a change. It is stressed that this is a pure

theory of production – the conditions under which the short-run full-employment level of output will in fact be demanded are not investigated. Constant returns to scale, competitive conditions and static expectations rule. Specific capital goods require fixed complementary amounts of labour to man them, though, because machines are divisible in Champernowne fashion, see above, chapter 1, p. 24, arguments which depend crucially on the ability to employ one more man may be used. A simple operating and scrapping rule of positive to zero quasi-rents presides.

An approach which is similar in some respects but which is designed for a different purpose, namely, to analyse the development through accumulation of an economy from the handicrafts industry stage to mechanized, capital-intensive industries, industry by industry, is used by Bensusan-Butt [1960] in *On Economic Growth*. This book is one of the really exciting contributions to the theory of economic growth in the post-war years. Charmingly written, and using apt quotes from Dorothy Parker's story, 'The Waltz', to head each chapter, it is one man's vision[1] of the historical process of growth over centuries, a process whereby techniques of production and institutions change endogenously and the macro aggregates which have become so fashionable in the post-*General Theory* era are shown to be the complicated outcomes of micro happenings in individual industries and firms. Indeed, Bensusan-Butt is properly sceptical of the role of these aggregates in growth theory, 'suspect[ing] that national income aggregates have, when stretched over centuries and not kept to their proper role in short-period analysis, little significance' (Bensusan-Butt [1960], p. 4). Again factor prices and competition are the means by which the processes occur and a slowly falling rate of profits, *the value of which at each moment is determined within the system*, plays a key role. Unless there is a shortage of land, the real wage rises as productivity in each industry, and in turn, rises.

Bensusan-Butt envisages an economy consisting, initially, entirely of handicraft industries in which labour alone is required. There are no capital goods and no accumulation. There exist, though, known

---

[1] 'Perhaps a mathematical idiot with neither time nor wit to keep up with the spate of contemporary literature should not tackle dynamic economics: but, once glimpsed, the vision of economic history as a largely determinate process is so obsessive that one must get it out of one's system,' preface, p. v. One could perhaps add, as a comment on Bensusan-Butt's work and adapting a view of E. H. Carr's on history (see Carr [1961], p. 37), that great economics is written precisely when the economist's vision of the past is illuminated by insights into the problems of the present.

mechanized techniques of production[1] which can be constructed by labour alone, i.e. the investment-goods sector is a handicraft industry, a very common assumption in this literature: see Solow [1962a], p. 207, for a justification. When these machines are manned by the appropriate team of workers, the productivity of the latter is raised. There is perfect competition in the goods and factor markets, perfect foresight and labour is homogeneous in all uses. It follows from these assumptions that if we inject an accumulation process into this economy, industries will become mechanized, labour both to man machines and to make them being absorbed from the handicrafts sectors, and prices of products will be forced down, and therefore real wages raised, in order that the additional products may be sold. (There will, however, be alternating phases of constant and falling prices, of one product only in turn, depending upon whether one industry's mechanization is being completed or another's just begun.)

The rate of profits at any moment of time is determined by the physical productivity of the machines in the industry which is on the margin of being mechanized, competitively determined factor and product prices being the agents by which this is achieved. In this way there emerges a recognizable process of accumulation, absorption of labour from handicraft to mechanized sectors, and falling rates of profits and rising real wages. (*There is as yet no population growth and, therefore, no land shortages and accompanying diminishing returns puzzles to worry about.* These are, however, introduced in the second model.) Coincident with these processes there occurs a falling general price level (measured in terms of current labour time, the standard of value in these economies), accompanied by a relative price structure which reflects the current rate of profits and the different productivities of the mechanized methods either existing or currently being introduced. At each step the author discusses the conditions of supply and demand in each industrial market. He considers the potential pitfalls which could interrupt the process, perhaps bring it to a close, and which

[1] Champernowne [1963] suggests in his review of Bensusan-Butt's book that technical progress could be introduced into the model by supposing that each mechanized technique became known shortly before it was introduced and that this would be preferable to assuming that the techniques were known from the beginning, especially as century-long processes are being analysed. This view is consistent with the approach taken by Atkinson and Stiglitz [1969] whereby changing factor prices induce the characteristics of the new 'best-practice' *points*; Bensusan-Butt's model would also then have a lot in common with Solow *et al.*'s analysis of 'quickening' except that (it is a big exception) he also considers *in detail* the nature of the demand for individual products, the inducement to invest and the supply of savings.

result from capitalists or workers, consumers or savers, not doing their things at the appropriate places.

Critics' corner

A number of criticisms of both malleable capital and vintage models, whether they serve entirely theoretical purposes or are the theoretical scaffolding for econometric exercises, have been made. To my mind, the most damning – and it applies to the whole structure of neoclassical thought – stems from Sraffa's 1960 book and is most conveniently dealt with in chapter 4 which is concerned with the double-switching and capital-reversing controversies. Suffice it to say here that it concerns a view of economic life and especially of the production process, price formation and income distribution that is more akin to that taken by the classical economists – Smith, Ricardo, Marx – than by the neoclassicals – Jevons, Marshall (though his long-run normal rate of profits is classical), Walras, Wicksteed, Wicksell – and the present group of 'modern theorists' at M.I.T., *et al.*

That much of the *technical* analysis in this field has been done by the attacked themselves (see, especially, Samuelson's work on linear programming in Stiglitz (ed.) [1966], part v, on the economics of Ricardo and Marx in Stiglitz (ed.) [1966], part iv, and on non-substitution theorems in Stiglitz (ed.) [1966], part vi) is a seeming paradox which disappears when the *objects* of the two groups are examined (see Bharadwaj [1963], Harcourt and Massaro [1964a, 1964b], Meek [1967], pp. 161–78, Nell [1967b]). (This also explains why Sraffa is *not* Leontief-come-lately – or early, for that matter.) The unifying principles which run through the works of Marshall, i.e. the principles of substitution and marginalism, allied with equilibrium (see Keynes [1933], pp. 223–4) and Samuelson [1947] – minimizing and maximizing behaviour under constraints and the existence of stable equilibria – are foreign to the ways of thought of both the classical economists and their modern descendants.

The second strand of criticism is especially associated with the works of Kaldor [1955–6, 1957, 1959a, 1959b, 1962, 1966]. It relates to a denial of the usefulness and the relevance of the assumptions of perfect (as opposed to *some*) competition, constant returns to scale, static expectations and perfect foresight, and marginalist and maximizing explanations of the choice of technique and factor rewards. For Kaldor, even the notion of a cost-minimizing choice of technique in a vintage model will not hold (see Kaldor and Mirrlees [1962]) and he substitutes, instead, a pay-off period criterion. Kaldor is, of course, an enthusiastic proponent of the embodied view of technical progress. He has himself produced technical progress functions of at least three vintages; he switched from a total one in Kaldor [1957] through a compromise in Kaldor [1959a] to a marginal one in Kaldor and Mirrlees [1962], following Black's impertinent reminder, Black [1962], that the first, when linear, implied a production function of a special form, Cobb–Douglas, no less! Kaldor did keep one strand of the original vintage approach, namely, the scrapping rule associated with the equality of the expected *price* and wage costs, though this is inconsistent, as Nuti [1969] points out, with an assumption of an imperfectly competitive market structure,[1] which no matter what its nature, will `always` ensure that prices are greater than the wage costs of *any* vintage operating (but see also, Robinson [1969c]).[2]

Kaldor also feels that a major contribution by Arrow [1962] – his work on learning by doing – puts a shaft through the pure form of neoclassical analysis, a view that reflects, presumably, Arrow's own summary of the implications of his article. Thus:

> The theorems about the economic world presented here differ from those in most standard economic theories: profits are the result of technical change; in a free-enterprise system, the rate of investment will be less than the optimum; net investment and the stock of capital become subordinate concepts, with gross investment taking a leading role. (p. 156.)

A third strand, whereby vintages themselves are the medium of criticism, relates to the use of CES production functions to estimate what in effect are the *ex ante* elasticities of substitution of capital for labour. It has been shown (see Robinson [1964a], also Robinson [1965b], pp. 30–5, Bardhan [1967], Harcourt [1964, 1966]) that if the neoclassical game is played in every sense *except* that vintages are taken into account, biases of measurement both enter and cannot adequately be allowed for.

The point may perhaps be most simply put as follows. To measure the *ex ante* elasticity of substitution, ideally we need observations on the *ex ante* production function itself, or, *if* we may assume that the choice of technique from the function is undertaken by cost-minimizing

---

[1] Kaldor is in excellent company on this one, see Sargent [1968], Harcourt [1968a, 1968b]. Solow *et al.* [1966] state the correct rule of *zero* quasi-rents, see pp. 111–12, where they tell of the price being the wage cost of the *no rent* vintage marked up by a profit margin.

[2] Kaldor [1970] admits the logic of Nuti's point but poses an hypothesis, as yet untested, that minimizes its importance empirically.

businessmen with static expectations, data on the labour productivity of the latest vintages and the current wage levels ruling in the same industries in different countries. We could then fit the regression equation

$$\log q = \log A + b \log w + \varepsilon \qquad (2.6)$$

to the data, see pp. 51–4 above.

In a vintage world, though, we have not observations on the labour productivity of the wage-earners on the latest machines, we only have observations on the *average* productivity of the *total* work force spread over *all* the vintages that are currently in use.[1] Moreover, the ratios of the productivity on the latest vintages to overall productivity in each industry and country are statistics which reflect the economic histories, and especially movements of wages and rates of accumulation, of each industry in each country for periods for which there are vintages operating in their respective capital stocks. If these ratios were random numbers (which they would be if technical progress could be regarded *as if* it had been completely disembodied – the ACMS procedure), this would not matter statistically. The coefficient, *b*, would be a less efficient but unbiased estimate of the *ex ante* elasticity of substitution. But as soon as we admit, as we must, the possibility that the ratios may be related in systematic ways to, say, wage levels and their rates of growth, or to the number of vintages in operation, or to past rates of gross investment, biases are introduced which cause the slopes of the regression lines which are fitted to the obtainable data to diverge from the slopes of regression lines fitted to the ideal data (if only we had them). Moreover, subsequent investigations of the nature of the biases suggest, first, that they are substantial and, secondly, that the discrepancies between the observed and desired slopes could go *either* way, depending upon which *a priori* and equally plausible story is told, see Harcourt [1966]. Bardhan [1967] is able to predict the direction – it's up – but only by telling an implausible story, 'one special, albeit interesting, case' (p. 329).

With some *people for friends you don't need enemies*

Finally, mention should be made of what, perhaps, is the most unkindest cut of all,[2] namely, the work of Jorgenson and Griliches [1966,

---

[1] Or, rather, to obtain the former data we would need to do some hard work in the form of sample surveys, see Salter [1962].
[2] Readers who object to this phrase should brush up their Shakespeare.

1967] on overall factor productivity and technical change. Though neoclassical to their finger tips – they assume perfect competition and constant returns to scale, factors are paid their marginal products and price ratios of commodities equal marginal rates of transformation – they argue that the finding that the bulk of the rise in output per man is due to 'technical progress' results from the faulty measurement of input services in the aggregate production function. Correcting for this they advance the (refutable) hypothesis that the rise in total output is largely explained by the growth of total inputs and not by improvements in them (or, rather, that the improvements are subsumed *within* the inputs by correct measurement). Their measure of the rate of growth of total factor productivity (which on their hypothesis should be approximately – nil) is a quantum index of growth in outputs, each weighted by its value share in total output, *less* a similar index of the rates of growth of input services, weighted in a similar fashion. A shift in the aggregate production function occurs if this rate of growth is greater than zero, otherwise all growth is due to movements *along* a given production function (in *n*-dimensional space).

The wheel has turned 360°: an implication of Solow's findings in 1957 was that the traditional economic factors, capital accumulation and deepening, had bit parts only in the growth saga. The backlash, foreseen and partly cheered on by Hicks [1960], has come, first, through embodied technical progress and, now, through the Jorgenson–Griliches script. The traditional economic factors and neoclassical processes are again the stars and the other factors have been left with virtually no role at all – they have been written out of the script. A comment by Smithies [1962] on Solow's [1962b] paper on investment and the rate of economic growth seems relevant here:

> Perhaps the whole problem is too complicated for adequate reflection in a formal model. In that event, we could do worse than re-read Adam Smith (or possibly read him for the first time). In Book I, he said that the division of labour was the mainspring of economic progress; and in Book II, that accumulation was a necessary condition for increased division of labour. How far have we got beyond that? (p. 92.)

The essence of the approach of Jorgenson and Griliches is the hypothesis that all *observed* relative product and factor prices may be interpreted as pairs of marginal rates of transformation, such as would be thrown up by the workings of competitive markets containing utility-maximizing consumers and profit-maximizing, cost-minimizing businessmen. If this identification of observed with theoretical variables is accepted, we may use the quantum index of the growth in total output and total inputs (or their 'dual', the indexes of their respective total prices) to test the hypothesis that the growth is nil. It must be stressed that this *is* a refutable hypothesis and not, as Denison [1966], p. 76, argued, a consequence of national-accounting identities. His confusion arose because he viewed the change in the inputs (and the outputs) as the sum of the increases in *both* prices *and* quantities whereas the essence of Jorgenson and Griliches's definition is that *either* the (changes in) quantities *or* (those in) prices (*but not both together*) are combined into aggregate indexes and compared one with another. It is therefore possible to start with the national-accounting identity, total output (in value terms) equals total input (similarly measured), and yet end with a refutable hypothesis, one which reflects moreover Jorgenson and Griliches's views as to how the values of the observed prices arose in the first place.

Thus, we first write the national-accounting identity

$$\sum_{i=1}^{n} p_i \bar{q}_i = \sum_{j=1}^{m} x_j y_j \tag{2.43}$$

where p_i = price of good, i, $i = 1, \ldots, n$
$\bar{q}_i$ = quantity of good i
x_j = price of input, $j, j = 1, \ldots, m$
and y_j = service of input j
Then a quantum index of the rate of growth of total output ($\bar{Q}$) is

$$\bar{Q} = \sum_{1}^{n} \frac{p_i \bar{q}_i}{\Sigma p_i \bar{q}_i} \frac{\dot{\bar{q}}_i}{\bar{q}_i} \tag{2.44}$$

The corresponding index for total input (Y) is

$$Y = \sum_{1}^{m} \frac{x_j y_j}{\Sigma x_j y_j} \frac{\dot{y}_j}{y_j} \tag{2.45}$$

and the first part of the basic hypothesis is

$$\frac{\bar{Q}}{Y} = 1 \quad \text{(i.e. } \bar{Q} - Y = 0) \tag{2.46}$$

which, clearly, is *not* a truism.

Now write the aggregate production function implicitly as

$$F(\bar{q}_1, \bar{q}_2, \ldots, \bar{q}_n; \quad y_1, y_2, \ldots, y_m) = 0 \qquad (2.47)$$

The second part of the hypothesis whereby observed prices are married to the equilibrium production relations and marginal rates of transformation is that

$$\begin{aligned}
\frac{\partial \bar{q}_i}{\partial y_j} &= -\frac{F_j}{F_i} = \frac{x_j}{p_i} \\
\frac{\partial \bar{q}_i}{\partial \bar{q}_k} &= -\frac{F_k}{F_i} = \frac{p_i}{p_k} \\
\frac{\partial y_j}{\partial y_l} &= -\frac{F_l}{F_j} = \frac{x_l}{x_j}
\end{aligned} \qquad (2.48)$$

The estimates of the capital services (which, in principle, should be, say, machine hours) have to be done by chains of inference and the use of assumptions, the most dubious of which are that competitive producer equilibrium conditions were in fact satisfied and that all machines worked to the same proportion of their capacities, as given by the power industries' performance. (The latter assumption is devastatingly criticized by Denison [1966], who gets his own back with interest.) The price of the capital service of each good is the price of each investment good multiplied by the rate of return on *all* capital *plus* the rate of depreciation and an adjustment for any capital gains on each capital good. The rate of return on *all* capital is the non-wage share of value added inclusive of capital gains divided by the value of the accumulated capital stocks; the whole procedure is a statistical reflection of the neo-classical procedure as outlined by Champernowne [1953–4] and Swan [1956]. This approach makes explicit the important point that flows of services, not stocks of factors, actually *produce* output, a point with which no one would disagree (but the practical significance of which is much reduced by* the assumption of uniform capacity working). Whether they would accept the method of aggregation of the services is another matter.

Lydall [1969] has developed a measure of technical progress which is similar to that used by Jorgenson and Griliches but which is statistically tractable and which does not depend upon assumptions about the natures of producer equilibrium and market structures. Indeed Lydall's approach is an excellent compromise between the so-called NBER approach of 'measurement without theory' and the over-reaction to this which in recent years has produced ultra-refined and -rigorous theories that have no hope ever of being tested against the rough, error-full data of even our most advanced economies. Lydall looks for simple categories and concepts and when he makes a simplifying assumption, he has an economic statistician's feel for the orders of magnitude of the errors that are likely to be introduced. If they are peanuts he presses on, as is right and proper.

Mention should also be made in this context of the work of Rymes [1968, 1971]. Rymes has spelt out the dynamic implications of Sraffa's implied criticism of marginal analysis for the neoclassical measures of technical progress, i.e. of the relevance of Sraffa's concentration on the *interdependence* of the economic system for the concept of capital as a primary input: see Sraffa [1960] and the appendix to chapter 4 below. Rymes shows that Joan Robinson and Harrod's measure of neutral technical progress – also Read's [1968] – reflect Sraffa's view, whereas the neoclassical measures do not. Essentially, if commodities are produced by commodities, measures of technical progress that treat the production process as a one-way flow from factors to products will fail to pick up the feed-back effects of technical progress from one activity to another.

The point may be put in terms of Solow's all-purpose one commodity model of disembodied technical change: see Solow [1957], and pp. 47–51[1] above. Consider an economy which has a constant saving ratio and in which technical progress occurs in the sense that output per head at a given capital–labour ratio rises. More is now saved than would have been otherwise so that the capital–labour ratio rises *more than it would have*, had the saving ratio been the same but the technical advance not occurred. Should we attribute the extra rise in capital per head to accumulation or to technical advance? It is achieved by saving more but the economy can save more because the technical advance has occurred. (Moreover, the impact of a given amount of saving on output per head is now greater because of the technical advance.) Solow's measure of technical progress would attribute the rise *solely* to saving and the rise in productivity per man *due to deepening* would be assessed by the increment of output per head along the *initial* production function, with the residual change being due to technical progress (see fig. 2.1 above). This robs technical progress of some of its contribution by failing fully to take into account its impact on capital *as an input* whereby the latter is improved, i.e. made more efficient. Read [1968] and Rymes [1968, 1971] show that by measuring capital *in real terms*,

[1] The following argument is due to Joan Robinson (1970a], p. 316.

this error may be avoided in both one- and two-commodity models.

We have not heard the last of vintage models, the measurement of technical progress nor, indeed, of malleability: see, for example, Katz [1968a], a paper in which productivity growth in Australia and Argentina is compared, using Solow's 1957 method, and Sampson [1969], in which, though the starting point is Salter's work, the author nevertheless sturdily ignores Salter's major contribution of vintages.[1] These assumptions have great analytical and mathematical convenience and the hold of them on econometric methodology is still fast. There is no reported instance, as there is of one man's confrontation with the binomial theorem, of anyone being reduced to tears by the sight of Cobb–Douglas 'because it is so beautiful' – but clearly many members of the trade have had lumps in their throats, even as seasoned a campaigner as Phelps Brown: see Phelps Brown [1968], Phelps Brown with Browne [1968], pp. 337–8.

After a masterly survey of alternative theories of distribution and of the distribution of the product (of manufacturing industry) between pay and profits in five advanced industrial economies, he selects as the best explanation of the stylized facts thrown up by his researches – a constant rate of profits of 10 per cent per annum, a share of pay in product of 75 per cent, and a steady capital–output ratio of two and a half – a Cobb–Douglas constant-returns-to-scale aggregate production function allied with neutral technical progress. He couples them with a new twist – a perfectly elastic supply curve of savings at a rate of profits of 10 per cent. The exponents of the Cobb–Douglas are such as to give a marginal product of capital (equals the rate of profits) of 10 per cent and also the values of the other observed 'great ratios'. The wage of labour (equals its marginal product) grows at the same rate as average productivity. The rate of profits is determined, along with the capital–labour ratio, by the intersection of the demand curve for investment (with a little juggling and licence, the marginal product of capital curve) with the perfectly elastic supply curve of savings. The rate of profits therefore remains constant, thus suggesting that the fruits of progress go entirely to labour. This, however, is an anti-wage-earner way of putting it; if the profit-receivers breed less fast than the wage-earners, because they have either more sense or less vitality, their *income* per head will rise faster than that of the lower classes.

---

[1] It would be unfair, however, to make only this comment on Sampson's work since it is, overall, excellent, especially the very neat tie up that he provides between the models of Salter, Solow and ACMS.

The perfectly elastic supply curve of savings reflects Phelps Brown's vision that liberal capitalism provides the appropriate environment in which enterprise may flourish and produce this response. His model – if correct – provides the justification for Johansen's factual assumptions (see, especially, p. 68 above). It is, however, a little surprising that Phelps Brown should have such faith in the present hypothesis, especially when we consider the formidable arguments of his earlier paper on the Cobb–Douglas, see Phelps Brown [1957], arguments which subsequently have been reinforced by the recent work of F. M. Fisher, see F. M. Fisher [1969, 1970], and chapter 4, pp. 173–5 below.

The reasons for the fast hold of this methodology on theoreticians and practical men alike, apart from those already covered, are examined in the next chapter, which is on the rate of return on investment. This is the other main stream that flowed from Joan Robinson's original strictures against the production function approach and the impossibility of measuring capital outside worlds of stationary or growing equilibria – her fabulous but mythical Golden Ages.

3 Solow on the rate of return: tease and counter-tease

Preliminaries to the main bout

Another offshoot of the criticisms of the use of the concept of malleable capital both in theoretical analysis and in the aggregate production function is the work on the social rate of return on investment, which is associated especially with Solow. His views are set out in the 1963 De Vries Lectures, Solow [1963a], in his contribution to the Dobb *Festschrift*, Solow [1967], and in the subsequent exchanges with Pasinetti in Solow [1970] and Pasinetti [1970]. (In the company of Tobin, von Wiezsäcker and Yaari [1966], he added further thoughts in the analysis of 'quickening'.) These sources, together with Joan Robinson's review article of Solow [1963a] (Robinson [1964b], reprinted as Robinson [1965b], pp. 36–47), help to crystallize the nature of the approach and to highlight some of the causes of the controversies between Cambridge, England, and Cambridge, Mass.

Partly the debate is about definitions and the meaning of tautologies; partly it is about whether any positive or normative significance may be attached to results that imply that the rate of return on investment is equal to the rate of profits. Here, as elsewhere, though, there seem to be legitimate doubts as to whether one side really understands what the other is supposed to be saying. But if one side may be said to be guilty of setting up straw men of their own making, the better and more effectively to knock them down again, the other is equally as guilty of employing dodges and feints which, in typical 'learning by doing' fashion, were acquired as a result of the experience gained in previous rounds.

In this chapter we discuss the exchanges between Solow and Joan Robinson, postponing our account of the Pasinetti–Solow bout until the discussion of the reswitching and capital-reversing controversies in chapter 4, where it more naturally belongs. Joan Robinson [1970a, 1970b] subsequently added some further thoughts, in the light of the double-switching debate, on the issues specifically discussed in this chapter.

Solow wished to analyse the empirical relationship between capital accumulation and economic growth in industrialized countries today. (His two examples are the United States and West Germany, a choice dictated as much by limitations of data as by a desire to compare maturity with vigour.) He argues that the appropriate (or only) theoretical tools are 'a modernized version of neoclassical or late-Wicksellian capital theory' (Solow [1963a], p. 8), elsewhere described 'as a modern amalgamation of Wicksell and Irving Fisher' (p. 17).[1] Solow believes the key concept of capital theory to be *the rate of return on investment.* His own contribution is to introduce technical progress and to consider the relationship between saving and investment and the long-run growth of productive capacity.

The analysis is prefaced by a discussion of *why* there are recurring controversies in capital theory. Solow gives two reasons, one of which is ideological – the social function of providing an ideological justification for profit (Joan Robinson [1971] would argue that it was rentier income) which in the nineteenth century was the non-Marxist backlash; the other reason is analytical – it's difficult. The first reason is not supposed to impugn in any way and by itself either the motives of the economists who provided it or the scientific validity of their doctrine. (No doubt the same will be said of the value-free, scientifically objective analysis of the anonymous compilers of *The Report from Iron Mountain*, Lewin [1967].)

I suspect that here at least some participants in the debate part company, as they would also over his view that the elegant show-piece of modern economics, the resource-allocation implications of a system of prices or shadow prices, is free of ethical overtones: on this, see, for example, Dobb [1940] and Dobb [1967], p. 162. Dobb argues convincingly that even such a seemingly ethically innocuous concept as the elasticity of demand positively bristles with values and preconceived 'pictures of the real world'. Stigler [1941], p. 297, makes a similar point to Solow's when he deplores the fact that J. B. Clark's marginal pro-

---

[1] The best modern account of Fisher's theory (apart, that is, from Fisher's own, see Fisher [1930]) is to be found in Hirshleifer's well-known article, Hirshleifer [1958]. Dewey [1965] gives a simplified version which, while technically sound, is marred by his method of presentation, which is unfair to Fisher's predecessors or rivals and to those of Dewey's contemporaries with whom he happens to disagree. Blaug [1968] has an excellent chapter on Wicksell, as has Stigler [1941], provided that the reader can work out for himself Stigler's rarely explicit statements of what to Stigler is truth. The relevant portions of the appendix to Swan's [1956] article have been cited already as things of beauty ...

ductivity theory contained 'prescription as well as ... analysis', an ethical system 'of dubious merits', an exposition which 'more than that of any other eminent contemporary economist, afforded some grounds for the popular and superficial allegation that neoclassical economics was essentially an apologetic for the existing economic order' – but he hurries on to applaud Clark's scientific contributions. No doubt, both Solow and Stigler would agree that 'the less, therefore, man clogs the free play of his mind with political doctrine and dogma, the better for his thinking' (quoted by E. H. Carr [1961], p. 39) – but which of them would it make the Sir Lewis Namier of economics?

To escape from the first reason for controversy, all that is necessary, according to Solow, 'is to draw a conceptual line between the imputed return to capital and the income of capitalists', to have 'a theory of distribution among factors of production, if not among persons'. I rudely commented at this point in my survey: 'As the baby said, move over, bathwater, here I come', a comment which I stick to. It is possible to accept the logic of Solow's distinction without accepting the implication that controversy will thereby vanish. Moreover, economists ought to ask: 'Is profit justified?' – as well as the equally valid questions: 'How does it arise and what determines its size?' Indeed the answers to the last two questions may be extremely relevant for the answer to the first question. Economists ought to examine the institutions of particular societies and, in addition to analysing their implications for the *workings* of the economy, ask whether they are good or bad, just or unjust and what may be done about them. The purging of economics (and economists) of questions of this sort, ostensibly in order to sharpen our senses (which is good) but also in order to produce that never-was animal, a value-free, objective science, may go so far that in ridding ourselves of rubbish we may also remove, as repeated doses of castor oil do, the vital bacteria which alone allow the large intestine and, ultimately, the body, to flourish – and survive. Values should be recognized honestly, stated explicitly (as should opponent's arguments) – and defended stoutly. Faulty logic is to be deplored in any approach.

As a corollary of his viewpoint, Solow believes that, sometimes, the best way to understand capitalism is to think about socialism. There would be more agreement about the reverse proposition: see Robinson [1960], part 5, Robinson [1964b], also Robinson (1965b), pp. 36–47. Thus:

... the notion of factor allocation in conditions of perfect competition makes sense in a normative theory of a planned economy rather than in a descriptive theory for a capitalist economy, and . . . the notion of the marginal productivity of investment makes sense in the context of socialist planning. (Robinson [1964b], p. 410, also Robinson [1965b], p. 36.)

Solow goes on to argue that only someone who is naively identifying the many aspects of capitalistic production with one of them (he mentioned the Austrian's 'time' as 'an inspired simplification' which did not come off) would believe that the theory could be summed up by defining something called 'capital' and calling the rate of interest the marginal product of 'it'. But a head count of articles in the relevant literature surely would show that this is *just* what a large proportion of the trade is doing.

Solow's basic puzzle concerning a simple, unique measure of capital which in fact has many dimensions and characteristics has been put splendidly by Swan [1956] as follows:

That there should be great difficulties in handling the concept of Capital in a process of change is not surprising. A piece of durable equipment or a pipe-line of work-in-progress has dimensions in time that bind together sequences of inputs and outputs jointly-demanded or jointly-supplied at different dates. The aggregation of capital into a single stock at a point of time is thus the correlative of an aggregation of the whole economic process, not only in cross-section (which gives rise to the ordinary index-number problems), but also in time itself: in other words, the reduction of a very high-order system of lagged equations – in which each event, its past origins and its future consequences, could be properly dated and traced backward and forward in time – to a more manageable system with fewer lags. This second kind of aggregation introduces a further set of ambiguities, similar in principle to those of index-numbers, but as yet hardly investigated . . . From the idea of capital as a single stock there is in principle no sudden transition to 'the enormous who's who of all the goods in existence'. Between the two extremes lies an ascending scale of *n*th-order dynamic systems, in which capital like everything else is more and more finely sub-divided and dated, with ascending degrees of (potential) realism and (actual) complexity. In fact, most of us are left at ground-level, on ground that moves under our feet. (p. 345.)

As a self-confessed middlebrow, Solow sees the rate of return on investment as the link between highbrow capital theory – the micro-economic theory of resource allocation and prices which allows for the fact that commodities can be transformed into others over time and which is only complete when it also explains the distribution between factors – and lowbrow theory, which is concerned with aggregation and approximation and relates to the empirical implications of saving and investment decisions. By analysing these problems in terms of a rate of return, i.e. a *price*, we take cognizance of the fact that 'the theory of capital has as its "dual" a theory of intertemporal pricing . . .' (Solow [1963a], p. 14.)

Solow classifies capital theories as either technocratic or descriptive. They are technocratic when planning and allocation questions (and so socialism) are discussed, descriptive when used in an explanation of the workings of capitalism. Joan Robinson and Solow are on common ground when he discusses a further reason for difficulty in descriptive capital theory, namely, that 'capital problems are inevitably bound up with questions of uncertainty, limited foresight and reactions to the unexpected' (p. 13), all areas in which no notable progress has, as yet, been made in economic analysis. Joan Robinson's reaction has been to argue that certain concepts, the value of 'capital', 'the rate of profits', for example, can only be given meaning when uncertainty is absent and expectations are realized – hence the concentration on Golden Age situations; Solow's reaction is candidly to ignore it in the analysis that follows. Finally Solow also warns us that by dodging the ideological overtones, we may destroy the bridge that leads to descriptive theory, especially that relating to the workings of capitalist economies, and be left with only technocratic answers about the consequences but not the causes, of saving and investment decisions.

Main bout, round one

The upshot of the preliminary discussion is that, in Solow's view, the central concept of capital theory should be the rate of return on investment, i.e. capital theory should be about interest rates, not capital.[1]

---

[1] Irving Fisher's theory is concerned principally with the determination of a rate of return on investment as the outcome of the interplay of the forces of productivity – the technical possibilities of transforming present goods into future goods as given by well-behaved investment-opportunity schedules – with those of thrift – the subjective rates, as given by their respective indifference curves, at which individuals swap present goods for future goods: see Hirshleifer [1958]. Capital is not mentioned explicitly though investment is. Borrowing and lending possibilities are also introduced so that individuals and, latterly, societies, are not confined to points of tangency of their indifference curves with investment-opportunity schedules alone: see N. C. Miller [1968].

This makes for clarity, while concentrating on 'time' or 'capital' or the 'marginal productivity of capital' (or labour) makes for confusion.

What, then, is the rate of return on investment? Consider a planned economy which has a stock of heterogeneous capital goods, produces a certain volume of one consumption good and is at full employment with its inputs efficiently allocated. (Efficient means only that it is impossible to have more of anything without less of something else.) Compare this situation with possible neighbourhood efficient arrangements in which there is a little less consumption and therefore more capital goods (in physical, not necessarily in value terms). Now change over to an alternative arrangement by saving, i.e. reducing consumption. This allows a one-period gain (the next) in consumption *over what it would have been*. Make sure that the *biggest* gain is chosen for a given reduction in consumption now. Finally suppose that in the period after the next the economy reaches the position that it intended to be at by that period anyway. That is, the economy over the three periods has had decided for it – we are all technocrats now – a consumption stream

$$C_0 - h, \ C_1 + j, \ C_2, \ldots$$

instead of one of

$$C_0, \ C_1, \ C_2, \ldots$$

Then a natural definition of the *one-period* rate of return on investment (R_1) is

$$R_1 = \frac{j-h}{h} = \frac{j}{h} - 1 \tag{3.1}$$

... perfectly natural usage. If by saving an extra \$1.00 of consumption this year society can enjoy at most \$1.10 of consumption next year without endangering its later prospects, then one would certainly want to say that society has earned 10 per cent on its investment. (Solow [1963a], p. 19.)

At the other extreme is the average rate of return in perpetuity (R_∞) whereby a reduction of consumption now (h) adds p per period *extra* consumption for ever *over what it would have been otherwise*, in which case

$$R_\infty = \frac{p}{h} \tag{3.2}$$

In between these two, we may distinguish, conceptually, 2-, 3-, ..., n-period average rates of return (though Solow feels that, in practice, the one-period, ten-period and perpetuity rates of return may be all we know and all we need to know). Nor need we always think of a rise in saving (equals investment) followed by a temporary or permanent mini-orgy; we could just as easily consume now, pay later, always remembering that with not-so-smooth though often well-behaved technologies even small rises in current consumption may differ from small falls as far as the sizes of their rates of return are concerned. Solow is especially attracted to the one-period rate of return 'because, in a highly developed and complex growing economy, saving-investment decisions come up for reconsideration every period and can easily be changed or even undone' (p. 21).

The measure is intimately associated with displacements from basic situations. In the nineteenth century the situations would have been stationary states from which small displacements were made – the classic neoclassical procedure incisively described by Swan [1956] (see also chapter 1, p. 38 above). The modern equivalent is the balanced growth path. We should note the vital importance in all these definitions of an implicit assumption either that saving may be transformed into investment *without affecting relative prices* or that we are analysing a one-commodity model. Without these assumptions, saving, in the sense of consumption forgone, will not necessarily add the additional consumption because, depending on *how* prices change, it will be associated with different amounts and types of investment. Hence Solow concentrates on *small* changes – the notional changes of the neoclassical procedure – and, as we shall see below in chapter 4, p. 168, the prices corresponding to a switch-point rate of profits: see Solow [1967, 1970].

Solow claims that calculating the rate of return requires no measure of the stock of capital, not even necessarily a mention of it, although in some of his theoretical examples and in his empirical work he is unfaithful to himself. He also claims that neoclassical theory, in so far as it centres around the rate of return, can escape from the malleability assumption and 'can accommodate fixity of form and proportions both' (p. 27). As an aside but very much related to the malleability assumption, he comments that J. B. Clark's jelly assumption (see Stigler [1941], chapter XI, and Samuelson [1962]) makes the analysis easier (it does, even when jelly is butter, see pp. 99–109 below). Moreover it contains the important kernel of truth that substitution possibilities are easier over longer periods of time even though at any moment of time capital goods may be highly specific and substitution possibilities *ex post* (if not *ex ante*) limited: see Hicks [1932], pp. 19–21.

This seems to be literally true only if we are considering the working out in *actual* time of the possibilities which exist at the beginning of a Marshallian long period, while not allowing anything to change, other than what was expected to change at the start of the period. The application of results from this analysis to real-world happenings is, therefore, suspect, as Salter [1960, 1965], for example, has so clearly shown.

It is much better, especially when dealing with the problems that Solow has in mind in the present context, to get away from the neo-classical stationary state with its given *total* factor supplies and into the vintage world where *investment* decisions are made on the basis of the *ex ante* production function, at the margins of the capital stock, which does not, however, have to be measured. It is in this world, as we have seen, that Marshall's long-period analysis properly breathes and moves and has its being.[1] Ferguson [1969], however, sees the malleability assumption as a convenient way of analysing tendencies associated with substitution possibilities untrammelled by the constraints of the short period. This highlights a fundamental disagreement between the two sides. One argues that a grip on the real world must always be kept in analysis, though simplifications are, of course, needed, while the other argues that tendencies may be analysed in isolation even though they will not, of necessity, ever show up in their pure form in actual situations. Hence Joan Robinson, for example, stresses that, by definition, actions always take place in the short run, so that only rarely should it be abstracted from.

Rates of return on investment are calculated by Solow for two 'poles apart' models of planned economies. The first is an all-purpose one-commodity model with a smooth, well-behaved, constant-returns-to-scale production function; the second is Worswick's stockade dictator version of Joan Robinson's model of accumulation (see Worswick [1959]). One-period and perpetuity rates of return are obtained and these are shown, in the neoclassical case, to equal the *net* marginal product of capital.[2] The two extreme cases are chosen in order to show '. . . that the rate of return . . . does not depend for its existence and meaning on the possibility of defining "marginal productivities" or having smoothly variable proportions between the factors of production' (Solow [1963a], p. 30). For the record, Solow's real-life appropriate

---

[1] Stigler [1941], p. 303, makes the same point as Solow in his discussion of J. B. Clark's concept of capital. See also Hicks [1932], pp. 19–22.

[2] The neoclassical case is illustrated below, see pp. 105–9, where it fits more conveniently into the development of the argument.

assumption would be near fixed technical coefficients in the short run and a 'fairly wide range of substitutability . . . in the long run'. (See also, Hicks [1932], p. 20.) The results in both models are then whipped over to market economies where the only possible outcome of competitive conditions in *both* models is that, in equilibrium, 'the rate of interest must equal the rate of return on investment'. (This is illustrated for Worswick's model, see pp. 97–9 below.) These results are offered as the answer (or, rather, an answer) to the important question: What is the pay-off to society from an extra bit of saving transformed into capital formation?

In Worswick's model there is no *direct* substitution between capital and labour, but, overall, proportions may be varied by changing the distribution of the total work-force between the three sectors of the economy. These are the two consumption-good sectors, one of which is handicrafts, the other, mechanized, and the capital-good or machine-making sector, which is also a handicrafts sector. For simplicity we assume that machines last for ever.[1] We now derive an expression for the perpetuity rate of return and show that it is equal to the rate of profits (equals the rate of interest) if the economy is a competitive market one and *if* – a big one – the collective outcome of the behaviour of atomistic businessmen coincides with the outcome that the dictator may consciously plan for.

In the handicrafts part of the consumption-good sector, *one* man working for *one* period produces *b* units of the consumption good (there is only one).

In the mechanized part of the consumption-good sector *n* men working on *one* machine for *one* period produce *nc* units of the consumption good. In the machine-making sector *m* men working for *one* period produce *one* machine.

At the start of the analysis there are M machines and L men allocated as follows

L_h to consumption handicrafts
L_c to mechanized consumption production
L_m to machine-making

i.e.
$$L = L_h + L_c + L_m \tag{3.3}$$

Clearly
$$L_c = nM \tag{3.4}$$

(and we assume that $L_c < \{L - L_m\}$, i.e. $L_h > 0$). Suppose that at the start

---

[1] Solow assumes radioactive depreciation but this does not significantly affect the argument, so, for simplicity, we drop it.

of the analysis, i.e. in period 0, $L_m = 0$, so that total consumption (C_0) is

$$C_0 = ncM + bL_h$$
$$= cL_c + b(L - L_c) \qquad (3.5)$$

Now suppose that the dictator decides in period 0 that saving is a 'good thing' and moves one man from consumption handicrafts to the machine-making sector, so sacrificing, i.e. saving, b units of the consumption good. Consumption in period 0 now becomes: $C_0' = C_0 - b$, and $1/m$ machines are added to the capital stock by the end of the period, i.e. $1/m$ is the investment of the period. In period 1 (and ever after if the dictator decides that he has had enough of a good thing), consumption (C_1) will be

$$C_1 = nc\left(M + \frac{1}{m}\right) + b(L - L_c') \qquad (3.6)$$

where

$$L_c' = n\left(M + \frac{1}{m}\right)$$

The increase in consumption as between the 'otherwise' situations ($\Delta C_i, i = 1, 2, \ldots, \infty$), starting with period 1 and continuing for ever is

$$\Delta C_i = C_1 - C_1' \qquad (3.7)$$

where $C_1' = C_0$ (in *amount*, not in *time*)

i.e.

$$\Delta C_i = \frac{nc}{m} - \frac{bn}{m} \qquad (3.8)$$

and, by definition,

$$R_\infty = \frac{\Delta C_i}{b} = \frac{n}{m}\left(\frac{c}{b} - 1\right) \qquad (3.9)$$

We may note in passing that, because machines last for ever, we have ΔC_i for ever, not just for one period, and whether we like it or not, so that R_1 does not exist. Or, at least, it does *only* if we leave the new machines idle in period 2 and go back to where we would have been then, had no saving been done in period 0. It may be shown that R_1, thus calculated, equals R_∞.

One machine and n men working for one period produce nc units of the consumption good. In a competitive economy this amount, nc, must be sufficient to pay the wages (w per man) of n men and provide the rate of profits, r, on the value of the machine, wm, supposing wages to be paid at the *end* of the gestation period of production of the machine,

i.e.
$$nc = wn + rwm \tag{3.10}$$

But as long as there *is* a consumption handicrafts sector, $w = b$ (shades of Bensusan-Butt [1960]), because one man, unaided, can produce b per period, which is, therefore, the opportunity cost of transferring him to the machine-making sector and the wage payment needed to do so. It follows that

$$nc = bn + rbm \tag{3.11}$$

and, so, from expressions (3.10), (3.11) and (3.9), that

$$r = \frac{n}{m}\left(\frac{c}{b} - 1\right) = R_\infty \tag{3.12}$$

We are, of course, in a very funny sort of economy (as Solow would be the first to admit). Handicraft workers dutifully transfer from their branch of the consumption-good sector to the machine-making sector whenever atomistic businessmen sense profit opportunities in the mechanized branch of the consumption-good sector and so invest (according, however, to an unspecified investment function). The consumption habits of businessmen and workers (if they save) adjust just sufficiently to absorb total consumption output, which is at a level that provides just enough employment for that part of the total workforce which is not employed currently in the machine-making sector, so ensuring full employment each and every short period.[1]

View from the red corner

Joan Robinson [1964b] (also [1965b], pp. 36–47) interpreted Solow's first lecture as an attempt to justify the marginal productivity theory of distribution and, in particular, the macroeconomic application of the microeconomic proposition that in a competitive capitalist economy labour is paid its *full-employment* marginal product. (This is a corollary of Solow's neoclassical example cited on pp. 96–7 above, in which there are constant returns to scale and full employment, and in which the marginal product of capital equals both the social rate of return on investment and the rate of profits.) Whether this was the purpose or not – and Solow certainly would deny it – Joan Robinson's argument

[1] This theme is developed more fully on pp. 99–105 below.

highlights in a very simple way the heart of the controversy. Especially does it show the difficulties which must develop in post-Keynesian times when some tackle distribution puzzles within the context of a *fully employed* neoclassical model while others are sceptical of the relevance of the model, preferring to concentrate on the Keynesian saving–investment relationship and the parameters of the saving functions of the different classes in the economy.[1]

To illustrate the controversy, consider a very simple one-commodity (butter) economy with a smooth, well-behaved, constant-returns-to-scale production function which relates butter output to homogeneous labour and butter input, i.e. malleable capital. If this were a planned economy in which full employment were decreed, the wage rate (w_b) would bear the same proportion $(1-\alpha)$ to the full employment average product of labour (AP_f) as consumption (C) does to total output (B'). (C is total butter output *less* that set aside for the next period, i.e. saving equals (is) investment.) That is to say

$$\frac{w_b}{AP_f} = (1-\alpha) = \frac{(1-\alpha)B'}{B'}\left(\equiv \frac{C}{Y}\right)$$

(Employment devoted to the production of butter for consumption would be $(1-\alpha)$ of the total, fully employed, labour supply as well.) With these conditions prevailing, all the butter produced would be sold, supposing socialist workers to consume all that they earn and that managers are workers too.[2] But the short-run marginal product of labour could be zero (capacity working of the existing stock, if we may momentarily leave the world of butter) or equal the average product

---

[1] Solow and Stiglitz [1968] return to these issues in a later paper where they argue that the essential difference between the two approaches is that the real-wage rate is regarded by neoclassicals (and neo-neo?) as a *labour*-market-clearing price while, for the neo-Keynesians, it is a *goods*-market-clearing price – a view that is consistent with Joan Robinson's criticisms. The latest statements of Joan Robinson's views, fortified by the aftermath of the double-switching debate, are in her two reviews of Ferguson [1969], see Robinson [1970a, 1970b].

[2] If consumption goods differ from investment goods (as they must outside a butter world) and if workers in the two sectors are treated alike, the real wage must bear the same *ratio* to the average product of the workers in the consumption goods sector as does employment in that sector to total employment: see Robinson [1964b], p. 411, also Robinson [1965b], p. 37. This argument ignores the use of ingenious fiscal policies which, for example, would allow labour to be paid its efficient shadow price as decreed by the planners and, simultaneously, allow this to be adjusted by taxation and/or subsidies, so that both effective demand puzzles and social ethics concerning both the absolute level and the relative levels of different workers' standards of living could be catered for.

(idle machines of the same quality as those in use) or it could equal the wage, if investment were the 'right' proportion of total output (and we have returned to the butter world).

We now compare our planned economy with a competitive capitalist market economy in which there is the same level of investment expenditure but also in which, initially, there is paid a wage which equals the *full-employment* marginal product of labour (MP_f). We consider, first, a

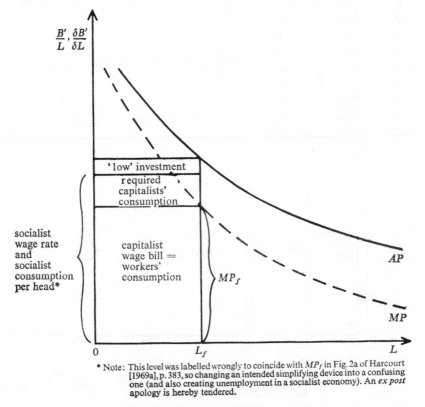

* Note: This level was labelled wrongly to coincide with MP_f in Fig. 2a of Harcourt [1969a], p. 383, so changing an intended simplifying device into a confusing one (and also creating unemployment in a socialist economy). An *ex post* apology is hereby tendered.

Fig. 3.1a. The case of 'low' investment

'low' level of investment. In the planned economy the real-wage rate exceeds the full-employment marginal product of labour, being just great enough when spent to absorb that proportion of total butter output that has not been set aside as 'low' investment (see fig. 3.1a). Then, in the capitalist economy, *unless* capitalists' consumption were such as to just fill in the gap between total output produced and the sum of the expenditure of the total wage bill ($MP_f L_f$) and butter put to stock for the next period, there will be, initially, unintended stocks, i.e. disequilibrium. Employment will fall until, with an unemployment rate of $L_e L_f$ and a wage payment that equals the (now higher) marginal product of labour, aggregate demand for butter from all sources just matches the (now lower) aggregate supply (see fig. 3.1b, in which for simplicity we ignore capitalists' consumption).

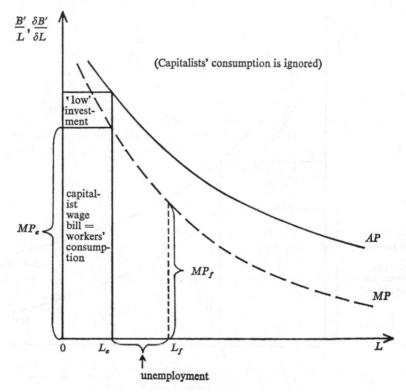

Fig. 3.1b. Unemployment equilibrium

If investment were very 'large' so that in a socialist economy, the wage rate would be less than MP_f (and workers 'exploited', no doubt for their own good), in the capitalist economy there would be excess demand for butter and labour.[1] (The outcome of the processes thereby set in motion may be found by consulting Solow and Stiglitz [1968].) It is only when, given the consumption functions of the workers and

[1] A similar analysis may be found in Eltis [1965], pp. 1–3.

capitalists, the level of investment is such as to give full employment without excess demand for labour that paying a wage rate equal to the *full-employment* marginal product of labour clears, simultaneously, both the goods and the labour markets (see fig. 3.2). Hence the general need, if the real wage is viewed as a labour-market-clearing price, for an all-wise government to set either the appropriate rate of interest (Meade [1961] and Swan's [1956] solution) or to conduct an appropriate fiscal policy.

In the butter economy, the rate of profits – a ratio of butter to butter – equals the marginal product of the existing butter stock (in this instance, the *full-employment* marginal product), as we are, in effect, back in Swan's world. Moreover, the assumption of malleable-butter-capital is absolutely vital, for only then can the existing capital stock be instantaneously moulded into the form that is appropriate for co-operating with the existing, fully-employed, labour force. In fact, as we saw on pp. 100–1 above, in the short run with given specific equipments, relatively fixed technical coefficients of production and full capacity working, the marginal product of labour is indeterminate, being equal either to the average product (if employment is reduced) or close to zero (if it is increased).

The analysis has been conducted in real terms but it is easy and more in keeping with Keynesian (without quotes) analysis (see Leijonhufvud [1968]) to repeat it in money terms, i.e. with a money wage and price. Let w_m be the *money* wage rate, ignore capitalists' consumption and let wage-earners consume all that they earn. Consider the 'low' investment case and suppose, initially, that there is full employment. The market-clearing price of butter *to be consumed* (P) would be the total money wage bill divided by the butter available for consumption,

i.e.
$$P = \frac{w_m L_f}{(1-\alpha)B_f'} = \frac{w_m}{AP_f}\left\{\frac{1}{1-\alpha}\right\} \tag{3.13}$$

(This requires that firms use (or be treated *as if* they use) a mark-up of $\alpha/(1-\alpha)$, which is the ratio of the employments (and outputs) in the two sectors.) This is not, however, the profit-maximizing price, for it is easy to show that, with the circumstances postulated, the *full-employment* value of the marginal product, VMP_f, is less than w_m, so that the full-employment marginal cost,

$$MC_f\left(=\frac{w_m}{MP_f}\right) > P$$

This implies, of course, that output and employment must be lower – total proceeds at full employment are not great enough to get the economy onto its aggregate supply curve. Thus

$$\frac{VMP_f}{w_m} = \frac{P\ MP_f}{w_m} = \frac{P}{MC_f} = \frac{MP_f}{AP_f}\left\{\frac{1}{1-\alpha}\right\} \tag{3.14}$$

Expression (3.14) will be less than unity,

i.e. $$MC_f > P \text{ if } \frac{1-\alpha}{1} > \frac{MP_f}{AP_f}$$

Now $(1-\alpha)/1$ is the ratio of the full-employment production of butter available for consumption to the total, full-employment, production of butter, a ratio which, because investment is 'low', we know exceeds MP_f/AP_f (see figs. 3.1a and 3.1b).

Therefore $$\frac{VMP_f}{w_m}\left(=\frac{P}{MC_f}\right) < 1 \tag{3.15}$$

If we assume that the butter production function is Cobb–Douglas, say, $B' = L^{1-\beta}B^\beta$, then we know that

$$\frac{\delta B'}{\delta L} = (1-\beta)\frac{B}{L} \quad \text{so that} \quad \frac{MP}{AP} = 1-\beta$$

If, therefore, firms use a mark-up of $\beta/(1-\beta)$, P will equal

$$\frac{w_m}{AP}\left\{\frac{1}{1-\beta}\right\} = \frac{w_m}{MP} = MC$$

and employment and production will be at such levels that their *composition* is $\beta/(1-\beta)$ also. These are the characteristics of the under-employment equilibrium position towards which the economy will tend to move, and, at which, the real-wage rate will again clear the goods market. The attainment of full employment therefore imposes two conditions in this model: not only must investment bear to consumption the ratio $\beta/(1-\beta)$, but the level of investment must also be such that when this ratio holds, the full-employment output is both produced and sold under *profit-maximizing conditions*.[1]

The analysis brings out the emphasis on effective demand which the

---

[1] It is to the short-run dynamics of an economy with characteristics of this nature (though the production function need not be Cobb–Douglas) that the article by Solow and Stiglitz [1968] is especially addressed.

neo-Keynesians are always conscious of, well, nearly always, but which tends to get lost sight of in the technocratic neoclassical approach to distribution theory – what Joan Robinson [1970b] calls pre-Keynesian theory after Keynes.[1] This does not imply that in the latter approach demand is ignored; it is, however, *relative* demands, not effective demand, which get star-billing. Of course, once the real wage is known,

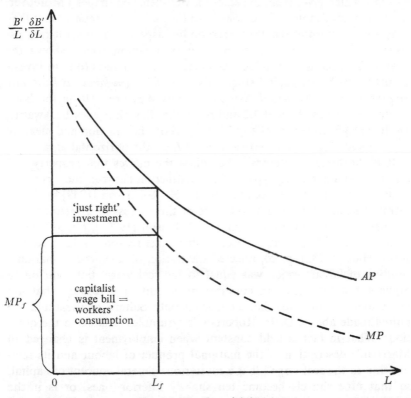

Fig. 3.2. The 'just right' story

with *given technical conditions* and in a non-butter world, the rate of profits, relative prices and the value of capital may be determined by calculating the 'Sraffa' prices of the system: see Sraffa [1960], part I, chapter 4, and the appendix to chapter 4 below.

The average and marginal product curves in figs. 3.1 and 3.2 above

[1] On this, see two earlier papers by Solow [1962a, 1963b] and Joan Robinson's comments [1962b].

are very special, i.e. neoclassical, cases of what Joan Robinson calls 'utilization functions', i.e. short-run production functions. They show the variations in average and marginal products which occur when, according to the level of effective demand and given a constant stock of butter capital, varying levels of employment are offered in the short run to labour. (It is, of course, the property of butterness – instant substitution – which gives them the smooth, well-behaved shapes.) Moreover, in the butter economy, the curves have the *additional* property that they may also be interpreted as the corresponding aspects of a constant-returns-to-scale *long-run* neoclassical production function which shows the average and marginal products associated with changes (due to investment) in the butter-capital stock–labour *ratio, when labour is kept fully employed period by period.* We would now measure L/B on the horizontal axis in figs. 3.1 and 3.2 and remember that time goes backwards, i.e. from right to left, *or* change directions on the function and measure $\delta B'/\delta B$ and B'/B on the vertical axis, B/L on the horizontal axis.

It is, however, 'butterness' that gives the curves this property and allows both a complete bypass of the distinction between short run and long run, as raised, for example, by D. H. Robertson [1949] in 'Wage Grumbles', and the merging into one of the process of investment and the use of capital in production, see Robinson [1970a], pp. 311–13. It could be noted here that, for exactly the same reasons as Joan Robinson's, Hicks [1932], p. 20, rejected the notion of a short-run marginal product of labour which was equal to the real wage, but went on to argue for a full long-run equilibrium equality for reasons that are vulnerable to criticisms that stem from both Salter's analysis and the points made above. D. H. Robertson's 'grumbles' related to the question: What in fact is held constant when employment is changed in Marshall's description of the marginal product of labour and its relationship to the real wage? Is it a mysterious general concept of capital, so that nine shovels become ten slightly inferior ones, or is it the existing equipment, in which case what does the tenth man work with? In the long run, Marshall supposed that suitable adjustments were made so that the wage was equal to the *net* marginal product of labour. This, however, introduces a joint production puzzle and leaves unexplained the level of the normal rate of profits that is earned on the adjusted stock of capital. Moreover, long-period comparisons are *only* comparisons since each *point* is an equilibrium position with its own (realized) past, as far as the values of r and w are concerned, and its own confidently expected future. To attempt a transition from one point to another could both rupture one equilibrium and not allow the economy to enter another. Time may only run at right angles, as it were, through each point.

'Butterness' overcomes these puzzles but only by supposing that they may be viewed 'as if' they never existed. Nevertheless, it is this butter property which makes this particular form of the production function so attractive to econometricians in their work on aggregate production functions and which explains the tenacious grip of its users in the face of considerable onslaughts by the critics. For if real world observations may be treated 'as if' they came from such functions, there are available actual data – observations from short-run utilization functions – which allow estimates of the characteristics and parameters of the 'as if' longer-run production functions: see Solow [1957], ACMS [1961], Minhas [1963], Samuelson [1962]. Technical progress, of course, complicates the methodology – destroys it, some might say – but there are no shortages of ingenious devices for coping with this puzzle also, as we have seen already and shall see again below, pp. 111–17.

In fig. 3.3 the *total* product variant of this approach[1] is used to show that the one-period rate of return on investment in this world equals the marginal product of butter capital. For simplicity I assume a constant labour force and that butter lasts for ever. A planned economy is examined in order to escape from effective demand puzzles. Solow [1963a] is *most* insistent on this, i.e. the effective demand proviso. Thus:

> The qualification about near-full employment is important. The rate of return . . . is primarily a technological concept unaffected by the possibilities of deficient effective demand . . . subjective rates of return on real investment were zero or negative in the U.S. during the depression of the 1930s . . . a consequence of hardened expectations of poor markets. In my technocratic sense the real social rate of return at full employment could not have been very different in 1933 from what it had been five years earlier. (pp. 69–70.)

Technocratic analysis thus consists of working out necessary relationships without always asking what sort of behaviour by the various economic actors in the community would be needed to establish them in fact.

B_0', B_1' and B_2 are prime butter outputs produced by L_f labour co-operating with butter capital stocks of B_0, B_1 and B_2 respectively in three succeeding periods. ΔB_0, the investment in period 0, establishes

---

[1] Divide by L on both axes and we enter the well-known world of Hahn and Matthews [1964], part I, p. 788.

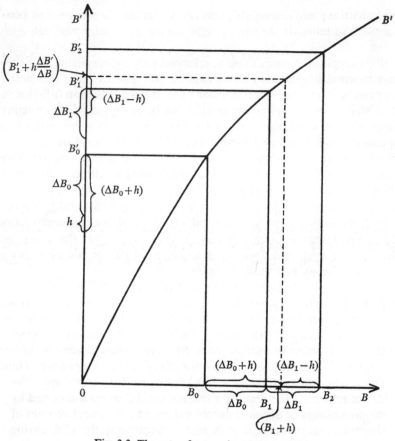

Fig. 3.3. The rate of return in a butter world

the butter capital of stock of B_1 for period 1; similarly, ΔB_1 gets the stock to B_2 for period 2. If investment in period 0 were $\Delta B_0 + h$, the capital stock in period 1 would be $B_1 + h$ and total output would be $B_1' + h(\Delta B'/\Delta B)$, where $\Delta B'/\Delta B$ *is the marginal product of butter capital in period 1.*[1] Investment in period 1 now need be only $\Delta B_1 - h$, in order that B_2 be the capital stock and B_2', the output of period 2.

The one-period rate of return, see pp. 93–4 above, is

$$R_1 = \frac{j}{h} - 1 \tag{3.1}$$

---

[1] Notice that the Δs associated with $\Delta B'/\Delta B$ refer to completely different orders of magnitude to those associated with, for example, ΔB_0.

We calculate j as follows. In period 1, in the first situation, the consumption of butter is

$$C_1 = B_1' - \Delta B_1 \qquad (3.16)$$

In the second situation it is

$$C_1' = B_1' + h\frac{\Delta B'}{\Delta B} - (\Delta B_1 - h) \qquad (3.17)$$

Thus

$$j = C_1' - C_1 = h\left(\frac{\Delta B'}{\Delta B} + 1\right) \qquad (3.18)$$

i.e. society gets as additional consumption in period 1, not only the *whole* of the increment of output associated with the investment of the extra saving of the period before, $h(\Delta B'/\Delta B)$, *but* also, for good measure, it gets the extra saving back as well, see Solow [1963a], p. 30.

$$R_1 = \frac{h\{(\Delta B'/\Delta B) + 1\}}{h} - 1$$

i.e.
$$R_1 = \frac{\Delta B'}{\Delta B} \qquad (3.19)$$

– the marginal product of butter capital.

Joan Robinson [1964b], p. 410, also [1965b], p. 37, takes Solow mildly to task for setting up the (one-period) rate of return in this way.

The purpose of investment is to increase productive capacity. Why work out what would happen if it were disinvested again next year? ... The planner, who must be concerned with long-lived installations, has to think in terms of alternative paths to be followed over the next twenty years or so, and even a small change in the amount of investment decided upon this year may require extensive changes in the physical specifications of the plan over a long future as well as for this year. And so does the consumption to be permitted next year.

Mouth guards out while we arrange a return bout

Joan Robinson closes her comments on Solow's first lecture by arguing that in a competitive capitalist economy, expected rates of profits guide the investment decisions of individual businessmen and that there will be a Marshallian tendency for them to approach equality. (Presumably they guided the investment expenditure of the utilization functions of the capitalist economies above.) The expected rate of profits, however, is of no interest to the planner, though the rate of return on investment is, while the latter is of no interest to the capitalist! This bait (which was also dangled by Dobb) was too much for Solow to resist, despite his own eminently sensible comments on it in Lecture 3 in Solow [1963a], pp. 70–2, and it is the subject of his paper, Solow [1967], in the Dobb *Festschrift*.

Dobb [1960] argued that there was a gap between the (private) profitability of investment and its (social) marginal productivity, because the former excludes payments to factors other than capital while the latter should reflect the *total* resulting addition to national output without any deductions of the values of other factors. He was, however, discussing the case of surplus labour (whose cost to society when employed in investment – but not to the businessmen who pay them – is zero, see Robinson [1964b], p. 410, also [1965b], p. 36) and changing employment levels. He explicitly conceded the point, which Solow tries rigorously to establish, that there is *no* gap when all other factor supplies are constant and the real-wage rate does not change.[1]

Solow uses a Ricardo–Sraffa system with circulating capital (see the appendix to chapter 4 below); he shows that the rate of interest is an accurate measure of the social rate of return on investment, provided only that the economy is at full employment and uses competitive pricing, and that we are comparing one stationary state with another which has the same labour force but uses, *at the given rate of profits*, a different equi-viable technique, namely one that requires more circulating capital, commodity by commodity. Both stationary states are in long-run competitive equilibrium; their net products consist entirely of consumption goods. In order for one economy to move (technocratically) from its technology to the other's, consumption must be cut in one period (or for a number of periods in more complicated cases). Solow shows that the *extra* consumption per period obtained in perpetuity as a result of this move, when expressed in terms of the common set of prices at the *given* rates of interest (and wages) and as a proportion of the consumption forgone, similarly measured, equals the

---

[1] Ng [1970] also enters the lists but makes his points by means of a butter model, so that the wage rate *rises* when accumulation occurs – and he misses his mark by a mile.

rate of interest. This ratio, as we saw on p. 94 above, is Solow's measure of the rate of return in perpetuity, $R_\infty = p/h$.

We have already met this result in a very simple guise in the discussion of the real Wicksell effect in chapter 1, pp. 44–5 above. Consider a positive real Wicksell effect whereby at a rate of interest just below the switch-point rate, the technique with the higher output per head and value of capital per man at the switch point prevails. Then at the switch point, the extra output *in perpetuity*, i.e. the difference between the two outputs per head – we are considering stationary states – expressed as a proportion of the extra capital, also valued at the switch-point prices, using the common r and w, i.e. the differences in the two capital values, equals the externally given, equilibrium rate of profits. (Pasinetti argues that the equality is a *definition*, i.e. an identity: see Pasinetti [1969, 1970] and chapter 4, pp. 168–9 below.) But the value of the extra capital may be considered equivalent to the value of consumption that would need to be forgone *in order to create it at the common set of prices*, i.e. the saving (or dissaving) needed for the investment (or disinvestment) for one economy to change over from one position to the other,

i.e.
$$\frac{q_b - q_a}{k_b - k_a} = r_{ba}$$

remembering that $q_b = w_{b\,\text{max}}$ and $q_a = w_{a\,\text{max}}$. Thus, while, as we saw, we must resist the temptation to call the ratio the marginal product of capital, may we nevertheless call it, *in this special case*, the social rate of return on investment (all the benefits of which go, of course, to the profit-receivers)?[1] Perhaps we may, provided that we note that it has a limited and special meaning, that it is a definition, and, further, that we are treading, backwards and forwards, a very slippery path indeed between technocracy and the workings of competitive market economies, see Nell [1970]. The sequel to this analysis – the recent exchanges between Pasinetti [1970] and Solow [1970] – is discussed in chapter 4, pp. 157–8, p. 162, p. 168 and pp. 172–3 below.

Round two

So far we have been discussing deepening, in so far as it is relevant to the rate of return. Now Solow adds his own contribution, the role of

---

[1] It is also an example of a situation in which the values of Irving Fisher's two concepts of the 'rate of return on sacrifice' happen to coincide, see Pasinetti [1969, 1970], Solow [1970] and chapter 4, p. 163 below.

technical progress and its effects on the measurement of the rate of return. With technical progress occurring, saving and accumulation are twice blest; not only is society's productive capacity raised by saving, because it provides more capital, but also because it now provides 'better' capital. This applies to the lot if technical progress is dis-embodied, at the margin if it is embodied. With disembodied technical progress (which is illustrated by Cobb–Douglas, see pp. 112–13 below) there emerges the possibility that the rate of return, especially the one-period one, which, in this case, equals the *net* marginal product of capital at the level ruling in the appropriate period, will get greater and greater, unless capital deepening is occurring at the same time and at approximately the same rate as (neutral) technical progress.

We again assume that capital lasts for ever. Neutral technical progress occurs at a rate of a per cent per period.

In period 0

$$Q_0 = A(0)L_0^{1-\beta} K_0^{\beta} \tag{3.20}$$

and, in the first situation, in period 1,

$$Q_1 = A(0)(1+a)L_1^{1-\beta}K_1^{\beta} \tag{3.21}$$

Now suppose that an extra amount, h, were to be saved in period 0, so that in period 1, we have

$$Q_1' = Q_1 + h\frac{\delta Q_1}{\delta K_1}$$

i.e.

$$Q_1' = Q_1 + h\beta A(0)(1+a)\left(\frac{L_1}{K_1}\right)^{1-\beta} \tag{3.22}$$

where

$$\beta A(0)(1+a)\left(\frac{L_1}{K_1}\right)^{1-\beta}$$

is the marginal product of capital *in period 1*. (It is useful to recall at this point that $\delta Q/\delta K = \beta(Q/K)$ as well.) Suppose that saving (equals investment) in period 1 in the first situation were to have been I_1. In the second situation it now need be only $I_1 - h$. It follows that

$$\begin{aligned} C_1 &= Q_1 - I_1 \\ C_1' &= Q_1' - (I_1 - h) \end{aligned} \tag{3.23}$$

so that j, the *extra* consumption that the economy may have in the second situation, is

$$j = C_1' - C_1$$

i.e.
$$j = h\{\beta A(0)(1+a)\left(\frac{L_1}{K_1}\right)^{1-\beta} + 1\} \tag{3.24}$$

and
$$R_1 = \frac{j}{h} - 1 = \beta A(0)(1+a)\left(\frac{L_1}{K_1}\right)^{1-\beta} \tag{3.25}$$

which is the marginal product of capital in period 1.

Suppose, though, that we were measuring the *one-period* rate of return n periods on, i.e. between periods $n-1$ and n. Then

$$R_1 = \beta A(0)(1+a)^n\left(\frac{L_n}{K_n}\right)^{1-\beta} \tag{3.26}$$

If L/K remains constant, i.e. if

$$\frac{L_1}{K_1} = \frac{L_2}{K_2} = \ldots = \frac{L_n}{K_n}$$

and if a has any push at all, it seems as though society has only to sit still for a few periods in order to achieve a fantastically high rate of return on investment.

The crucial proviso is the constancy of L/K. We are dealing with a process which is akin to the impact of a change in the saving ratio (s) in Swan's model in Swan [1956], pp. 337–8 (which this model is, after all). In Swan's model we know that following a change in s, the economy will approach a new equilibrium level at which both Q and K will again grow at the same constant rate of $\{a/(1-\beta)\}+l$, where $l = \dot{L}/L$, a rate which is, moreover, independent of the value of s. Thus

$$\frac{\dot{Q}}{Q} = a + \beta\frac{\dot{K}}{K} + (1-\beta)\frac{\dot{L}}{L}$$

When $\dot{K}/K = \dot{Q}/Q$, we get a rate of growth of $\{a/(1-\beta)\}+l$. 'After a transitional phase, the influence of the saving ratio on the rate of growth is ultimately absorbed by a compensating change in the output–capital ratio' (Swan [1956], p. 338). A constant Q/K implies a constant marginal product of capital, and, thus, deepening at the rate of $a/(1-\beta)$. Something like this is happening to L/K during, as Solow [1963a], p. 46, puts it, 'the planned evolution around which we are contemplating variations'. It also follows that the greater is the rate of growth of neutral technical progress, the greater is the value of R_1, both in the short run with given stocks of labour and capital and also in the long run when the economy, given its saving ratio, has fully adapted itself, in Swan-like fashion, to the higher rate of technical progress.

As a digression Solow derives the factor–price frontiers for the Cobb–Douglas and Worswick cases and analyses the shifts which technical progress causes in them. The analysis is neat, but what is it supposed to teach us? The order of magnitude of the rise in real wages that may be expected if the rate of profits is kept constant while technical progress occurs? Then these neighbourhood islands of long-period equilibrium, despite frequent changes in technique, hardly seem the appropriate tools to use (though the Phelps' [1966] have tried them out).

Solow's analysis of embodied technical progress uses a model that we have met before in chapter 2, pp. 69–72 above, in which both *ex ante* and *ex post* substitution is possible. His illustration is Cobb–Douglas – all vintages have the same exponents and retain *ex post* the substitution possibilities open to them *ex ante*. However, once installed, the machines are immune to technical progress – it is not catching. Solow thus retains malleability – 'butterness' – and embodiment both. Expected obsolescence (absent, of course, in the disembodied case, where *all* capital shares in the dispensation of grace) reduces social and private rates of return below the corresponding marginal products of capital as ordinarily measured *but does not disturb, in the cases examined, their own equality one with another*. 'The return to current saving is reduced by the fact that current saving adds less to future consumption-potential than next year's saving would.' (p. 62.)

Solow's production function has as one input an '*effective*' stock of capital which is obtained by summing together all profitable vintages, each layer weighted by its respective productivity (which due to technical progress will rise as we go from earlier to later vintages, see chapter 2, p. 69 above). This avoids the need to calculate the contribution to total output of each layer of 'fossils' in the stock. It also makes it unnecessary to distribute labour (or to know its distribution) over the range of vintages in use. It is, of course, assumed, though, that the actual labour supply may be treated *as if* it had been distributed so that marginal and average products were equalized, vintage to vintage, so maximizing total output, with earlier vintages worked less labour-intensively than later ones.

We obtain Solow's result by using his example of 'purely capital-augmenting' technical progress: what one unit of capital and x men could produce last year, $1/(1 + \lambda)$ units of capital, where λ is the rate of embodied technical progress, and x men can do this year. Again we assume that capital lasts for ever and we look at periods 0, 1 and 2. In period 0, inherited from history, the 'effective' capital stock is J_0 and, in the first instance, I_0 of Q_0 ($= F(J_0, L_0)$) will be saved and invested. In period 1, we have Q_1 ($= F(J_1, L_1)$, where $J_1 = J_0 + I_0$), of which I_1 will be invested. In period 2, $J_2 = J_1 + I_1(1 + \lambda) = J_0 + I_0 + I_1(1 + \lambda)$, because investing one unit in period 1 is the equivalent, *for production purposes*, of investing $(1 + \lambda)$ units in period 0. In the 'otherwise' situation, or second instance, therefore, we need to have added to J_0 by the beginning of period 2, the equivalent of $\{I_0 + I_1(1 + \lambda)\}$.

We do the usual exercise, i.e. save an extra amount, h, in period 0, so getting $Q_1' = Q_1 + h(\delta Q_1 / \delta J_1)$ in period 1. Because of embodied technical progress, though, we can reduce investment in period 1 by $h/(1 + \lambda)$, i.e. to $I_1 - h/(1 + \lambda)$ (for the *amount*, $h/(1 + \lambda)$, would be *effectively* $(h/(1 + \lambda))(1 + \lambda) = h$ in period 2). The change in 'effective' capital between period 0 and period 2 in the second instance is therefore

$$I_0 + h + I_1(1 + \lambda) - \left(\frac{h}{1 + \lambda}\right)(1 + \lambda) = I_0 + I_1(1 + \lambda)$$

as it should be. Following the usual procedure

$$C_1' - C_1 = j = h\left(\frac{\delta Q_1}{\delta J_1} + \frac{1}{1 + \lambda}\right) \tag{3.2}$$

and

$$R_1 = \frac{\delta Q_1}{\delta J_1} - \frac{\lambda}{1 + \lambda} \tag{3.28}$$

i.e. the marginal product of 'effective' capital reduced by an allowance for expected (and realized) obsolescence. But the private rate of return on a unit of up-to-date capital in a competitive economy with perfect foresight, etc., is $\delta Q_1 / \delta J_1$; in order that the return per dollar on all vintages is the same, their price must fall by an amount that reflects the increase in capital productivity since they were installed (for simplicity suppose only this year's and last year's). Then the price of last year's capital goods must fall to $1/(1 + \lambda)$, giving a capital loss of $1 - \{1/(1 + \lambda)\}$ $= \lambda/(1 + \lambda)$. The net private return is therefore $(\delta Q_1 / \delta J_1) - \{\lambda/(1 + \lambda)\}$, as above.

Solow's emphasis on the equality of private and social rates of return, especially in the embodied case, is not intended to give the impression that they *are* equal. (Most of his analysis, though, in *Capital Theory and the Rate of Return*, the Dobb *Festschrift* paper and his subsequent reply to Pasinetti's criticisms, is directed to this end, while his wise asides continue to deny it.) The emphasis is meant, rather, to demonstrate 'the much weaker proposition that if the private and social marginal products of capital coincide, then the private and social rates of return will coincide', Solow [1963a], p. 65. Two puzzles then arise: first, are marginal products of aggregate capital definable and important after all? Secondly, what *is* the significance of the equalities: could we – should we – in fact without qualms leave investment decisions to private businessmen (and saving to private individuals)?

TKO in the third and final round

The aggregate production function model just described is the basis for the empirical estimates given in Lecture 3 of Solow [1963a] of the rates of return on investment in the United States and West Germany. Solow first estimates, for a plausible range of values of λ and by econometrically fitting Cobb–Douglas,[1] the exponents of the production functions, i.e. the elasticities of output with respect to 'effective' capital and labour in the two countries. Combining the estimates of 'effective' capital with the corresponding estimates of the output – 'effective'-capital elasticities and the output – 'effective'-capital ratios give estimates of the marginal products of 'effective' capital. These are then adjusted by the orders of magnitude of λ (and physical depreciation, d) to give the values of the empirical counterparts to equation (3.28) above.

It is at this point that Solow's warning (in Lecture 1) that dodging uncertainty is a major limitation of the current theory of capital is most relevant – and where his (explicit) assumptions are strained to breaking point, as he himself says. Realized expectations and perfect foresight are needed strictly to justify *all* Solow's results. Capital, rates of profits, etc., cannot be measured unless this is so, for past investments could not be weighted by their appropriate λs (which themselves might no longer be appropriate). The calculations of the man of words would have irretrievably – and forever – parted company with those of the man of deeds, as Joan Robinson would say. Comparisons taken from pseudo-production functions bear not at all on the out-of-equilibrium processes that have occurred. This approach to analysis is not, of course, confined to one side alone. And it should also be pointed out that the calculations are carefully hedged round with appropriate qualifications and a fine sense

---

[1] Provided that it is assumed that the exponents of the Cobb–Douglas functions of each vintage are the same, technical progress may always be treated as purely capital-augmenting and a one-number measure of the 'effective' capital stock obtained, basically because, when the labour supply is distributed so that the total output is maximized, the *average* products of labour on all vintages are the same.

of the empirical orders of magnitude involved. Nevertheless, the analysis *is* an illegitimate extrapolation of results that hold only for a one-commodity, malleable capital world in which the short run and the long run collapse into one and perfect foresight and realized expectations are guaranteed.

Solow (p. 96) estimates social rates of return of the order of 15 to 20 per cent and comments: 'If the whole economy can be thought of as a bank paying 15 to 20 per cent interest, then it would seem to be in society's interest to find ways of making somewhat larger deposits.' With this we can all agree, especially if in the American case it leads to full employment.

The shade of Irving Fisher hovers, as promised, over the last pages where many Americans are found to have marginal rates of time preference no greater than 4 or 5 per cent a year – they 'save voluntarily to buy riskless assets' paying these rates. Businessmen on the other hand require target rates of return of the order of 20 per cent per annum or more. (A pay-off period of five years leads to much the same conclusion.) With social rates of return somewhere in between, the inevitable implication is that something or someone needs to give a nudge to bring them all closer together. Otherwise the divergencies between social and private risks will continue to have unfortunate consequences for the social well-being of the economies concerned. Fisher's ghost also raises the spectre of diminishing returns to investment in the United States – this is suggested slightly in Solow's figures, see Solow [1963a], p. 94. But, again, though Fisher duly makes his appearance, rather like a battered old warrior who, as an ex-champ, is introduced to the crowd when the main bout is over, Solow's best intentions are not realized, for *capital* as well as the rate of return on investment has been mentioned – and used.

4 A child's guide to the double-switching debate

Setting the stage

As we have seen in the preceding chapters, the results of neoclassical marginal productivity theory have played a key role in both the theory of economic growth and the econometric studies of the post-war period. The easiest illustration of this proposition is the essential part which the equality of marginal products with factor rewards plays in the development of the arguments in Swan's famous model of economic growth (Swan [1956]), and in Solow's influential – and equally famous – article on technical progress and the aggregate production function, Solow [1957]. This methodology has been continuously under attack and the latest (and sharpest) arrows in the quivers of the neo-Keynesian critics are the results of the double-switching debate. Not all of these are, however, related to the phenomenon of double-switching itself; a related phenomenon, capital-reversing, also plays a key role: see, especially, Garegnani [1970a, 1970b], Bliss [1970], Pasinetti [1969, 1970] and below, *passim*.

To the neo-Keynesians, the results of the debate represent a triumph for their point of view and signal if not the re-emergence of classical economics, then the need for it. By destroying, as they believe they have, both the concept of the aggregate production function *and* the underpins of the traditional demand curves for capital goods and labour, at both economy *and* industry levels, the neo-Keynesians feel that the marginal productivity theory of value and distribution has also been discredited, especially the traditional demand and supply approach to distributive questions. The theory of value, from being all-embracing (as it has tended to be since the days of the first neoclassicals – Jevons, the Austrians, Marshall, Walras, Wicksell, Wicksteed, *et al.*) is now to be confined to its rightful place, *à la* Ricardo, of 'the study of the *relations* between the wage, the rate of profits and the system of relative prices'. These 'relations would then provide the basis for studying the circumstances on which depend the distribution of the product between classes' (Garegnani [1970], p. 427). Thus we are called to ponder anew Ricardo's distinction between 'commodities, the value of which is determined by scarcity alone' and the value of those 'commodities only as can be increased in quantity by the exertion of human industry, and on the production of which competition operates without restraint' (Ricardo, Sraffa with Dobb edition [1951–5], p. 12).

To the neo-neoclassicals, on the other hand, though the results of the debate destroy the wider application of certain simple parables, they leave unscathed the marginal productivity theory of distribution, *which, the neo-neoclassicals argue, has nothing to do with the existence or not of an aggregate production function.* Neither would they wish to limit the scope of the theory of value to the areas outlined above nor to give up basic neoclassical methodology and views. They, or rather their new frontiersmen, do wish, however, to hasten away from stationary states and equilibrium comparisons into the richer worlds of processes and dynamic adjustments in growth models, what Stiglitz [1968] calls 'true dynamics', in which specification errors associated with neoclassical theorems may be investigated – if only we ourselves were new frontiersmen. It is to a discussion of these views that the present chapter is addressed.

It ought also to be said that outside of the two Cambridges, these discussions, which, *technically*, relate to simple (!) questions such as: 'Can factor-price frontiers cross more than once?' and 'What is the shape of the factor-price frontier?', have been regarded as 'a little silly'. How can grown men (and women) get so cross over matters like these? Such an attitude only serves to illustrate anew how far, in the search for scientific purity, economic analysis has been removed from economic and social *questions*. Logic rarely begets polemics; so it is healthier to search for the causes than to deplore their existence. The discussions *do* relate to fundamental problems. The controversies arise because of political and ideological differences between the two sides, differences which are thrown into sharp relief when the implications of the results of certain logical exercises become apparent.

Both sides of the debate have examined heterogeneous capital-goods models in which any *one* technique of production does not allow substitution between factors, i.e. fixed input–output coefficients prevail and proportions of factors may vary only by going over to another technique as a result of changing factor prices.[1] The objects of the exercises dif-

---

[1] When input–output coefficients vary as between *activities* in any *one* technique, the *aggregate* factor proportions associated with a given technique may change *in value*

fered as between the two groups. To the neo-Keynesians they represent an attack on the marginalist method, an attack which has been led, in spirit anyway, by Sraffa, who, as we noted in the Introduction, see p. 7 above, subtitled his book, *Prelude to a Critique of Economic Theory*, by which he meant marginalist theory. In the preface of Sraffa [1960], p. vi, we read:

It is, however, a peculiar feature of the set of propositions now published that, although they do not enter into any discussion of the marginal theory of value and distribution, they have nevertheless been designed to serve as the basis for a critique of that theory. If the foundation holds, the critique may be attempted later, either by the writer, or by someone younger and better equipped for the task.[1]

To the other side, the object was to justify neoclassical marginalist procedures, an object which is *not* identical with one of providing a *rigorous* defence of the concepts of an aggregate production function and the associated input of 'capital'. A puzzle that arises, nevertheless, is whether the stories associated with smooth, one-commodity, malleable capital models can 'stand in' as analogies for comparisons using these more 'realistic' models. The aggregate production function must now refer to the relationship between value capital and other variables within the whole set of techniques (though Bruno, Burmeister and Sheshinski [1968] have argued recently that the term, 'production function', should be confined to the engineering aspects of each technique, which seems to me a fudge based on hindsight). If the neoclassical stories as told, for example, by Swan [1956] and Solow [1957] did in fact hold for heterogeneous capital-goods models, this would be an enormous simplification for economic theory and econometric specification alike (see Brown [1968, 1969]). It is to this question that the double-switching debate is especially addressed.

In order to preserve perspective we should note, at this point, that

---

terms when *r* and *w* do. Changing the composition of demand could also have the same effect on aggregate factor proportions, even though relative prices would remain unchanged in these models. These exercises are not, however, a description of substitution as it occurs as an actual process; they are merely the logical implications of the comparisons of different equilibrium positions, logical relations only.

[1] The recent work of some of his contemporaries at Cambridge, and, also, by some of his younger and well-equipped fellow countrymen – Garegnani, Nuti, Pasinetti and Spaventa – as well as by a young Cambridge-trained Indian economist, Bhaduri, may be interpreted as attempts to provide this critique, the foundation having held. Of course, the elder statesmen of Cambridge, Mass., are also not without younger enthusiasts on the ramparts with them.

both Samuelson and Solow have argued that heterogeneous capital-goods models analysed by modern programming techniques are the appropriate tools for a rigorous development of capital theory. Thus:

> Repeatedly in writings and lectures I have insisted that capital theory can be rigorously developed without using any Clark-like concept of aggregate 'capital', instead relying upon a complete analysis of a great variety of heterogeneous physical capital goods and processes through time. Such an analysis leans heavily on the tools of modern linear and more general programming and might therefore be called neo-neoclassical. It takes the view that if we are to understand the trends in how incomes are distributed among different kinds of labor and different kinds of property owners, both in the aggregate and in the detailed composition, then studies of changing technologies, human and natural resource availabilities, taste patterns, and all the other matters of microeconomics are likely to be very important. (Samuelson [1962], p. 193.)

Samuelson stands by this approach 'as the best tool for the description and understanding of economic reality, and for policy formulation and calculated guesses about the future'. The simpler stories are then used to overcome communication problems with the more peasantish, albeit poetic, members of the trade – 'one's easier expositions [simplified models involving only a few factors of production] get more readers than one's harder' – and because economic statistics are often too crude to warrant the use of more refined methods (see Solow [1963a], p. 8, also Solow [1970]).

> ... Solow, in the interest of empirical measurements and approximation, has been willing occasionally to drop his rigorous insistence upon a complex-heterogeneous-capital programming model; instead, by heroic abstraction, he has carried forward the seminal work of Paul H. Douglas on estimating a single production function for society and has had a tremendous influence on analysts of statistical trends in the important macroaggregates of our economy. (Samuelson [1962], p. 193.)

The econometric methodology then becomes: We know we've been naughty but we don't think it makes much difference to our estimates of the values of key concepts; if it does, it's up to the critics to tell us the orders of magnitude involved rather than smack our bottoms for our lack of principle – which would be fine, if only some notice were taken of the critics when they do *just that*, see chapter 2, pp. 81–2 above. But perhaps more notice will be taken in the future now that sympathetic 'insiders', as it were, are also performing these exercises, see Newbery [1970].

The neoclassical tradition, like the Christian, believes that profound truths can be told by way of parable. The neoclassical parables are intended to enlighten believers and non-believers alike concerning the forces which determine the distribution of income between profit-receivers and wage-earners, the patterns of capital accumulation and economic growth over time and the choice of the techniques of production associated with these developments. Four truths which, before the revelations of the false and true prophets in the course of the recent debate, were thought to be established were:

(1) an association between lower rates of profits and higher values of capital per man employed;

(2) an association between lower rates of profits and higher capital–output ratios;

(3) an association between lower rates of profits and (through investment in more 'mechanized' or 'round-about' methods of production) higher sustainable steady states of consumption per head (up to a maximum);

(4) that, in competitive conditions, the distribution of income between profit-receivers and wage-earners can be explained by a knowledge of marginal products and factor supplies.

The 'explanation' referred to in parable (4) relates to expressions for the equilibrium values of factor prices and supplies, in a general-equilibrium situation in which demand factors, e.g. consumer tastes constrained by incomes, also play a role. That these truths *were* accepted seems to be a fair inference from the topics that Samuelson [1966], for example, chose to discuss in his summing-up of the debate. The references to the views of earlier writers given by Garegnani [1966, 1970a] and Pasinetti [1966a, 1969, 1970] are further evidence, as is the climax to Stigler's account of neoclassical economics, the discussion of the marginal productivity theory of distribution itself, in Stigler [1941], chapter XII.

I have avoided the temptation to write these as, for example, 'falling rates of profits lead to higher values of capital per head' – a temptation that has not always been avoided in the literature. Following Joan Robinson's strictures that it is most important not to apply theorems obtained from the analysis of differences to situations of change (or, at least, to be aware of the act of faith involved in doing this), modern writers usually have been most careful to stress that their analysis is essentially the comparisons of different equilibrium situations one with another and that they are not analysing actual processes.[1] Nevertheless, in their asides, they sometimes speak as if their results were applicable to a world of change and as if 'back-of-an-envelope' excursions into the statistics can provide 'realistic' orders of magnitude to try out in their theorems.[2]

Thus, the following quote from Samuelson [1966a] is *not* atypical:
It is no longer literally true to say, 'Society moves from high interest rates to low by sacrificing current consumption goods in return for more consumption later, but with each further dose of accumulation of capital goods resulting in a lower and lower social yield of in-cremental product'. Actually, society can go from *B* to *E* in Figure IVb [*B* and *E*, though not shown in Samuelson's figure, are points on the factor-price frontier envelope which correspond to the *same* technique at widely different rates of profits] without making any physical changes at all: a reduction of profit from a 200 per cent rate per period to a 5 per cent rate, merely lowers what a critic might call the 'degree of exploitation of labour' prevailing. In Figure Va [the well-behaved Austrian case, see p. 150 below] the apologist for capital and for thrift has a less difficult case to argue. (p. 577.)

This quote is all the more significant because it comes from the article in which Samuelson sums up the double-switching debate and in which he handsomely admits the logic of the neo-Keynesian criticisms. Pre-sumably, therefore, either he has been careless in his exposition (though several other passages to like effect in the same paper could be quoted) or certain habits of thought have become so ingrained as for him to be unconscious of their presence.

Moreover, Samuelson's 1962 paper on the surrogate production function, which is a watershed on the way to the main debate, was written *partly* as a defence of the methodology and analysis used by Solow in his work on aggregate production functions. The object of his paper was to show

---

[1] They do, of course, analyse processes in other contexts and the spate of phase diagrams and dynamic processes now so common in the literature owes something, surely, to Joan Robinson's original paper: see, for example, Cass and Stiglitz [1967], Hahn [1966]. These papers are typical members of a rapidly growing tribe, one which, moreover, looks back with contempt rather than with nostalgia to the static and comparative static analyses, uninteresting propositions all, on which most of them – and us – were brought up. Hahn's recent affirmation of doubt in Hahn [1970] could also be mentioned in this context.

[2] See, for example, Samuelson [1966a], pp. 568, 569, 577; Bruno, Burmeister and Sheshinski [1966], p. 545 n2; Meade and Hahn [1965], p. 448 n1; Samuelson and Modigliani [1966b], p. 329.

that a new concept, the 'Surrogate Production Function', can provide *some* rationalization for the validity of the simple J. B. Clark parables which pretend there is a single thing called 'capital' that can be put into a single production function and along with labor will produce total output (of a homogeneous good or of some desired market-basket of goods). In so doing, I may also be providing some extenuations for Solow's holiday high-spirits. (p. 194.) The latter is a reference to the 'two Solow's – the orthodox priest of the M.I.T. school and the busman on a holiday who operates brilliantly and without inhibitions in the rough-and-ready realm of empirical heuristics', ... 'both ... of vintage quality' (p. 193). One might also ask, what *is* the point of these exercises, if they are *not* meant to throw some light on the second way of phrasing propositions? Be that as it may, the outcome of the double-switching debate is to put a shaft through the above four propositions. Even as parables they must be expunged from the Bible proper (or, at least, propositions (1) to (3) must), though no doubt they will continue to be told in the commentaries and Sunday School Lessons for a long time to come.

Lesson 1: what it's all about

The phenomena of double- (or re-) switching and capital-reversing were first noticed in the literature by Joan Robinson [1953–4, 1956], Champernowne [1953–4] and Sraffa [1960] (whose book, it will be remembered, though published in 1960, had an enormously long gestation period dating back at least to the mid-1920s). Double-switching is associated essentially with the possibility that the same method of production may be the most profitable of a number of methods of production at more than one rate of profits (r) even though other methods are more profitable at rates in between. Capital-reversing is the value of capital moving in the *same* direction, when alternative rates of interest are considered, so that a technique with a *lower* degree of mechanization, as measured, for example, by its level of output per head and value of capital per head, is associated with a lower rate of profits. That is to say, it is the most profitable technique at this rate of profits and, in particular, is *more* profitable than a more mechanized technique (in the two senses above) which was either equi-profitable or more profitable than this one at *higher* rates of profits. (All these comparisons must be taken to occur in the neighbourhood of a switch point.) Joan Robinson [1956], pp. 109–10, called this a 'perverse' relationship, a curiosum, and acknowledged

Ruth Cohen for pointing out the possibility to her, so that it has become known in the literature as the Ruth Cohen curiosum (RCC). In the same passages she describes (but does not name) double-switching (which is *not* the same thing as capital-reversing) but the implications of the phenomena were neither realized nor spelt out: see Robinson [1970a], pp. 309–10. We have commented already, in chapter 1, p. 30 above, on Champernowne's clear descriptions of double-switching and capital-reversing and his analysis of them.

Both phenomena imply that the same physical capital goods may have more than one value, because a different real-wage rate and set of relative prices will be associated with each rate of profits and the capital goods associated with the method have to be valued at their appropriate set of prices. Double-switching and capital-reversing may occur in an industry (Sraffa's example in Sraffa [1960], chapter XII) and in an economy (the original cases discussed by Joan Robinson [1953–4, 1956] and Champernowne [1953–4] in a context, one ought to add, that goes back at least to Wicksell and probably to Ricardo: see Sraffa [1960], part III).

Before entering the realm of controversy, it may clarify the subsequent arguments if we give now some very simple examples of the two phenomena. We use the model of chapter 1, pp. 40–5, with which we analysed price and real Wicksell effects. In the top half of fig. 4.1, we show the w–r relationships of two techniques, one of which is a straight line (bb), the other, concave to the origin (aa). Technique b has a higher output per man than technique a, i.e. $q_b(=w_{b\max})>q_a(=w_{a\max})$. It will be recalled that the value of k_b is constant (the price Wicksell effect is neutral), no matter what are the values of r and w, and that k_a is smaller, the smaller is the value of r (a negative price Wicksell effect).

At a rate of profits greater than r_{ba} technique b is the more profitable; at r_{ba} the two are equi-profitable, while below r_{ba} (and above r_{ab}) technique a is the more profitable. In the lower half of the figure we plot in an unbroken line the values of capital per head (in terms of the consumption good) of the technique that would actually be in use at each value of r. (The dotted lines show the values of k of each technique associated with *their* respective equilibrium rs and ws. Straight lines are used solely for simplicity.) It can be seen that at r_{ba} *capital-reversing* occurs, in the sense that $q_a<q_b$ and $k_a<k_b$, and that as we consider lower and lower values of r, k_a gets more and more so. At the rate of profits r_{ab} the two techniques are equi-profitable again and at values less than r_{ab} technique b is the more profitable, i.e. 'comes back' or 'reswitches'. (There is, of course, *no* capital-reversing at r_{ab}.)

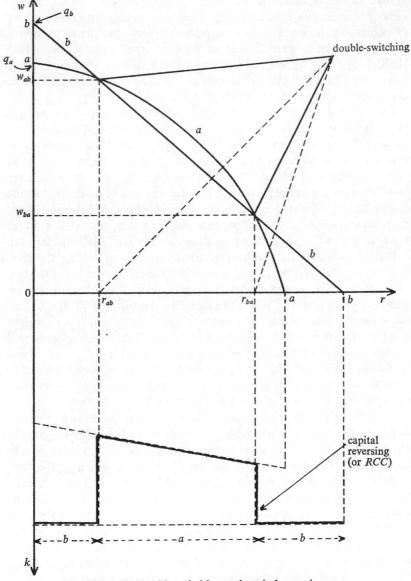

Fig. 4.1. Double-switching and capital-reversing

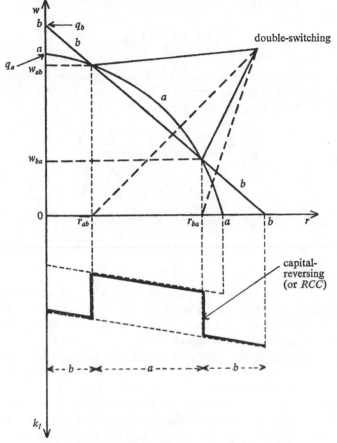

Fig. 4.2. Real double-switching and capital reversing

We repeat the analysis, this time measuring capital in terms of labour time per head, i.e. as real capital per head, k_l. With our present assumptions, the value of k_l *of any given technique*, no matter what is the shape of its *w-r* relationship, is smaller, the smaller is the value of *r* (see fig. 4.2). This is obvious when k_l is defined, for example, as

$$\frac{K}{L_c w} = \frac{L_g(1+r)^t}{L_c}$$

(see chapter 1, p. 24 above), for then

$$\frac{dk_l}{dr} = \frac{L_g t(1+r)^{t-1}}{L_c} > 0$$

In general, if $k_l = F(r)/L_c$, where $F'(r) > 0$, then

$$\frac{\mathrm{d}k_l}{\mathrm{d}r}\left(=\frac{F'(r)}{L_c}\right)>0$$

It may also be shown (in my case, by my colleagues, A. J. Fischer and N. F. Laing) that when we view k_l as $(q-w)/wr (\equiv F(r)/L_c)$, $\mathrm{d}k_l/\mathrm{d}r$ still equals $F'(r)/L_c$, as is to be expected. Thus

$$\frac{\mathrm{d}k_l}{\mathrm{d}r} = \frac{\mathrm{d}}{\mathrm{d}r}\left(\frac{q-w}{wr}\right) = \frac{\mathrm{d}}{\mathrm{d}r}\left(\frac{q}{wr}-\frac{1}{r}\right)$$

$$= -\frac{q}{wr^2}+\frac{1}{r}\frac{\mathrm{d}w}{\mathrm{d}r}\frac{\mathrm{d}}{\mathrm{d}w}\left(\frac{q}{w}\right)+\frac{1}{r^2}$$

which, after a number of steps, simplifies to

$$\frac{F'(r)}{L_c}$$

When only two techniques are considered, and we are comparing stationary states, capital-reversing implies double-switching and vice versa. However, when more than two are considered, it is possible to have capital-reversing without double-switching, i.e. any one technique is the most profitable of all for a self-contained range of values of r and once it retires it *never* makes a comeback. The example shown in fig. 4.3 is based on Pasinetti's example in Pasinetti [1966a], p. 516. In the bottom half of the figure, the unbroken lines show values of k and the dotted lines, k_l. It may be seen that capital-reversing occurs at rates of profits of r_{dc} and r_{ca} (but not at r_{ab}) *and that no technique ever comes back*.

Lesson 2: two offsetting errors cancel, so don't make three

So much for preliminary analysis, now for controversy. Levhari [1965] claimed to show that while double-switching may occur in an industry, it could not occur in an economy. Thus

> If we change the interest rate and we want to compare the techniques used in the different stationary states, we may encounter what Joan Robinson calls the 'Ruth Cohen Curiosum'. This refers to the possibility that as we change the interest rate producers switch the process of production from α to β, but as we change it further in the

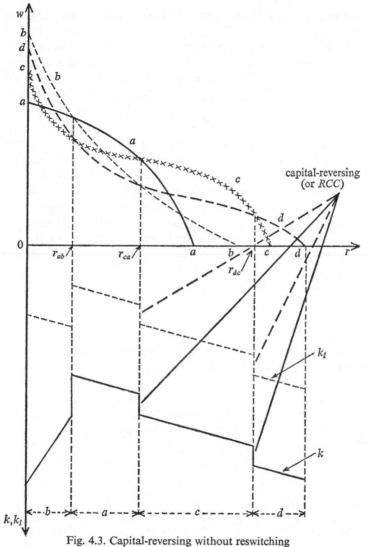

Fig. 4.3. Capital-reversing without reswitching

same direction they return to α.[1] This would have the unfortunate consequence that we could no longer say that the lowering of the interest rate brings about a process of 'deepening' and each process

[1] Levhari's terminology is wrong: *capital-reversing* is the RCC. What he is describing here is *double-switching*: see Robinson [1956], pp. 109–10, Robinson [1970a], pp. 309–10.

is more capital-intensive than its predecessors. This curiosum is also discussed by Piero Sraffa in chapter 12 of his book. He shows that producers may shift from one activity to another as the interest rate changes but return to the first activity as it changes further in the same direction. *The phenomenon may indeed be observed in the production of a single good. But in the second part of this discussion we show that it is impossible with the whole basis of production.* We cannot switch from one matrix to another in response to a change in the interest rate and then return to the first matrix in response to further changes in the same direction. So even though we cannot order the activities according to 'degree of mechanization', we can do so with the matrices. (Levhari [1965], p. 99 (emphasis added).)

That is to say, Levhari claimed to have shown that double-switching was impossible in an 'indecomposable' or 'irreducible' technology, 'a situation in which *every single* output requires, directly or indirectly as input for its production something . . . of *every single* other output'. (Levhari and Samuelson [1966], pp. 518–19.)[1] This proposition was shown conclusively to be false (except under very special conditions) in a series of papers in the 1966, 1967 and 1968 issues of the *Quarterly Journal of Economics* by Pasinetti [1966a], Levhari and Samuelson [1966], Morishima [1966], Bruno, Burmeister and Sheshinski [1966], Garegnani [1966], Samuelson [1966a], Robinson and Naqvi [1967], Bruno, Burmeister and Sheshinski [1968].[2]

The analysis has been conducted in terms of *w–r* relationships. Basically it consists of equilibrium comparisons, at different, arbitrarily given rates of profits, of Ricardo–Sraffa[3] systems in which labour and

---

[1] Pasinetti was the first to provide a counter example, originally in his paper to the Rome Congress of the Econometric Society in 1965 – an example which had its roots, moreover, in Sraffa's book. Subsequently, Levhari's three 'mates', Bruno, Burmeister and Sheshinski [1966], p. 527, argued that 'indecomposability of the technique matrix is essentially irrelevant for the reswitching discussion' anyway! (But on this, see Levhari and Samuelson [1966], pp. 518–19.)

[2] Following the 1966 Symposium in the *Quarterly Journal*, further excellent papers have been written: Stiglitz [1966], Brown [1968, 1969], Bhaduri [1969], Garegnani [1970a, 1970b], Pasinetti [1969, 1970], Spaventa [1968, 1970], Bliss [1970], Ferguson and Allen [1970].

[3] Sraffa was concerned to analyse, in the classical tradition, those properties of an economic system that are independent of changes in scale and proportions of factors. The production process is regarded as a circular one in which intermediate goods get star-billing rather than as 'a one-way avenue . . . from "Factors of Production" to "Consumption Goods".' Sraffa [1960], p. 93. An important consequence of Sraffa's view is that the marginal product is ruled out, 'it just would not be there to be found' (p.v.). See the appendix to this chapter where these themes are elaborated.

commodities are used to produce commodities, one commodity (in the absence of joint production) being produced by each method of production. Suppose that there is more than one method available for producing directly or indirectly a commodity which will be in surplus and therefore part (or even the whole) of the net product of the year's production, after account has been taken of the amount of commodities used up as means of production in the production process.[1] The forces of competition are assumed to ensure that the same rates of profits and wages will be paid in all industries. (Samuelson [1966a], p. 575, attributes this result to the workings of ruthless competition, allied with geometry.) Notice that this implies *nothing* about what determines their actual sizes or the distribution of income.

Then the neoclassical parables lead us to believe that as we arbitrarily consider lower rates of profits, methods associated with higher outputs per head become eligible, values of capital per head and per unit of output become greater and the distribution of income may be obtained by multiplying the quantities of factors by their respective marginal products which may be treated *as if* they were equal to the equilibrium real wage and rate of profits. Or, rather, the distribution of income, which, under very special circumstances, equals the simple Marshallian elasticity of the factor-price frontier envelope, may be treated as *equivalent* to that which would be obtained by this alternative procedure. The latter may, therefore, be dodged, see pp. 142–3 below.

Lesson 3: 'I come to praise Solow, not to bury him', P.A.S., 1962

Indeed, it was exactly these stories which Samuelson told in his 1962 article. He started with a heterogeneous capital-goods model whereby there were many different ways of producing the consumption good, methods which required different inputs of direct and indirect labour, i.e. labour applied after being transformed into commodities, and therefore different inputs of the same good *treated as a capital good*, into itself. (When producing itself, its form and the quantities used varied from method to method, so that we have in effect heterogeneous capital goods.)

I want to consider a special subclass of realistic cases, to present

---

[1] Those who find this an unfamiliar way of looking at the economic system may like to read an outstanding article by Nell [1967b]. They may also find helpful two papers by Massaro and myself [1964a, 1964b] and an article by Lowe [1954]. See, also, the appendix to this chapter.

certain valid results which hold rigorously for such models ... it would serve no purpose ... to consider a model in which there were not diverse physical capital goods ... it would evade the issue to consider a model in which capital goods were not highly specific to one use and to one combination of co-operating labour. None of these issues will be dodged in the slightest. (Samuelson [1962], p. 196.)

Taking each method in turn he 'costed' them up at different rates of profits to find the maximum equilibrium real-wage rate that could be associated with each. The range of rate of profits is from zero to a maximum which is determined by the commodity's own rate of growth when the real-wage rate is zero and radioactive depreciation is allowed for. (We ignore the latter in what follows.)

We may illustrate the procedure in the most general sense by using the general example given by Joan Robinson and Naqvi [1967], pp. 585–6. (The simplest way is based on Champernowne's example: see Champernowne [1953–4], and equation (1.4) on p. 25 above.) Consider two activities, 1 and 2, each producing a quantity (gross output) of one commodity (X_1 and X_2 respectively) and using in its production, *itself*, the other commodity and direct labour (l_{0i}, $i = 1, 2$, is the input of labour per unit of output). We may also suppose, as Joan Robinson and Naqvi do (also Garegnani [1970a] and Samuelson [1962]) that the activities are in such a proportion to one another that they form a sub-system with a *net* product of one unit of commodity 1 so that we are in effect considering again a stationary state in which the consumption good is the entire national product.

If we let commodity 1 be the *numéraire*, we may write the price equations as:

$$(1+r)(x_{11}X_1 + p_2x_{21}X_1) + wl_{01}X_1 = X_1 \qquad (4.1)$$

$$(1+r)(x_{12}X_2 + p_2x_{22}X_2) + wl_{02}X_2 = p_2X_2 \qquad (4.2)$$

where x_{ij} is the input per unit of output of commodity i into commodity j, $i = 1, 2$, and p_2 is the price of commodity 2 in terms of commodity 1.

Equations (4.1) and (4.2) may be rearranged so that each forms an expression for p_2. Equating these, we derive the following expression for w as a function of r: it is, of course, the w–r relationship, the basic relationship of the analysis.

$$= \frac{(x_{11}X_1x_{22}X_2 - x_{21}X_1x_{12}X_2)(1+r)^2 - (X_2x_{11}X_1 + X_1x_{22}X_2)(1+r) + X_1X_2}{(l_{02}X_2x_{21}X_1 - l_{01}X_1x_{22}X_2)(1+r) + l_{01}X_1X_2}(4.3)^1$$

Brown [1969], Garegnani [1966], Hicks [1965], and Spaventa [1968] use a simpler formulation of expression (4.3), namely, that capital and labour are inputs into consumption and capital goods respectively in the two activities. However, this, while it fits happily into the literature on two-sector growth models (see Hahn [1971]), nevertheless obscures some of the technological factors here made explicit. The present procedure is also more faithful to Sraffa's basic point of view. (Solow [1963a] derives w–r relationships for the Cobb–Douglas and Worswick models in Lecture 2. Brown [1969] has a most interesting analysis of the double-switching issues in terms of a composite production co-efficient – the amount of labour required to produce a machine which in turn produces a unit of consumption good: see below, p. 172.)

In general all that can be said of expression (4.3) is that the greater is r, the smaller is w,[2] Joan Robinson and Naqvi (and other writers, e.g. Hicks [1965], Brown [1969], Garegnani [1966, 1970a], Spaventa [1968], and pp. 40–3 above) have systematically examined the conditions under which expression (4.3) is concave or convex to the origin, or a straight line, a very special but·crucial case, as we see below. The w–r relationship, expression (4.3) version, is a straight line if, when $r = 0$, the ratio of the *labour* value of the means of production to the direct labour used in the production of commodity 1 is the *same* as the corresponding ratio associated with the production of commodity 2, and the time patterns of the inputs are uniform, so that the relative prices of the two commodities are *independent* of the rate of profits, *even when* it is positive. (They are in fact equal to the ratio of the direct labour inputs per unit of output of the two commodities.) *It follows that the value of 'capital' – means of production – is similarly independent of the value of r, in the sense that it does not change when we consider different values of r.*

Students of Marx will prick up their ears here for this is, if you like, the pure labour theory of value case – uniform organic compositions of

---

[1] I have corrected a printing slip in the version of expression (4.3) shown in Robinson and Naqvi [1967], p. 586. My definition of x_{ij} differs from that of Joan Robinson and Naqvi, and I have not cancelled X_1X_2 in expression (4.3) (which, irony of irony, is shown as x_1x_2 in Harcourt [1969a]) so that readers may translate my version into theirs.

[2] Samuelson [1966a], p. 574, uses this result to poke fun at Marx for backing one horse too many. I suspect that they went to different race tracks.

capital. 'Pure' is perhaps an unfortunate word since it may be taken to imply that the labour theory of value is simply the proposition that prices are proportional to embodied labour whereas, in fact, it implies that prices are determined by embodied labour. In this sense, Sraffa has a labour theory of value: see Harcourt and Massaro [1964b], Meek [1967], pp. 161–78.

We may illustrate the propositions above by the following example from Joan Robinson and Naqvi [1967], p. 585, *passim*: Consider a technique which produces a net output of one unit of wheat, using, in total, one unit of labour, i.e.

1 t. wheat $+\frac{14}{5}$ t. copper $+\frac{3}{5}$ labour $\rightarrow$ 3 t. wheat

1 t. wheat $+\frac{6}{5}$ t. copper $+\frac{2}{5}$ labour $\rightarrow$ 4 t. copper

(It may be seen that total labour is one, and that when we allow for the copper and wheat used up in production we have exhausted all the copper produced and are left with one ton of wheat in the net product.) When $r = 0$, the *net* product of one wheat is entirely wages, in this case, the wage *rate* per unit. There is, therefore, only one unknown – the price of copper in terms of wheat (p_{cw}) which may be obtained by solving *either* of the equations

$$1+\tfrac{14}{5}p_{cw}+\tfrac{3}{5} = 3$$
$$1+ \tfrac{6}{5} p_{cw}+\tfrac{2}{5} = 4p_{cw} \qquad (4.4)$$

both of which are measured in wheat units. We obtain

$$p_{cw} = \frac{5(3-1-\tfrac{3}{5})}{14} = \frac{1+\tfrac{2}{5}}{4-\tfrac{6}{5}} = \tfrac{1}{2} \qquad (4.5)$$

Notice that this equals the ratio of the direct labour inputs per unit of output, i.e.

$$\frac{2}{5\times4} \bigg/ \frac{3}{5\times3} = \tfrac{1}{2}$$

The means of production–labour ratios, measured as wheat per unit of labour, are

$$\frac{1+\tfrac{7}{5}}{\tfrac{3}{5}} = \frac{1+\tfrac{3}{5}}{\tfrac{2}{5}} = 4 \qquad (4.6)$$

To show that the *w–r* trade-off relationship is *now* a straight line, we take either price equation, convert the copper–wheat and copper–copper inputs to their equivalents in wheat and express *w* as a function of *r*. For example, using the price equation for wheat, we have

$$(1+r)(1+\tfrac{14}{5}\cdot\tfrac{1}{2})+w\tfrac{3}{5} = 3 \text{ so that } w = 1-4r \qquad (4.7)$$

In the appendix to the chapter we further examine this example in order to show the special conditions under which expression (4.6) holds. The following quote from Sraffa [1960], pp. 12–13, is a splendid intuitive example of why relative prices are now constant and independent of r.

Starting from the situation in which the whole of the national income goes to labour, we imagine wages to be reduced: a rate of profits will thereby arise.

The key to the movement of relative prices consequent upon a change in the wage lies in the inequality of the proportions in which labour and means of production are employed in the various industries. It is clear that if the proportion were the same in all industries no price-changes could ensue, however great was the diversity of the commodity-composition of the means of production in different industries. For in each industry an equal deduction from the wage would yield just as much as was required for paying the profits on its means of production at a uniform rate without need to disturb the existing prices.

For the same reason it is impossible for prices to remain unchanged when there is inequality of 'proportions'. Suppose that prices did remain unchanged when the wage was reduced and a rate of profits emerged. Since in any one industry what was saved by the wage-reduction would depend on the number of men employed, while what was needed for paying profits at a uniform rate would depend on the aggregate value of the means of production used, industries with a sufficiently low proportion of labour to means of production would have a deficit, while industries with a sufficiently high proportion would have a surplus, on their payments for wages and profits.

In the Hicks, Brown, Garegnani and Spaventa versions of the w–r relationship – also Samuelson's (see pp. 136–7 below) – we get a straight line when each activity has the *same* physical capital input to labour ratio. If there is concavity (to the origin) this implies that the capital–labour ratio in the capital-good activity is greater than that in the consumption-good one (and vice versa for convexity). This may be seen most easily by noting first that the changes in the slopes of the chords joining points on the w–r relationship of a technique to its w_{max} intercept (see fig. 4.4) measure the changes in the price of the capital good in terms of the consumption good (p_k) provided that the net product consists of one good only. Thus the slope of the chord is

$$k = \frac{w_{\max} - w}{r} = p_k \bar{k} \qquad (4.8)$$

where $\bar{k}$ is the physical amount of the capital good per head.

If $\qquad\qquad k_2 - k_1 \gtreqless 0 \quad$ then $\quad \bar{k}(p_{k_2} - p_{k_1}) \gtreqless 0 \qquad (4.9)$

Consider the bottom inequality (which corresponds to fig. 4.4); as we consider lower values of r, the fall in capital costs will affect the capital good more than the consumption good if the former's capital-intensity is greater than the latter's and, *overall*, $p_k \bar{k} (= k)$ gets less: see Garegnani [1970a], pp. 409–10.

Samuelson, in fact, assumed that the physical capital to labour ratios of *each* activity in a technique were the *same* and that the net product consisted of the consumption good. As a result, he could order tech-

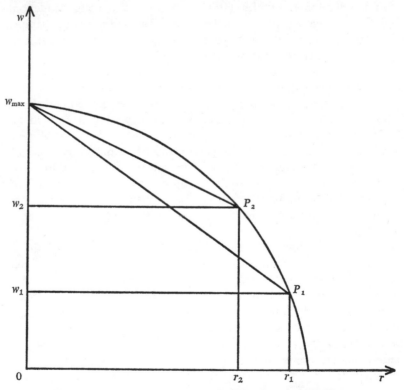

Fig. 4.4. Concavity of the *w–r* relationship and the value of k

niques according to the maximum real-wage rates (physical outputs per head when $r = 0$). The three (straight-line) $w–r$ relationships corresponding to techniques a, b and c (each one of which may be interpreted as a stationary state in the manner of chapter 1) are shown in fig. 4.5.

That Samuelson's $w–r$ relationships are straight lines (see Samuelson [1962], pp. 204–5) may be shown as follows: Consider a constant-returns-to-scale technique of two activities which produces two goods, a capital good (k) and a consumption good (c), using inputs of labour (l_i, $i = c, k$) and capital (k_i) in each activity. p_c, the price per unit of the consumption good, is unity, i.e. the *numéraire*; p_k is the price of the capital good in terms of c. In Ricardo–Sraffa systems, the following price equations[1] hold

$$rp_k k_c + wl_c = 1$$
$$rp_k k_k + wl_k = p_k \qquad (4.10)$$

(As always we ignore depreciation.) The $w–r$ relationship may be obtained by eliminating p_k from the expressions (4.10) to give

$$w = \frac{1 - rk_k}{r(k_c l_k - k_k l_c) + l_c} \qquad (4.11)$$

Samuelson assumes that

$$k_c = k_k = k^*, \ l_c = l_k = l$$

(which implies that $p_k = p_c = 1$!). Expression (4.11) thus becomes

$$w = \frac{1 - rk^*}{l} = \frac{1}{l} - \frac{k^*}{l}r \qquad (4.12)$$

a downward-sloping straight line with a vertical intercept of $1/l$, i.e. *productivity, and a slope of* k^*/l, i.e. *the physical capital–labour ratio.*

In fig. 4.5 there are two switch points, $e(r_{ab}, w_{ab})$ and $d(r_{bc}, w_{bc})$, where two methods are equi-profitable. As r gets smaller, one method either survives or at a critical value of r (a switch point, for example, r_{ab}) gets ready to swap over to another, *but it never reappears once it is gone.* As we know, Sraffa [1960] and Champernowne [1953–4] were the parents of the outer envelope, $cder_{a\,\text{max}}$, which Samuelson christened the factor-price frontier (*FpF*). But, we should remind ourselves, since

---

[1] Sraffra always avoids the terms, 'cost of production' and 'capital', because in neoclassical theory they sometimes carry the supposition that their quantities are independent of and determined prior to the prices of products, see Sraffra [1960], p. 9. Otherwise we might have been tempted – as others have been – to call expressions (4.10) cost-of-production equations.

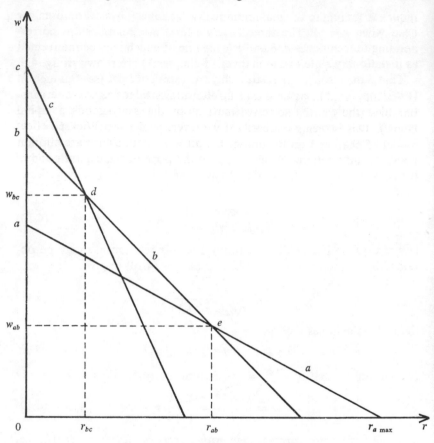

Fig. 4.5. Samuelson's straight-line *FpF*s

the neo-Keynesians do not regard 'capital' as a primary factor on all fours with labour and land, or, indeed, as a factor at all, they would decline to be the godparents of the child so named.

Clearly, by increasing the density of techniques, 'increasing the number of pages in the book of blue-prints', a virtually continuous change from one method to another will occur, though each point on the envelope is associated with a specific method of production (or two at switch points) in which there is no substitutability of commodities – 'capital' – for labour. Garegnani [1970a], for example, has shown that if we make the changes in the coefficients defining each technique change *continuously* rather than discretely from technique to technique, i.e. make them all functions of a continuous variable (a device also used by Champernowne [1953–4] and Pasinetti [1969]), each point on the *FpF* envelope will be associated with a *single* method or technique instead of there being segments associated with one and 'corners' (switch points) associated with two, as occurs in the discrete case.

We may note in passing that fig. 4.5 allows us to tell the first three parables (the fourth, however, must await the analysis of pp. 141–3 below). This is seen most easily if we revert to the real Wicksell effect model of chapter 1 and suppose that all *w–r* relationships are straight lines, see fig. 4.6. Thus lower rates of profits *are* associated with higher

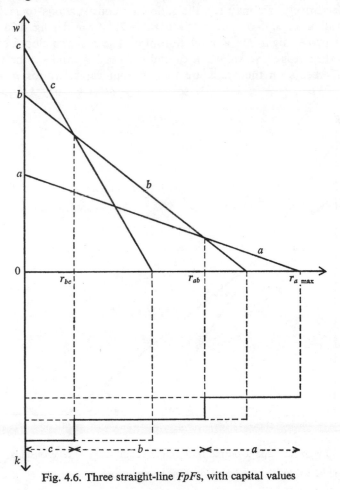

Fig. 4.6. Three straight-line *FpF*s, with capital values

values of capital per man, for technique b is chosen at lower rates of profits than technique a and $k_b > k_a$; also

$$q_b(= w_{b\,\max}) > q_a(= w_{a\,\max})$$

Similarly, $k_c > k_b$ and $q_c > q_b$. Higher capital–output ratios *are* associated with lower rates of profits, for

$$\frac{k_c}{q_c}\Big/\frac{k_b}{q_b} = \frac{k_c q_b}{k_b q_c} = \frac{q_c - w}{q_b - w}\frac{q_b}{q_c} = \frac{q_b q_c - w q_b}{q_b q_c - w q_c} > 1 \qquad (4.13)$$

as $wq_b < wq_c$, for common values of w and r, i.e. at switch points.

Alternatively, we may use the following constructions to make the point about capital–output ratios (parable 2).[1] Consider fig. 4.7a which shows two straight-line w–r relationships. The *absolute* slopes of each equal their respective values of capital per head, k_a and k_b; the respective intercepts on the r axis are their output–capital ratios, q_a/k_a and q_b/k_b. (When $w = 0$, $k = q/r$, so that $r = q/k$.) Clearly $k_b/q_b > k_a/q_a$.

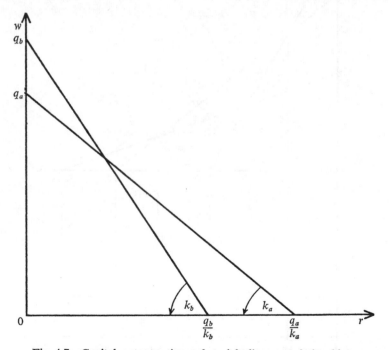

Fig. 4.7a. Capital–output ratios and straight-line w–r relationships

[1] I am indebted to Ian Steedman for these constructions.

With a curved w–r relationship, the output–capital ratio corresponding to each point on it may be found by drawing chords from the respective w_{max} points on the w axis through the relevant point – from q_a through P in fig. 4.7b – to cut the r axis at a distance which equals q/k. Thus $q_a/k_{a,1}$ corresponds to the rate of interest, r_1, and wage rate, w_1, in fig. 4.7b. We note that $(q_a - w_1)/r_1 = k_{a,1}$ from which it follows that

$$\frac{q_a}{k_{a,1}} = r_1 + \frac{w_1}{k_{a,1}},$$

which is the value of the distance from the origin to the point where the chord through q_a and P meets the r axis. Thirdly, higher sustainable steady states of consumption per head *are* associated with more 'mechanized' methods of production, for $q_c > q_b > q_a$ and $k_c > k_b > k_a$.

Samuelson then shows that the FpF envelope may be approximated to, as close as we like, by using a simple, all-purpose, one-commodity model in which 'capital' and output are jelly (J), the production function showing the various combinations of labour and jelly which produce jelly is homogeneous of order one, and factors are paid, through the

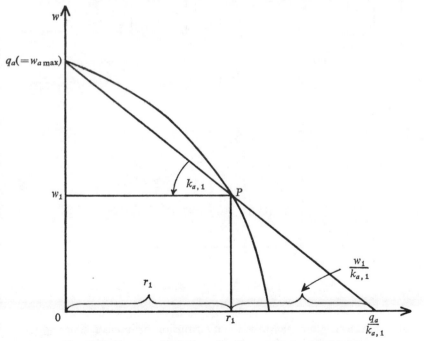

Fig. 4.7b. The capital–output ratio of a curved w–r relationship

workings of competition (and static, realized expectations), their marginal products measured in jelly. In figs. 4.8a and 4.8b we show the relationships between these rates and the jelly capital–labour ratio (j). The factor payments are obtained by partially differentiating the expression for the production function with respect to jelly and labour and putting the resulting marginal products equal to r and w respectively. Corresponding to each value of j is an equilibrium rate of profits and wage rate which, together, make up a point on an *FpF* (see the two points, r_1, w_1, and r_2, w_2 in fig. 4.8c).

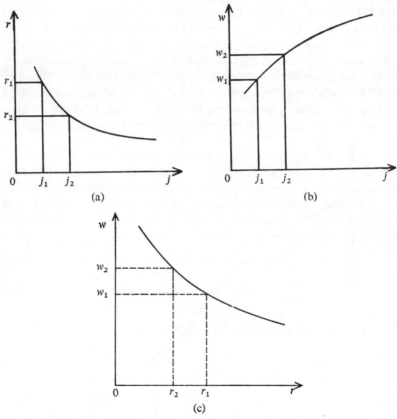

Fig. 4.8. The world of jelly

It can be easily shown that the simple Marshallian elasticity at each point on the frontier measures the distribution of income. Corresponding to any point it will always be true that

$$q = rk + w \qquad (4.14)$$

where q, k and w are all amounts of jelly per head, and that

$$dq = rdk + kdr + dw \qquad (4.15)$$

Divide expression (4.15) by dq *and remember that* $r = dq/dk$ *by assumption*, to obtain

$$1 = 1 + \frac{kdr + dw}{dq}$$

This implies that

$$k = -\frac{dw}{dr} \qquad (4.16)$$

where $-dw/dr$ is the (value of) the slope of the *FpF*. The elasticity of the frontier at each point (E) is

$$E = -\frac{r}{w}\frac{dw}{dr} = \frac{rk}{w} \qquad (4.17)$$

which is the distribution of income and, thus, the fourth parable.[1]

A more orthodox derivation of this result, one which, however, is less germane for our present purposes, is due to ACMS [1961], p. 229. If the production function exhibits constant returns to scale and if factors are paid their marginal products, the elasticity of w with respect to r can be shown to be rk/w. Thus

$$w = f(k) - f'(k)k \quad \text{and} \quad r = f'(k) \qquad (4.18)$$

$$\frac{dw}{dk} = -f''(k)k \quad \text{and} \quad \frac{dr}{dk} = f''(k) \qquad (4.19)$$

$$\frac{dw}{dr} = \frac{dw}{dk}\Big/\frac{dr}{dk} = -k$$

and
$$E = -\frac{r}{w}\frac{dw}{dr} = \frac{rk}{w} \qquad (4.20)$$

Of course, knowing E, we are only one step short of the implied *FpF* which we may obtain by integrating $E(= d \log w / d \log r)$. It follows that if we know the *FpF* in the first place, and *if* the above assumptions hold, we should be able to go from it to the underlying production function by reversing our steps.

[1] These sections draw heavily on two excellent papers by Bhaduri [1966, 1969].

Parables (1) to (3) may also be shown to hold in the jelly world. Moreover, the correspondence between the jelly world of parable and the 'real world' of heterogeneous capital goods may be made as close as we like by choosing the suitable brand of jelly to use in the surrogate – *as if* – production function, the name given by Samuelson to the function from which the figures 4.8 are derived. What is more, *if* we view the values of r and w of an *FpF as if* they were observations taken from a jelly production function, Samuelson also shows that we have a ready-made method by which to estimate, from our knowledge of the *FpF*'s slope and the amount of labour in the economies *alone*, the value of J (jelly capital) corresponding to each and every point on the *FpF* – instant jelly, if you like.

Thus Samuelson writes the jelly production function as

$$J' = F(J, L) = LF(1, \frac{J}{L}) \equiv LF(j) \tag{4.21}$$

Now
$$w = \frac{\delta J'}{\delta L} = F(j) - jF'(j)$$

$$\tag{4.22}$$

and
$$r = \frac{\delta J'}{\delta J} = F'(j)$$

$$\frac{dw}{dr} = \frac{dw}{dj}\frac{dj}{dr}$$

$$= [F'(j) - F'(j) - jF''(j)]\left[\frac{1}{F''(j)}\right]$$

$$= -j \tag{4.23}$$

so that
$$-L\frac{dw}{dr} = Lj = J \tag{4.24}$$

(We have shown already that the slope of Samuelson's *FpF* is the (physical) capital–labour ratio, see p. 137 above.)

Nevertheless, we must remind ourselves again that straight-line w–r relationships only allow the construction of a pseudo-production function whereby equilibrium comparisons *seem* to tell the 'right' story and to be 'well-behaved'. The dynamic out-of-equilibrium process of the substitution of capital for labour is *not* being analysed. It may be in a jelly world but only by dodging *all* the real puzzles that heterogeneous capital goods in fact throw up.

Lesson 4: jelly may shed light – but it can't take heat

Unfortunately, for the neoclassical revivalists, all these results disappear when we drop our very special assumption (which is, however, related to Marx, vols. I and II, in which the organic composition of capital is uniform in all uses) that each *w–r* relationship is a straight line.[1] For now the *possibility* that the same method will be the most profitable at *two* (or more) values of *r*, while others are more profitable in between, becomes inevitable. (Note, though, that it is the *possibility* which is inevitable: curved *w–r* relationships do *not* automatically imply that double-switching will occur.) A case where it *does* occur is shown in fig. 4.1 above; technique *b* (which has a straight-line *w–r* relationship) comes back after giving way to technique *a* (which has a curved one) between the rates of profits of r_{ba} and r_{ab}. It will be noticed that q_b – output per man of technique *b* – exceeds q_a. If, therefore, we were to compare the sustainable steady states of consumption per head at different rates of profits, instead of obtaining the neoclassical parable – investment in more roundabout methods of production as *r* falls allows higher sustainable standards of living in the long run – we would have instead a 'dip' over the range $r_{ba}–r_{ab}$ (see fig. 4.9).

While reswitching will do the trick, capital-reversing is *all* that is needed to obtain 'perverse' steady-state movements: see Bruno, Burmeister and Sheshinski [1966], Pasinetti [1966a]. In fig. 4.10, we show the steady-state consumption per head levels that correspond to the *FpF* envelope of fig. 4.3 above, in which capital-reversing *alone* occurs. So bang goes parable (3). It should also be obvious, all too painfully so, perhaps, that either reswitching or capital-reversing, or the two combined, destroy parables (1) and (2) as well.

As the destruction *by capital-reversing* of parable (1) – the *necessary* association between lower rates of profits and higher values of capital per head, themselves associated with techniques of greater output per head – plays an important part in the subsequent controversies, we ought to remind ourselves of it by referring to fig. 4.3 above and by quoting Pasinetti's views on its significance from Pasinetti [1966a], pp. 516–17.

---

[1] It would be ironic if, nearly 100 years later, the rival theory of value to that of Ricardo and Marx should founder on the assumption which Böhm-Bawerk found so objectionable in Marx's theory. On this, see Dobb [1940], p. 74 n1, and generally for a brilliant – and highly relevant – account of the historical and analytical background to the present debate.

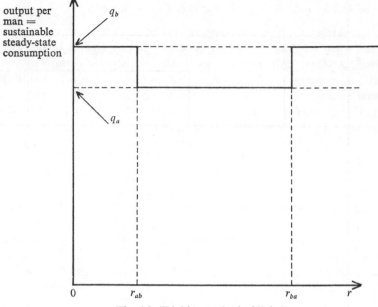

Fig. 4.9. 'Dip' in standard of living

The conclusion simply is that, on this problem, the whole theory of capital seems to have been caught in the trap of an old mode of thinking. Without any justification, except that this is the way economists have always been accustomed to think, it has been taken for granted that, at any given state of technical knowledge, the capital goods that become profitable at a lower rate of profits always entail a higher 'quantity of capital' per man. The foregoing analysis shows that this is not necessarily so; there is no connection that can be expected in general between the direction of change of the rate of profits and the direction of change of the 'quantity of capital' per man.

(I have changed 'higher' to 'lower', and vice versa, in the appropriate places to make the passage better fit the present context.) Indeed, Garegnani [1970a], p. 421, describes parable (1) as 'the basic premise of the traditional theory of distribution *in all its formulations*: the notion that a fall of r will cheapen the more capital-intensive processes of production' (emphasis added) – a proposition to which we return below, pp. 158–69.

It may also be shown that the elasticities of points on the *FpF* envelope

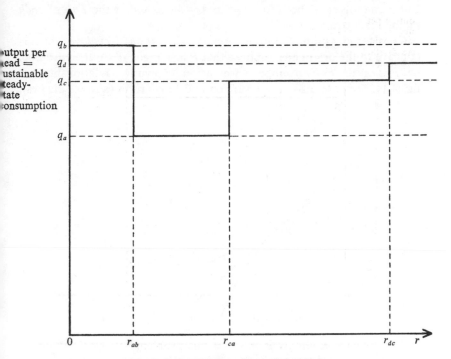

output per
head =
sustainable
steady-
state
consumption

Fig. 4.10. Capital-reversing and the 'dip'

no longer give the distribution of income, essentially because non-straight-line w–r relationships are inconsistent with the neoclassical parable that $r = \mathrm{d}q/\mathrm{d}k$. It follows that the 'as if' production function will not in general do the trick. Thus it is *always* true, as we have seen, that income per head may be written as

$$q = rk + w \qquad (4.14)$$

and therefore, by definition, that

$$k = \frac{q - w}{r} \qquad (4.25)$$

We have already seen that, when $r = \mathrm{d}q/\mathrm{d}k$

$$k = -\frac{\mathrm{d}w}{\mathrm{d}r} \qquad (4.16)$$

But k cannot equal both $(q-w)/r$ and $-\mathrm{d}w/\mathrm{d}r$ *unless* the *FpF* of *each* method is a straight line.

Consider any point P on a w–r relationship *of one technique* which is concave to the origin and suppose that P has 'made it' on the envelope, i.e. P is on the *FpF* envelope as well as on its own w–r relationship, see fig. 4.11. Suppose also, as Samuelson and Levhari do (and we always),

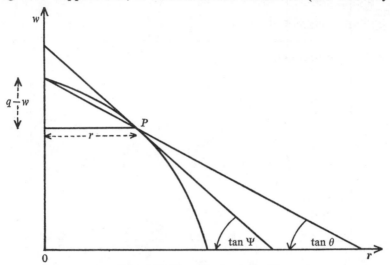

Fig. 4.11. The end of parable (4)

that stationary states are being compared. Tan θ measures $(q-w)/r$ and tan ψ, $\mathrm{d}w/\mathrm{d}r$. Tan θ and tan ψ are equal *only* when the relationship is a straight line. As the former is always true by definition, the latter cannot also equal the value of capital per head, r is *not* equal to $\mathrm{d}q/\mathrm{d}k$, and the value of E at P is *not* a measure of the distribution of income. (Nor may we obtain the value of K (via J) from our knowledge of $\mathrm{d}w/\mathrm{d}r$ and L.)[1] When $k = -\mathrm{d}w/\mathrm{d}r$, so that each w–r relationship is a straight line, we have in effect a measure of capital within each technique which *is* independent of distribution and prices. But as each technique produces the *same* all-purpose commodity, albeit with different proportions *as* between techniques, though not within them, it is *as if we had never really left the malleable capital or jelly world, within* the boundaries of that which no one has ever doubted the validity of the parables: on this, see especially Robinson and Naqvi [1967], Spaventa [1968], Garegnani [1970a], Pasinetti [1969].

[1] Figure 4.11 is due to Garegnani (1970a] and is used by Bhaduri [1969].

When we leave stationary states and enter steadily growing ones, revaluation puzzles associated with changing prices of capital goods in terms of consumption goods arise, Garegnani's diagram as used by Bhaduri (and myself, see Harcourt [1969a]) is no longer appropriate, and there is another (very special) case where the neoclassical parables hold, namely that associated with the neo-neoclassical theorem or Golden Rule of Accumulation: see, for example, Koopmans [1965], Pearce [1962], Bhaduri [1966], Nell [1970], Harcourt [1970a]. Here,

$$q \equiv w + rk \equiv c + gk \qquad (4.26)$$

where c = consumption per head and g = rate of growth, *externally given and a constant.*

$$dq \equiv dw + rdk + kdr \equiv dc + gdk \qquad (4.27)$$

When the Golden Rule prevails, so that c is at a maximum, $dc = 0$. If, as well, $r = g$ (in the neoclassical case, $r = g$ *implies* that $dc = 0$),

$$\frac{dq}{dk} = g = r \qquad (4.28)$$

and, as before, $k = -dw/dr$ and $E = rk/w$.[1]

In all other cases, though, while $k = (q-w)/r$, it does not equal $-dw/dr$, $E \neq rk/w$ and $dq/dk \neq r$. Figure 4.11 (and fig. 9 of Harcourt [1969a]) are not applicable to the growing economy cases because the valuation of q depends on the relative prices of c and gk which in turn depend upon the values of r and w, so that q can no longer be *measured on the w axis as the w intercept* when $r \neq 0$.[2]

We should also mention a counter example *in the stationary state case* which was pointed out to me by Y. K. Ng: see fig. 4.12. To be a serious contender, though, Ng needs further to show that the point P alone is the contribution of *this w–r* relationship to the *FpF* envelope.

Lesson 5: why?

Why did the original neoclassical parables omit the double-switching and capital-reversing possibilities and why, essentially, must they be supposed to occur in comparisons of technologies such as those actually

---

[1] This extremely neat formulation is due to my colleague, N. F. Laing.

[2] I am indebted to Masao Fukuoka, N. F. Laing, Edward J. Nell and David Bailey for making me see these points. They are elaborated further in Nell's comment [1970] on my survey article.

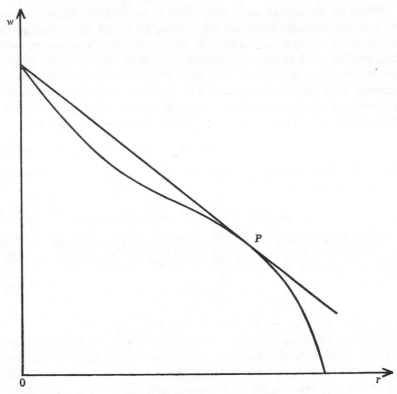

Fig. 4.12. Ng's counter example

used? The basic Austrian concept of capital may be expressed by supposing, first, that labour is applied uniformly through time to produce (say) a unit of output and, secondly, that the greater is the time taken for the final product to emerge, the smaller is the total amount of labour that is needed overall. This is the basis of the Austrian measure of 'capital' in terms of an average period of production.[1] It follows that at very high rates of profits (and low real-wage rates), techniques which use more total labour but less time will be cheapest; while at low rates of profits, the more time-intensive methods of production will be the most profitable. With discreteness in technology, one technique may be the most profitable for a range of values of r; but once it disappears, it *never* reappears again.

---

[1] This and the next paragraph owe much to Samuelson's 'summing up' of the debate, see Samuelson [1966a].

Notice the subtle way our stories have been told so far. Though we are only making comparisons of equilibrium positions, we nevertheless always start with a high rate of profits and move to situations with low ones and it is sometimes hard to remember that we are *not* being told about an actual process, for example, how an economy may move, through accumulation and deepening, from a high r, scarce capital position to a low r, abundant capital one – and what we may hope to achieve by this process. As we have seen, p. 123 above, Samuelson himself does not always remember.

Now consider the case where we compare two methods, in *neither* of which is labour applied uniformly over time. Then it is clear that the ratio of the costs of the methods of producing a unit of net output at different values of r can fall below and rise above unity.[1] Suppose, for example, that one method – method A – has a large input of labour at the beginning of its (two-period) gestation period, while the other – method B – has a larger gestation period (three periods) than A, a small input of labour at the start and a large one towards the end which is, however, *less* than the total input in A. The *total* input of labour in A is less than that in B. Then at very high values of r, interest on interest on interest on the cost of labour employed at the start of method B must exceed the wage and interest costs of method A, so that A is preferred to B. (If we ignore wage costs and talk instead in terms of real capital, we would say that the real capital cost of B is greater than that of A. Since both methods produce the same output, clearly A will be preferred.) At very low or zero values of r, A will also be preferred because it has the lower *total* input of labour (and time!). But there is an intermediate range of values of r where the investment of *most* of B's labour for a shorter period than A's at moderate rates of interest makes B's total cost less than A's. Hence B is preferred.[2]

The analogy between this result and the possibility of multiple rates of return to investment in present value calculations has been noticed by several writers, for example, Bruno, Burmeister and Sheshinski

---

[1] In Samuelson's example, w does *not* change as r does. Sraffa [1960], pp. 34–8, however, illustrates the same phenomena, though, admittedly, in a different context, in an example in which w does change (in a manner determined by its functional relationship with r) and the same result is obtained.

[2] Nobuo Okishio and Ian Steedman have kindly provided me with the conditions that ensure that the values of r at which A gives way to B and then comes back again, i.e. the switch points, are real and positive. They are that: (1) $l_a^2 - 4l_{b_1}l_{b_2} > 0$ (for two distinct *real* switch points), where l_a is the labour input in method A, l_{b_1} and l_{b_2} the labour inputs in method B, and (2) $l_a > 2l_{b_1}$ (for positive ones).

[1966], pp. 528 and 533. The following is perhaps the simplest way to put the point. In the example above, when r takes *two* particular values, say, r_{ab}, the capital costs of methods A and B are equal, i.e.

$$l_a(1+r_{ab})^2 = l_{b1}(1+r_{ab})^3 + l_{b2}(1+r_{ab}) \qquad (4.29)$$

Now view l_a and the two l_bs as the expected quasi-rents (QR) of two separate investment projects, A' and B', both of which entail the same initial outlay now of unity. The QRs will be received as follows: l_a, at the end of two periods; l_{b1}, at the end of one period; l_{b2}, at the end of three periods. Then it follows directly from expression (4.29) that the present values of their expected quasi-rents (and therefore their benefit-cost ratios) *at rates of interest of r_{ab}* will be equal also. Their present values may be obtained by dividing both sides of expression (4.29) by $(1+r_{ab})^4$ to give

$$\frac{l_a}{(1+r_{ab})^2} = \frac{l_{b1}}{(1+r_{ab})} + \frac{l_{b2}}{(1+r_{ab})^3} \qquad (4.30)$$

(At rates of interest in between the r_{ab}s, project B' would have the higher present values; outside the range, A' would have them.) It also follows, of course, that the use of the values, r_{ab}, as discount factors would reduce the present value of the differential QR stream: l_{b1}, $-l_a$, l_{b2} to zero, i.e. we have here an instance of multiple Fisherian rates of return over cost (Mark I): see Pasinetti [1969] and pp. 159–60 below.

Sraffa and Joan Robinson used this uneven distribution of labour through 'horizontal' or 'instant' time to describe the possibilities of double-switching and capital-reversing. Sraffa [1960], p. 81 *passim*, used his reduction to 'dated' labour examples (whereby the contribution of each input of labour to the value of a commodity is given by its wage cost accumulated forward at the appropriate rate of profits over the 'periods' between its input and the emergence of the product) as the analogy to make the point.

Joan Robinson's explanation in Robinson [1956], pp. 109–10, may be put as follows. Suppose that the gestation period of technique a is longer than that of technique b, but that the input of labour is concentrated at the beginning of the period while that of b is concentrated at the end. Consider their w–r relationships which, together with their respective capital values, are shown in fig. 4.13. We know that at the wage rate, w_{ba} (and the rate of profits, r_{ba}) the two methods are equiprofitable. Now consider the wage rate, w_a. Then both techniques will be associated with lower values of r, r_a and r_b respectively. But because the

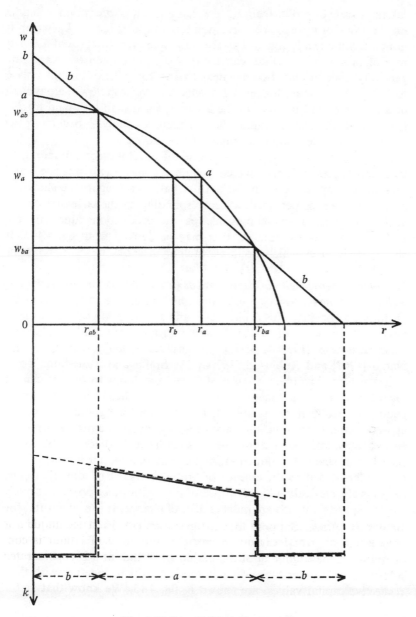

Fig. 4.13. Joan Robinson's example

fall in the rate of profits from r_{ba} to r_a has a much greater *relative* impact on the value of k_a than the corresponding fall to r_b has on k_b (which is none), technique a is able to pay the same wage rate – w_a – and a *higher* rate of profits $(r_a > r_b)$ than can technique b. But when the wage rate gets very high so that it comes near to absorbing *all* of q_a (but only a lot of q_b) there are no longer the profits left over to allow the payment of a higher *rate* of profits (on the lower k) for a than that paid for b – hence, first, the reswitching at r_{ab} and then, secondly, b becoming the more profitable technique at values of r below r_{ab}.

In fig. 4.14a we show the w–r trade-off envelope corresponding to three techniques, a, b, c, on which technique b makes two separate – and separated – appearances. In the bottom half of the figure we show the *real* capital values per head, k_l, corresponding to the envelope. In fig. 4.14b we show Joan Robinson's pseudo-production function – the relationship between q and k_l that may be derived from fig. 4.14a. It shows the impact which double-switching has on the q, k_l relationship.

It is *the heterogeneity of capital goods (whether fixed or circulating) as well as the time pattern of production* which gives rise to the possibility of double-switching. This is clear in Sraffa's description of the timelessness of the concept of 'dated' labour and has been made explicit by Champernowne [1953–4, 1966], Morishima [1966], Robinson and Naqvi [1967] and Robinson [1970a]. As Sraffa and Morishima point out, a process involving a lapse of time from input to output can be regarded as an instantaneous process requiring heterogeneous capital goods by introducing as many fictitious intermediate goods and sectors as we require. Each input then acquires its appropriate profits component, suitably compounded, on the way, with the 'earlier' inputs, not in time but in stage of production, being compounded more times. This, as I understand it, is the essence of Sraffa's concept of 'dated' labour. Sraffa is always dealing at an instant of time with those properties of an economic system which are independent of change. It is also natural for anyone thinking, as Sraffa is, in the Ricardian–Marxian mould, of 'divergences of prices from values' changing as the rate of profits changes, to sense the possibility of such double substitutions of machines for labour.[1]

---

[1] I am indebted to M. H. Dobb for this comment.

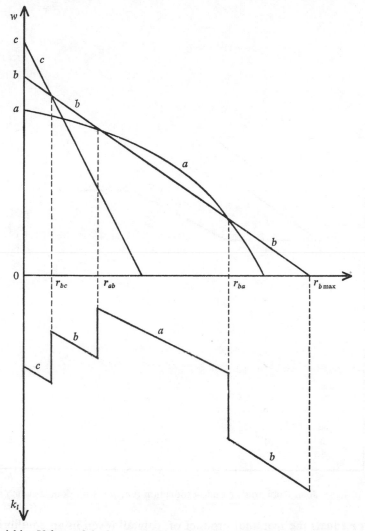

Fig. 4.14a. Values of k_i for an *FpF* envelope on which b makes two separated appearances

Lesson 6: nearly time to leave but what will we do in primary school?

Using comparisons of equilibrium positions we have seen that once heterogeneity of capital goods is introduced, the parables based on jelly no longer necessarily apply. In particular, it may no longer be argued

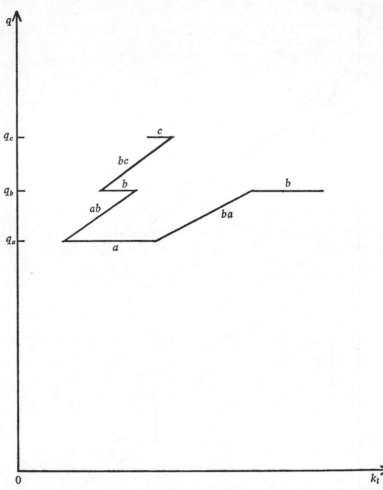

Fig. 4.14b. Joan Robinson's pseudo-production function with double-switching

that r equals the marginal product of 'capital' (even in an equilibrium situation), nor may the distribution of income be deduced from a knowledge of the elasticity of the *FpF* envelope alone. Furthermore, we are now unable in general to start from the *FpF* envelope and derive an 'as if', well-behaved, production function from it. This has led some writers to look elsewhere than to the concept and properties of an aggregate production function ('as if' or real) and marginal productivity concepts to explain the distribution of income (about which we shall say more below). The backlash to this argument has been the contention that the existence or not of an aggregate production function (in the sense of a unique relationship between *value* capital per head and output per head) and marginal productivity relations in distribution theory are not one and the same thing, as Champernowne [1953–4] showed long ago.

Bliss[1] [1968b], for example – but he is only the leading species of a large genus – argues that *if* we assume equilibrium (a most important proviso) and price-taking, cost-minimizing, profit-maximizing behaviour under perfectly competitive conditions in linear models, factors *as a matter of logic* must receive their marginal products, *suitably defined*, even though an aggregate production function may not be shown to exist. The key points of the argument are two: first, that we impose strict equilibrium assumptions; secondly, that businessmen are profit-maximizers and price-takers. A subsidiary point is that in linear models, marginal products at points (corners) may only be defined as lying within a range that is given by the partial derivatives that lie on either side of them. Within this range of indeterminacy, it is obvious that if any factor was *not* paid the value of its marginal product, a change in output consequent upon using more or less of it would add more to (or subtract less from) revenues than to (from) costs, so violating the assumptions that profits are maximized and that the economy is at equilibrium. (That the economy may not in fact get to an equilibrium position even if one can be shown to exist, that these relationships do not apply in out-of-equilibrium positions and that the real world is usually in the latter state, no one would deny.)

Solow makes the same point as Bliss in several of his papers cited earlier, Solow [1962a, 1963b] and Solow, Tobin, von Weizsäcker, and Yaari [1966], where typical marginal productivity results are obtained without *any* reference to aggregate capital – or *its* marginal product. His latest statement may be found in his reply [1970] to Pasinetti [1969]. Having stated that he does not hold 'a peculiar version of "marginal-productivity" theory' – 'peculiar because it seems to insist (as a matter of principle, not of convenience) on aggregating the whole stock of capital into one number, and because it means by marginal productivity the derivative of net output with respect to the *value* of this stock of capital' (Solow [1970], p. 424) – he concludes his article as follows:

 . . . nobody is trying to slip over on [Pasinetti] a theory according

[1] I am indebted to Christopher Bliss for a number of discussions and some correspondence on these and related points.

to which the rate of profits is higher or lower according to whether the existing 'quantity of capital' is lower or higher, and as such represents a general technical property of the existing 'quantity of capital'. That is just what neoclassical capital theory in its full generality can do without. (pp. 427–8.)

Garegnani [1966, 1970a, 1970b] and Pasinetti [1969, 1970] in particular, have come back strongly on this one (no suggestion of reswitching is implied). Garegnani points out that, in their formulation of marginal productivity theory, not all the neoclassical economists (early, late, or neo-neo) were either groping for or using an aggregate production function which could be interpreted 'as if' it behaved like a well-behaved, one-commodity one. Thus its destruction both at an economy *and* at an industry level (which he demonstrates in his paper [1970a]) is *not* a conclusive refutation of the marginal productivity theory of value and distribution. 'Expressing the conditions of production of a commodity in terms of a production function with "capital" as a factor is a feature of only *some* versions of the traditional theory . . .' (Garegnani [1970a], p. 422.) He mentions Marshall and J. B. Clark 'who thought that the principle of substitution, drawn from a reformulation of the Malthusian theory of rent in terms of homogeneous land and "intensive" margins, could be applied *without* modification to labour and "capital".' But this transition foundered on the fact that 'capital' cannot be measured in a physical unit but must be measured as a value, one which, moreover, changes whenever *r* and *w* change, i.e. one which is not independent of distribution. Moreover, it changes in such a way as *not* to allow us to say that the marginal products of 'capital' and labour are equal to their respective rates of remuneration.

All is not yet safe, because, Garegnani argues, 'traditional theory – reduced to its core as the explanation of distribution in terms of demand and supply – rests in fact on a single premise', what Pasinetti [1969], p. 519, calls 'an unobtrusive postulate'.

> This premise is that any change of system brought about by a fall in *r* must increase the ratio of 'capital' to labour in the production of the commodity: 'capital' being the value of the physical capital in terms of some unit of consumption goods, a value which is thought to measure the consumption given up or postponed in order to bring that physical capital into existence. (Garegnani [1970a], p. 422.)

This becomes the basis for the downward-sloping demand function for capital in a more general model.

As *r* falls, both the change in the system of production for each consumption good, and consumer substitution in favour of the more capital-intensive goods, would raise the ratio of 'capital' to labour in the economy. If we then assume that the quantity of labour employed remains equal to its supply, and the supply shows no drastic fall as *w* rises with the fall of *r*, it would follow that the amount of capital employed in the economy increases as *r* falls. This relation between *r* and the amount of capital employed could then be viewed as a demand function for capital; and competition in the capital market could be thought of as ensuring the absorption of 'net saving' through appropriate falls of *r*. (p. 423.)[1]

According to Pasinetti [1969], p. 508, Irving Fisher's concept of the rate of return over cost was an attempt to meet the criticism that he had earlier neglected the productivity aspects of capital goods in his explanation of the rate of interest. As we have already discussed Solow's attempted rehabilitation of the rate of return as the central concept of capital theory and as much of the recent work in capital theory has sought to bring Fisher up to date, it is appropriate to discuss the criticisms of the premise within the context of Fisher's work and Pasinetti's 1969 paper.

Pasinetti distinguishes two meanings of Fisher's 'rate of return on sacrifice' or 'rate of return over cost'. The first is the rate of interest at which two techniques (options, projects, going concerns, economic systems) are equi-profitable, i.e. that rate of interest which when used as the discount factor equalises the present values of two alternative streams of expected receipts (Fisherian incomes) and expenditures – call it R_{F1}. The second relates to the ratio of the expected increase in perpetuity in the production of a commodity to the withdrawal from consumption or other uses of the present annual flow of the commodity, the withdrawal or sacrifice being needed to make the investment that will make the increase in production possible. *If we assume that all prices and the rate of profits are given*, this may be expressed as a ratio of physical quantities – the expected increase in production over the necessitated withdrawal now from the current production stream, a *saving* which may then be

---

[1] Garegnani [1970a], pp. 418–21, also makes the excellent point that in a many-commodity model, we *must* distinguish between the real wage as seen by the workers, i.e. the wage made up of wage goods, and the product wage as seen by the businessmen, or, at least, examine the conditions under which one may be converted to the equivalent of the other, i.e. find the relative price system. Wage-rate – rate-of-profits trade-offs now relate to the relationships between *w* and *r* measured in wage goods and/or goods which are used directly or indirectly in their production.

translated *at a constant price ratio* into the necessary *investment*. Call it R_{F2} and notice that we get a choice of technique rule – the project is or is not worth doing according to whether or not R_{F2} is greater or less than the current rate of interest (or profits).

We may note in passing that we have already met R_{F2} in the discussion of the choice of technique in chapter 2, p. 63 above. At the point where the technique of production is chosen by the present value rule, the curve, VV, which shows the present value of the discounted expected net receipts, v', is parallel to the 45° line, ii, and therefore has a slope of unity, i.e. $\delta v'/\delta i = 1$. If capital lasts for ever, $\delta v'/\delta i$ is the (limiting) value of the discounted value of the annual increment of net receipts in perpetuity, $\Delta v''/r$, divided by the increment in investment expenditure, Δi. Thus we have

$$\frac{\Delta v''}{r\Delta i} = 1 \tag{4.31}$$

i.e.
$$r = \frac{\Delta v''}{\Delta i} \tag{4.32}$$

where $\Delta v''/\Delta i$ may be interpreted as R_{F2}.

In general $R_{F1} \neq R_{F2}$; R_{F1} is the rate of interest at which two projects (or options or going concerns or economic systems) are equi-profitable and R_{F2}, when compared with r, decides whether a change from one method to another should be made, *regardless of whether or not there is an R_{F1} at which the two are equi-profitable*. R_{F1} is, therefore, an accounting definition only, and so *explains* nothing. But R_{F2} is essentially associated with a change or transition – an out-of-equilibrium position; its value is intended to help decide whether or not to do something. R_{F1} is a definition – it defines *what* the rate of profits *is* in particular situations. It therefore explains nothing. It is especially when we apply Fisher's concepts to whole economies, however, that we get the discrepancy between the two, see pp. 162–3 below.

Pasinetti's distinction between the two concepts may be illustrated by the following example. Consider a going concern, say, an enterprise that produces a given rate of output using a given set of capital equipments and a given labour force. If we know the current level of prices, including the real-wage rate (and we make the usual assumption that current events are expected to continue into the future), clearly we could estimate the concern's current rate of profit. Now suppose a new opportunity arises. The enterprise uses some of its current output to save and invest in the equipment associated with the opportunity. We suppose – vitally – that all prices remain unchanged. As a result of installing the equipment the level of output rises. With unchanged prices, the increment of output per period may be related to the saving (equals investment) that brought it about and, thus, the value of R_{F2} calculated. In general the value of R_{F2} will not equal the rate of profit of the going concern before the opportunity arose.

Now it might be that *in the economic system as a whole* there exists a constellation of wages, prices and the rate of profits at which *both* the old and, now, the new situation of the enterprise would look equally profitable *to the enterprise*. There is no necessity about this and probably, in general, no such constellation exists. Even if it does exist, however, the rate of profit at which the two situations are equi-profitable would not coincide with the old rate of profit, or with the new one, or with the value of R_{F2} calculated for the change.

Fisher introduces the infinite options case in which diminishing returns prevail – given sacrifices now lead to successively smaller and smaller permanent increments of production – and suggests that we will choose the option at which the *marginal rate of return on sacrifice* equals the rate of interest. Moreover, his marginal rate of return on sacrifice when applied to the economy as a whole tends 'to the traditional notion of a marginal product of capital' and, Pasinetti [1969], p. 511, claims, 'represents something which is not only independent, but actually a *determinant*, of the rate of profits.' He refers the reader to the following passage in Fisher [1930], p. 176.

We can scarcely exaggerate the importance of the concept of 'rate of return over cost' and of its special variety '*marginal* rate of return over cost' as an element in our account of the conditions determining the rate of interest. It supplies, on the physical or technical or productivity side of the analysis, what the marginal rate of time preference supplies on the psychical side.

Fisher's examples relate to individuals but Pasinetti takes it that their application is to be wider, i.e. to the whole economy. Dealing with individuals in situations of perfect competition allows us, of course, to treat prices and rates of profits as given. The critics of neoclassical analysis suggest that this reasonable assumption ceases to be so when we deal with the whole economy because, then, any change of r, no matter how small, changes the whole pattern of relative prices, see Pasinetti [1969], p. 511. But *at a switch point* relative prices are constant, otherwise it would not be possible for two equi-profitable techniques (economies, islands of stationary states) to co-exist *in different proportions*: see Samuelson [1961]. But Pasinetti's interpretation of Fisher's arguments takes us *further* than a consideration of the switch-point case: see pp. 163–7 below, where it is shown that *one* technique only is the most profitable at any given value of r.

The objection to the switch-point cases is that while they are valid *comparisons* their results should not be applied to an analysis of the process of accumulation. Pasinetti [1969] criticized Solow for doing just this in the Dobb *Festschrift* article and Solow [1970] produces a *technocratic* example to justify his procedure, i.e. he sets out the necessary relations which allow the comparisons to become processes but ignores the question whether the behaviour of atomistic economic actors could be such as to allow this (double) transformation to occur. Nevertheless, he takes a punt both ways, for the equality of the interest rate and the rate of return means that 'there is an important relation between the competitive equilibrium interest rate and the technical possibilities of an economy . . . [though it] is only part of an explanation and no part of a "justification" of the rate of profits', Solow [1970], pp. 427–8.

Pasinetti compares, one with another, stationary states in which commodities are produced by commodities and labour in given technical proportions in any one technique and its activities. The relative prices of commodities and of one or other of the factor prices in this system are indeterminate until either r or w is given exogenously. Can either of Fisher's concepts supply the missing link and close the system? This is the basic question to which we now address ourselves.

Suppose that the labour forces are the same in the two economies, and consider a switch point, say, r_{ba} in fig. 4.1 above. Then (in our terminology)

$$R_{F1} = r_{ba} = \frac{q_b - q_a}{k_b - k_a} \qquad (4.33)$$

where it must be remembered that, in this and in more complex systems, all values are expressed in terms of the *common* set of prices corresponding to the switch-point rate of profits. (This is hardly surprising as r_{ba} is defined, in this instance, as the *extra* profit divided by the *extra* capital!)

When we come to R_{F2}, which essentially is to tell us whether or not to go over from one system to another, the extra outputs which are to be gained and the capital stocks with which they are to be associated (and in which, in general, there will be more of some commodities and less of others, *the latter becoming redundant*), *have to be valued at a set* *of prices in order that R_{F2} may be computed.* So, in general, R_{F2} is *not* independent of r and the accompanying set of relative prices. If we *arbitrarily* choose a value of r we may calculate R_{F2} and solve the problem of the choice of technique by seeing whether $R_{F2} \gtrless r$. In general, $R_{F2} \neq R_{F1}$, though there are cases where their values coincide (including Solow's examples in Solow [1967, 1970]), namely, in a one-commodity model, or when we consider an individual producer operating under perfectly competitive conditions, or at a switch-point. In the present context of stationary state comparisons, they coincide first, if R_{F1} exists, secondly, if R_{F2} is calculated in terms of the relative price system corresponding to the value of R_{F1} and, thirdly, if there is no redundancy of the commodities in the means of production when the transition is made from one state to the other (see Pasinetti [1969], p. 515). It is clear that in these special circumstances R_{F2} will be equal to R_{F1} as defined in expression (4.33) above.

Pasinetti constructs an abstract case in which the differences between two systems, α and β, consist entirely of extra 'corn' in their net products and their means of production – the greater amounts are in β. To go from α to β would, therefore, entail consuming *less* corn ($\bar{q}$) than previously (q_α) in one period in order that, forever afterwards, there would be more corn ($q_\beta - q_\alpha$). In this case

$$R_{F2} = \frac{q_\beta - q_\alpha}{q_\alpha - \bar{q}} \tag{4.34}$$

a ratio of physical quantities. Moreover, if $R_{F2} > r$, β, the more corn-intensive economy, has the more profitable technique; and vice versa, for $R_{F2} < r$. Thus

$$R_{F2} \gtrless r \text{ implies } \frac{q_\beta - q_\alpha}{q_\alpha - \bar{q}} = \frac{q_\beta - q_\alpha}{k_\beta - k_\alpha} \gtrless r \tag{4.35}$$

and, thus

$$q_\beta - rk_\beta \gtrless q_\alpha - rk_\alpha \tag{4.36}$$

At $R_{F2} = r$, we have a *unique* switch point – there cannot be more than one – and $R_{F2} = R_{F1}$ ($= (q_\beta - q_\alpha)/(k_\beta - k_\alpha)$, as we saw on p. 162 above).

We then compare β with γ (which has more corn than β in both its net product and its means of production) and compute the (lower) value of R_{F2} corresponding to γ. If we compare the R_{F2}s for all adjacent pairs of economies and order economies according to them, we also will have ordered them according to the increasing quantities of corn per head in their means of production, so that R_{F2} in this case represents 'the marginalists' ideal notion of a "rate of return" ', Pasinetti [1969], p. 517. If the number of techniques (economies) tends to infinity, switch points become irrelevant for now there always exists another *more* profitable technique in between two equi-profitable ones. Thus each rate of profits will be associated with a unique technique (and economy). (This is the basis of Pasinetti's contention that the traditional definition of the marginal product of capital is associated with situations in which only *one* technique is the most profitable at any given rate of profits: see chapter 1, pp. 44–5 above.) We thus arrive at an inverse monotonic relationship between a physical rate of return – R_{F2} – and an increasing quantity of (physical) capital. Moreover, it is an inverse relationship which permits 'an extension to the rate of profits of the marginal theory of prices' in which prices are 'indexes of scarcity' – as indeed they are here, for the smaller, i.e. the more scarce, is the existing quantity of corn, the higher is the physical rate of return (and of profits) to more savings. We may also construct a relationship between corn as net output per head and corn as capital per head which, as techniques thicken, approximates to the 'jelly' production function, the slope of which equals the Fisherian rate of return, R_{F2}, *which at the limit* becomes a derivative – the instantaneous rate of change of corn output with respect to corn input, or the marginal product of corn.

The next move is to show that if the 'unobtrusive postulate' holds – i.e. if at any given rate of profits two techniques are equi-profitable, at a rate of profits *less* than this, it is the technique with the higher value of capital per man and output per head which becomes the more profitable – *then R_{F2} becomes a surrogate for the physical rate of return that we met a moment ago*. Even though R_{F2} depends on the value of r and prices, in the sense that it may not be calculated without them, yet nevertheless it has all the essential properties of the physical ratio, especially in that we get the required inverse monotonic relationship. It is therefore 'as if' it were independent of r in all relevant respects.

We should add that there is no redundant 'capital', i.e. commodities in the means of production, when the change-over is made – the malleability assumption – and that the number of techniques is many, approaching infinity. The malleability assumption ensures not only complete adaptability but also that there should always be (in the long run anyway) *full employment* of 'capital' as well as of labour. That economists should cling to it in post-Keynesian times when, presumably, the misery of men's unemployment has been recognized and, to a large extent, overcome (unless they are black and young, or middle-aged and widowed, or have spouses in gaol, or have low IQs, or the prestige of being an international currency is at stake) is a fine index of their sensibility for all things, animate or inanimate. That the original neo-classicals should have introduced it in the first place is an index of their desire to get away from dangerous thoughts, especially Ricardian–Marxian ones in which labour played a key role, both in the theory of value and because of the primary importance of relationships between men in production, and of classes. It is also an index of their desire to get into a safe world in which all factors are on a par with one another, a world which reaches its (Schumpeterian) ideal of scientific advance when commodities become x, y, and z, factors a, b, and c, and algebra, rigour and elegance become the rage, see Meek [1967], p. 199 *passim*. This seems to me to be the outcome, though possibly not the intention, of the twists which Marshall, for example, and Wicksell gave to economic analysis. They were, themselves, men of 'warm hearts and cool heads' and it would be a supreme irony, if in their efforts to make their disciples and successors in a similar mould, and especially to avoid them being soft-headed, as Marshall anyway felt the socialists to be, they succeeded only in making them rigorous – and barren. It would also be a disaster, not least as a memorial to Wicksell, the most lovable of the 'great' economists: see Gårlund [1958].

The upshot of the argument is that R_{F2} is intended to form the basis *in a realistic heterogeneous capital-goods model* of a function which relates amounts wanted – values – to scarcity prices. The proof (for the discrete case) is very simple. The malleability assumption means that there are no discarded capital goods when one system supersedes another, so that

$$R_{F2} = \rho = \frac{\mathbf{p}(r)(\mathbf{Q}_\beta - \mathbf{Q}_\alpha)}{\mathbf{p}(r)(\mathbf{K}_\beta - \mathbf{K}_\alpha)} \qquad (4.37)$$

where $\mathbf{p}$ is the vector of prices corresponding to the rate of profits (r) and the $\mathbf{Q}$s and $\mathbf{K}$s are collections of heterogeneous goods treated as outputs and inputs respectively. But the 'unobtrusive postulate' implies that there can be only *one* switch point between any two techniques and that there is a *definite* ordering on either side of the switch-point techniques, properties associated with our physical rate of return above. Pasinetti states them as follows

$$\rho \gtrless r \quad \text{for } \mathbf{p}(r) \text{ corresponding to } r \lessgtr r^* \qquad (4.38)$$

where r^* is the switch-point rate of profits. This can only hold for switch points associated with the intersection of straight-line w–r relationships (at least, this is so when techniques are dense),[1] see those for techniques a and b in fig. 4.15 and revert, for a moment, to our very simple model

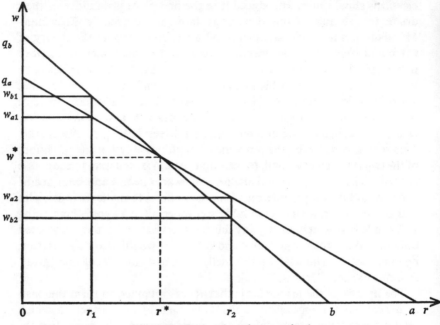

Fig. 4.15. The 'unobtrusive postulate'

where the value of k is independent of r and q is measured in physical terms. When $r = r_1 < r^*$, we may show that

$$\rho_1 = \frac{q_b - q_a}{k_b - k_a} > r_1 = \frac{q_b - q_a - (w_{b1} - w_{a1})}{k_b - k_a} \tag{4.39}$$

Thus

$$r_1 = \frac{q_b - w_{b1}}{k_b} = \frac{q_a - w_{a1}}{k_a} \tag{4.40}$$

i.e.

$$r_1(k_b - k_a) = q_b - q_a - (w_{b1} - w_{a1})$$

i.e.

$$r_1 = \frac{q_b - q_a - (w_{b1} - w_{a1})}{k_b - k_a} \tag{4.39}$$

[1] While *any* shape of individual w–r relationship will allow an *envelope* which has one method alone associated with each point on it (provided only that the change from method to method is continuous), it is only straight-line ones which allow the neoclassical parables to be told, see Garegnani [1970a], pp. 414–16.

Similarly, we may show that

$$\rho_2 \leqslant r_2 \quad \text{for } r_2 \geqslant r^* \tag{4.41}$$

Moreover, as we have seen, at switch points all the relevant magnitudes – values of capital goods, outputs per man, rates of profits and wage rates – move in the same way as in the artificial example and therefore *as predicted by the jelly parables*. 'Malleability' – no redundancy – gets rid of D. H. Robertson's grumble, see Robertson [1949]; all existing capital goods may be used and workers may remain, if they wish, teetotal. The high number of techniques confines the distance which ρ may move away from r^*. And, most striking of all, if we let the techniques become very many, approaching an infinite number, so that the change in the magnitude of r needed to go from one to another becomes infinitesimally small then, due to the 'unobtrusive postulate', the differences in values of capital goods and outputs per man likewise become smaller and smaller. In the limit, both change instantaneously, the switch point becomes irrelevant (as in the artificial case) and 'at any level of the rate of profits, there always is one technique which is the most profitable one ... at the same time any change in the rate of profits, no matter how small, always causes a change in the most profitable technique', Pasinetti [1969], p. 521.

Such, perhaps, is the post- (technical) revolution which lies behind Irving Fisher's pre-revolution investment-opportunity schedules, as brought into the modern era by Hirshleifer [1958]. I add 'perhaps' because Fisher's examples are always for individuals. It does, however, seem – and this is confirmed by Stigler [1941] – that the early neo-classicals were after bigger game than a partial analysis of an individual firm or industry and the scope of the questions examined by Dewey [1965] in the book he is pleased to call *Modern Capital Theory* confirms that this view still appeals to some. *What* Marshall was after we can never really be sure; for, characteristically, he always shied away from openly committing himself. (Keynes [1933], pp. 223–4, though, had no such scruples in *his* assessment of Marshall's stand – except on the subject of French letters, for which see Holroyd [1968], pp. 514–15, n1.)

But the results of the reswitching and capital-reversing debate show that there is *no* justification at all for the 'unobtrusive postulate', for we know that in a heterogeneous capital-goods model (where capital goods are really so and not just jelly in disguise), a lower rate of profits may well be associated with a lower output per head, with a lower value of capital per head and with a lower net output-capital ratio. Moreover, the same technique may be the most profitable at two widely separated rates of profits. Nearness of techniques as assessed by the rate of profits at which they are most profitable may tell us *nothing at all* about how close (or far apart) are their values of capital or outputs per head. And – most damaging of all for R_{F2} as a surrogate for a well-behaved physical rate of return, i.e. a marginal product which declines as the value of capital increases – the difference $(r - \rho(r))$ may become indifferently positive or negative at *any* level of the rate of profits, so losing the properties of a physical rate of return.

These results are as applicable to the industry case as to the economy one, as Garegnani has shown, thus providing an answer (but perhaps not *the* answer) to Samuelson's plea for an analysis based on microeconomic relationships, see p. 121 above. Pasinetti's conclusions led him to add:

> Continuity in the variation of techniques, as the rate of profits changes, does not imply continuity in the variation of values of capital goods per man and of net outputs per man [which] seems to reveal capital theory as a field unsuitable to the application of calculus and infinitesimal analysis, and thus of marginal analysis.
> (p. 523.)

Depending, as R_{F2} does, on predetermined prices which are taken as given, it serves as an aid to the choice of technique. But it cannot be used as the base on which to build 'the physical or technical or productivity side' of a theory of the rate of profits itself. And, as we have seen, R_{F1} is an accounting definition which is consistent with but may not (help to) explain *any* theory of the rate of profits.

We may note in passing that Solow [1967] analysed the case where R_{F1} and R_{F2} coincided, so laying himself open to the charge that he had shown that at the rate of profits at which two economic systems (techniques) are equi-profitable, that is the rate of profits at which they *are* so: see Pasinetti [1969], pp. 525–6. Solow's analysis reflects the fact that at switch points investment in either technique yields *by definition* a rate of return equal to the switch-point rate of profits, which is also the rate of profits at which prices have been computed. (That is *why* the techniques are equi-profitable.) R_{F2} is thus assured in this case of equalling r, as it equals R_{F1}.

We might perhaps sum up the argument to this point as follows: at a switch point, $\Delta q/\Delta k = r$ *by definition* and regardless of the shapes of the *w–r* relationships involved. However, on Pasinetti's interpretation, $\Delta q/\Delta k$ is *not* the *traditional* marginal product of capital. *If* we assume that $r = \mathrm{d}q/\mathrm{d}k$, we then imply (except for the special cases noted above, see p. 149) that $k = -\mathrm{d}w/\mathrm{d}r$ which requires that the $w\text{-}r$ relationships be straight lines. If they are not, $\mathrm{d}q/\mathrm{d}k \neq r$, essentially because we encounter revaluation puzzles associated with changes in r and relative prices. This is so whether we consider a given $w\text{-}r$ relationship, or the change from one to another, i.e. movements along the *envelope*, each point being the most profitable at its own value of r and therefore associated with its own set of relative prices, with the differences in the values of r being the infinitesimal increment, $\mathrm{d}r$. It is the implications of these revaluations which both the switch-point comparisons and the neoclassical procedure of concentrating on notional changes at a *point*, with its given constant equilibrium prices, seek to avoid.

Lesson 7: do we press on or drop out?

Some writers, for example, Bhaduri [1969], Joan Robinson [1965a], also [1965b], pp. 173–81, and Nell [1967b], look to Marx's theory of exploitation brought up to date in the guise of relative bargaining strengths, to explain the distribution of income, treated as a surplus, between profit-receivers and wage-earners. Competition's role, then, is to ensure the equality of profit rates in all activities and this, together with the technical coefficients of production, determine relative prices, i.e. the classical dichotomy between the theory of distribution and the theory of value is restored.[1] In this way capital goods in their role of aids to labour – a role common to all industrial societies, capitalist or socialist –

---

[1] We may sketch in an outline as follows. Capitalists compete among themselves as far as profit outlets are concerned, so bringing about a tendency towards equality in the various rates of profit (perhaps at a level determined by the forces examined by Kaldor, Pasinetti and Joan Robinson, see chapter 5 below), but gang up, tacitly or openly, on the workers when the wage bargain is made. *Its* level at any moment of time is determined in money terms but is influenced by the relative bargaining strengths and past experiences of the two groups, one on each side of the market. The level of effective demand is also relevant, it and overall activity themselves being simultaneous outcomes along with the distribution of income and prices when the wage bargain has been made and profit margins set such as to tend to achieve a uniform rate of profits. For what they are worth I have set out these ideas in Harcourt [1965b], in which I try to show how collective bargaining, the neoclassical forces, as exhibited in the choice of technique, and the Keynesian forces of aggregate demand and the equality of saving and investment, together with technical progress and population growth, all mesh together to determine simultaneously the short-run level of activity and distribution of income. The weakest, and yet the most vital, link in this chain of reasoning is the assumption of a uniform rate of profits; for, without it, the *relative* price system appears to remain undetermined.

can be separated from capital in its role of investible funds, belonging to those who own – have property in – the means of production and who obtain a share in the distribution of the net product or surplus because of their property rights.

The trouble with jelly is that it was meant to serve both purposes (it is after all the ideal medium by which the two concepts may be merged into one) and the theory of production relations and value was meant to be independent of the institutions of society; that is, relations between men were treated as irrelevant for an explanation of distribution. As J. B. Clark [1889], pp. 312–13, says:

> It [the principle of differential gain] identifies *production* with *distribution* and shows that what a social class gets is, under the natural law, what it contributes to the general output of industry. Completely stated the principle of differential gain affords a theory of Economic Statics. [Italics added.]

And as Joan Robinson [1970b] puts it, Walras' short-run stocks of physical inputs have been boiled down into a homogeneous, malleable commodity (leets) which can both produce output and purchase extra capital goods (through saving being investment) at an *unchanged price* of one to one. The owners of the capital goods receive a rate of return – leets over leets – equal to the marginal product of the existing (fully-employed and correctly formed) stocks at any moment of time. It was Marx's insight that the separation of value from institutions was invalid even in a world of pure logic, and the significance of the distinction for the case of more than one capital good has been emphasized by the modern critics of the neoclassical parables.

The neo-neoclassicals have produced a string of rebuttals. First, they argue that no one, these days, tries, or ever did try, to determine the rate of profits or other prices within the production system alone. After all, the neoclassical marginalist 'revolution' was concerned with first the prior, and then the equal, importance of the blade of scissors known as 'demand'. Secondly, they could refer to Bliss's arguments, see p. 157 above, and to the statements by Hahn and Matthews [1964] at the end of their survey of the theory of economic growth. Thus:

> As far as pure theory is concerned the 'measurement of capital' is no problem at all because we never have to face it if we do not choose to. With our armchair omniscience we can take account of each machine separately. Moreover the measurement business has nothing whatsoever to do with the question of whether imputation theory is or is not valid. In an equilibrium of the whole system,

provided there is perfect competition, no learning by doing and no uncertainty, the neoclassical imputation results hold. This should now be beyond dispute. It is also of little comfort to the empirically inclined. (p. 888.)

Returning once more to the question of the validity or otherwise of imputation theory there is a further, purely theoretical, point of some importance to be made. When an economy with many goods is considered, then we must also find the relative equilibrium prices of these goods. Whether these are determined *à la* Leontief–Samuelson–Sraffa or *à la* Walras, imputation is at once involved. If we abandon imputation entirely then the whole question of relative prices must be reconsidered afresh. Perhaps it ought to be, but recognition that this problem exists seems desirable. (p. 889.)

Following these, and no doubt warming to their task, they could refer to Samuelson's opening remarks in Samuelson [1962], see p. 121 above, and Solow's closing ones, Solow [1970], see pp. 157–8 above. That is to say, they would dismiss an aggregative approach to a rigorous theory of distribution – and capital – (though not, necessarily, one to econometrics). They could next invoke Swan's appendix, Swan [1956], and Champernowne's original paper [1953–4]. In the latter, when double-switching is allowed to occur, the production function is multi-valued, i.e. the same q is associated with two or more values of k. Nevertheless, factors *are* paid their marginal products. However, 'the question of which (r, w) and hence what income-distribution between labour and capital is paid is left in this model for political forces to decide' (p. 130) – surely one of the most perceptive comments of the whole debate? (At the (double) switch points, one technique is coming in at one point, leaving at the other, as it were; which, then, is the relevant one to determine distribution?) Champernowne adds: 'It is interesting to speculate whether more complex situations retaining this feature are ever found in the real world.'[1]

To the neo-neoclassical answer that the existence or not of an aggregate production function or of a well-behaved demand curve for capital at economy (or *industry* level) has nothing to do with marginal produc-

---

[1] Champernowne [1966] has discussed in an unpublished note his reasons for ruling out double-switching by assumption in his original article. He argues that his intuition at the time was that the probability of the input per unit of output coefficients being such as to allow it, i.e. to be consistent with ranges of r which allow positive real wages, was low. However, the very restrictive assumptions needed to rule it out, as established by Bruno, Burmeister and Sheshinski [1966], pp. 538–46, suggest that this intuition may be wrong.

tivity relations, *some* critics (Kaldor [1966], Nell [1967b], Sraffa [?])
might reply: Your logic *may* be impeccable but your results are, nevertheless, irrelevant for the world as we know it, and especially for an
explanation of distribution, i.e. they would reject maximizing behaviour
as a fundamental postulate of economic analysis (see Solow [1968]
also). This raises a puzzle in the analysis of choice of technique where
most writers, *including Sraffa*, explicitly assume maximizing behaviour.
Kaldor, of course, does not; his analysis is based upon the implications
of businessmen following rules of thumb such as the pay-off period
criterion.

Brown [1966], on the other hand, just because he wishes to retain
maximizing behaviour, has suggested neoclassical exploitation as a
compromise. Moreover, in his later papers [1968, 1969], while he accepts
the *logic* of the neo-Keynesian critics, as an econometrician, he, possibly
rightly and certainly understandably, tries to find common ground
between linear models and neoclassical ones. He works out the conditions which ensure capital-intensity uniqueness (*CIU*) at an *aggregate*
level in two two-sector models, one linear, the other neoclassical,
i.e. one in which each sector has a well-behaved production function.
The tools which he uses are substitution and composition effects (see
p. 133 above).

> The basic result that emerges from the neoclassical analysis is that
> the substitution and composition effects (as defined within that
> system) determine the uniqueness of the relationship between the
> aggregate labour-capital ratio and relative factor prices. The parallel
> is then taken: substitution-composition effects (as defined within
> the linear system) determine *CIU* as well as other things; and sub-
> stitution-composition effects (as defined within the marginal pro-
> ductivity system) determine, uniquely, the aggregate capital-labour
> and factor-price relationship. (Brown [1969], p. 355.)

This leads him to conjecture that answers to certain large questions may
not be substantially different, a philosophy and strategy which, for
obvious reasons, is akin to those of Solow on his busman's holiday.

The latest statement of Solow's philosophy, one which is entirely
consistent with his earlier ones, is as follows:

> So far as I know, I have never in rigorous work adopted Pasinetti's
> 'unobtrusive' postulate – which is intimately connected with his
> special version of orthodox theory – that if one of two techniques
> is more profitable than the other at a higher real wage and less
> profitable at a lower wage it will have a higher value of capital

goods per man. It is true that one-capital-good models behave that way, but they are merely cheap vehicles for interpreting data (which seem to behave that way). (Solow [1970], p. 424.)

Pasinetti [1970], p. 429, rightly points out the 'surprisingly high proportion of current economic literature [that is] carried out in terms of "neoclassical production functions" and one-commodity-models', which, whether rigorous or not, certainly do depend for their validity on the 'unobtrusive postulate'. Secondly, he points to the 'ancients' and 'moderns' who also have used the 'unobtrusive postulate' in order to get an index of scarcity in a general equilibrium system, and so a marginal productivity theory of capital. For:

It made 'capital' appear to be like a scarce resource, and the rate of profits to be like any other general-equilibrium price – an index of scarcity. It is this construction that has fallen down. For that unobtrusive postulate was essential to it. (Pasinetti [1970], p. 429.)

Ferguson and Allen [1970] have carefully analysed the conditions under which the construction *does* break down when changes in the composition of demand due to changes in relative product prices are taken into account. They derive some comfort from their results. Their approach seems open to at least two criticisms. First, as they candidly admit, they use a model which favours the neoclassical position, as intermediate goods are ignored and the capital good is the only basic. Secondly, they do not investigate whether the changes in the composition of demand are consistent with their assumption of full employment. Moreover, as their analysis consists only of comparisons, their appeal to the facts to decide seems to be beside the point.

Joan Robinson [1970a, 1970b], of course, would accept neither Brown nor Solow's approach, nor Samuelson's rationalization of it. To her, Samuelson's surrogate production function, even though it allows the simple parables to be told, does so *only in the form of comparisons*, so that it remains a spoof – a pseudo-production function. Only when capital is *actually* jelly (or leets) can substitution and the other neoclassical processes occur and full employment of all factors be maintained in competitive economies. But, in her view, such constructions assume away *all* the real difficulties associated with the existence of heterogeneous capital goods and the implications of the disappointed expectations of atomistic economic actors in competitive situations.

Mention should also be made in this context of F. M. Fisher's Irving Fisher Lecture, F. M. Fisher [1969], in which he surveys the current state of knowledge about capital aggregates. He does not come to grips with all the puzzles raised here (that was *not* his object). Nevertheless, his conclusions come a long way towards supporting the *implications* of the theoretical criticisms above, even though they were reached by a different route.

In short, it seems to me important to worry about aggregation and production functions because production functions are themselves important. They, and their implications, play central roles not only in empirical work but in theoretical analysis. Just because it is possible to use aggregate production functions for grand statements about long-run growth and technical change, it is important to be careful about the foundation for such statements. At present, that foundation seems solid only insofar as relatively small changes are concerned. The analyses which I have here summarized have convinced me that there is at least need for great caution in this area. It may be recalled that Solow's seminal article, Solow [1957], p. 312, called for 'more than the usual "willing suspension of disbelief" to talk seriously of the aggregate production function'. That suspension has clearly led to very fruitful results. I am, however, finding it increasingly difficult to maintain. The conditions for the existence of aggregate production functions, at least when widely diverse industries are included, seem very, very strong. (p. 576.)

We should also note the sequel to Fisher's paper, F. M. Fisher [1970], in which he reports the results of a simulation experiment. His main conclusion is that if the real world behaves in such a way as to throw up, say, a constant share of wages, or a linear relationship in the logarithms between productivity and wages, it is *these findings* which explain the 'apparent success' of the Cobb–Douglas and CES production functions respectively rather than the other way around.

> ... the view that the constancy of labour's share is due to the presence of an aggregate Cobb–Douglas production function is mistaken. Causation runs the other way and the apparent success of aggregate Cobb–Douglas functions is due to the relative constancy of labour's share. (p. 4.)

> The present results suggest ... that the explanation of that wage-output per man relationship may not be in the existence of an aggregate CES but rather that the apparent existence of an aggregate CES may be explained by that relationship. (p. 32.)

Fisher appears to have been too literal in his understanding of the nature of the econometric hypotheses involving the Cobb–Douglas and the CES functions. Their proponents have never believed that they *actually* existed, only that it may be useful to interpret trends in real world observations 'as if' they were observations thrown up by a jelly world of either the Cobb–Douglas or CES variety.

If, then, a small (but, I like to think, significant) section of the trade is convinced that the distribution of income and factor prices cannot be explained either within the system of production alone or, *relevantly*, as the outcome of a general equilibrium system even when (because) we use marginal productivity notions and modern programming methods, factors and forces elsewhere in the economic system – and other than these – must be introduced. Sraffa himself has suggested that the rate of profits may be related to the money rate of interest, or, sometimes, following Ricardo, he introduces the real wage which, however, *reflects* labour's share in the national income rather than the command of the *money wage* over subsistence goods. Thus, Sraffa [1960], pp. 8–11, takes the total annual labour of society as unity. The real-wage rate is then labour's share in the national income, which is, itself, the surplus of commodities over the means of production and the *numéraire* of the system.

Sraffa's procedure differs from the approach of both Adam Smith and the neoclassicals: see, for example, Hicks [1965], whereby the real wage is measured in terms of a *numéraire* of, say, corn, i.e. a subsistence standard. Sraffa's view reflects the proposition that the distribution of income is a matter of social conflict rather than a technical matter in which, in effect, 'the necessary subsistence of the workers' is not differentiated from 'the fuel for the engines or the feed for the cattle' (p. 9).[1] Given either of the rate of profits *or* the wage rate and the technological conditions of production, the other factor price and relative prices may be determined.

Other writers – Kaldor, Joan Robinson, Pasinetti – have suggested the overall rate of growth allied with the coefficients of the capitalists' saving function (and latterly, their borrowing function, see Kaldor [1966]). Which is correct seems to me a still unsettled question. What *is* clear is that the neo-Keynesians regard the marginal productivity and other neoclassical parables as set out, for example, by Samuelson [1962] as bankrupt in a world of heterogeneous capital goods and so have advanced these alternatives (which themes are taken up again in chapter 5).

We should add, as a final postscript (and especially as Champer-

---

[1] These themes are returned to in the appendix to this chapter. I have been greatly helped in writing these passages by reading an unpublished paper by Akyüz [1970].

nowne's paper [1953–4] contained much of what has been found out subsequently, so that it is fitting to at least go out where we *could* have both come in *and* gone out simultaneously), that if double-switching is ruled out by assumption and if the rate of profits and the real-wage rate are *parameters, given from outside*, the Champernowne chain index method of measuring capital will allow rp to equal the marginal product of capital (this is always true) and higher values of capital will be associated with lower rates of profits. But, even so, the conclusion that the rate of profits and the distribution of income cannot be solved for from within the production system itself still holds.

The last proposition may be put most simply as follows, see Bhaduri [1969]: Suppose that r *and* w are given from outside as $\bar{r}$ and $\bar{w}$, i.e. are constants. This is what the chain index method of measuring capital provides, for it gives a 'quantity' of capital *from which the effects of changes in the values of w and r have been removed*. Then totally differentiating $q = \bar{r}k + \bar{w}$ gives $dq = \bar{r}dk$ so that $\bar{r} = dq/dk$. In a general equilibrium model with fixed, i.e. equilibrium prices, the marginal product of aggregate capital is equal to the rate of interest (determined in conjunction with either the consumers' or the government's rate of time preference) but this relates only to one *point*: see, for example, Swan [1956]. That is to say, this is true of any point, i.e. stationary state, but, as Swan also argues, no one point may be compared with another because a *different* equilibrium dollar's work of capital is implied at each: see Swan [1956] and chapter 1, p. 38 above. (Laing [1969b] demonstrates this proposition in terms of an intertemporal production function.) As we have seen, it is the assumption (or the *deduction*) of the *fixity of relative prices* which is one key – and which is challenged most keenly by Pasinetti, Garegnani – and Joan Robinson.

Appendix to 4   Mr Sraffa's *Production of Commodities by Means of Commodities*[1]

Sraffa's *Production of Commodities by Means of Commodities* discusses a number of traditional issues of economic theory. It is concisely written but enough information is given to allow the reader to obtain the results which are presented. The main purpose of the book is to present the foundation for a critique of the marginal theory of value and distribution. Though the relevance of Sraffa's results for this purpose is not made explicit, keeping it in mind helps in understanding the degrees of abstraction adopted and the propositions developed by him. His earlier writings, in particular his well-known 1926 article and his Introduction to Ricardo's *Principles* [1951–5] (written in collaboration with M. H. Dobb) also provide some helpful hints to his method of analysis and main propositions.

The reviews of Sraffa's classic varied from banal to insightful (with one, the author of which shall be nameless, completely incomprehensible). In the former category must be placed the reviews by Quandt [1961] and Reder [1961]; one reviewer did not get his sums right and both missed the point. (Harrod got *his* sums right but read too much into them: see Harrod [1961] and Sraffa's reply [1962].) In the latter category we may place Joan Robinson's two reviews (Robinson [1961b], reprinted as Robinson [1965b], pp. 7–14, and Robinson [1965b], pp. 173–81), Meek's [1967], pp. 161–78, and Bharadwaj's [1963]. We should also mention, in this context, Nell [1967b]. Nell's article is not a review; nevertheless it spells out with insight what Massaro and myself [1964b] were groping for in our review article.

[1] This appendix is more specialized than the rest of the book and may be omitted, at the reader's discretion, without loss of continuity. The first section is a slightly amended version of the review article [1964b] of Sraffa's book which I wrote with Vincent G. Massaro. I am indebted to the editors of the *Economic Record* for permission to reprint it here, also to my co-author for allowing me to use it free.

In this appendix we outline in section I the basic structure of Sraffa's arguments, explain in section II his useful concept of sub-systems (in the context of Joan Robinson and Naqvi's example, see Robinson and Naqvi [1967] and chapter 4, pp. 132–5 above) and, in section III, indicate briefly the relevance and implications of his approach, as sketched by Nell [1967b], for the theory of economic growth. Few reviewers got past part I – the circulating capital model – and certainly the importance of part III in which double-switching and capital-reversing are discussed did not get the prominence which we can now see it merited. Nevertheless, the foundations for his critique of economic theory were securely laid in part I, a point which was emphasized by the perceptive reviewers (and missed by the others).

Sraffa begins with a warning that he is '. . . concerned exclusively with such properties of an economic system as do not depend on changes in the scale of production or in the proportions of "factors" ' (preface, p. v). The author writes 'factors' because he wishes to contrast the view that regards 'the system of production and consumption as a circular process' with what he regards as the view of modern theory – that it is 'a one-way avenue . . . from "Factors of production" to "Consumption goods" ' (p. 93).

It is true that the emphasis on circularity in modern theory is found more in discussions of the expenditure, income-creation process than in the theory of price-formation. Nevertheless, some modern theories, for example, those associated with the work of von Neumann, Leontief and Morishima, are more akin to the first view. But, as Nell [1967b], p. 25 n8, rightly says, Leontief's system 'must be sharply distinguished from Sraffa's' because the former never deals 'with a uniform rate of profits nor with the effects of changes in distribution upon prices'.

Sraffa's analysis starts at a level of abstraction which excludes the continuous change characteristic of actual economic systems. Or, we may regard the analysis as concerned with any actual economic system during one 'year', a 'year' being defined as the time taken to produce commodities and distribute them. The economic relationships examined, therefore, occur within, *and are only true of*, the period of time contained within Sraffa's 'year'. (Nevertheless, the author is not prevented from examining, for this period, many questions which are analysed within the context of the theory of economic growth – for example, the distribution of income, the value of capital and the choice of techniques.) Thus Sraffa does not find it necessary to assume constant returns, and the apparent 'changes' examined in the text (the varying proportions of basic equations, the sub-system analysis) are merely different ways of viewing the given, non-changing, basic data.

The author's point of view has the important consequence that by ruling out variations in scale and in 'factors', marginal product is ruled out as well – 'it just would not be there to be found' (preface, p. v). This is true. However, it should be noted that prices in the marginal theory of value are related to notional instantaneous rates of change which can be thought of as occurring at the margins of the levels of production of the actual economic systems examined here. In other words, there need not be an actual marginal product in order to have a determinate system of prices which is based on marginalist notions.

Sraffa may be hinting that the assumption of mathematical continuity is inappropriate for the analysis of price-formation in an economic system; that is to say, it is impossible to use the device of notional movements along a schedule which shows a relationship between two economic variables and which assumes that everything else remains constant. This is because the very fact of change necessarily implies that the changes in these other things are such that it just cannot be assumed that they remain constant. (Such is the basis of his criticism of supply and demand analysis in Sraffa [1926].) Alternatively, he might be interpreted as meaning that there is not enough information in any actual economic system to tell us what the marginal (as opposed to the average) product is. Even if it is a valid procedure to derive a system of prices from notional changes, it might still be that the prices associated with the technical conditions of production and with self-replacement are more fundamental than those associated with notional changes.

Meek [1967], pp. 161–78, whose review article is entitled 'Mr. Sraffa's Rehabilitation of Classical Economics', provides an interesting explanation of the rationale of Sraffa's approach. Thus,

Mr Sraffa's important book ... can be looked at from various points of view. It can be regarded, if one pleases, simply as an unorthodox theoretical model of a particular type of economy, designed to solve the traditional problem of value in a new way. It can be regarded as an implicit attack on modern marginal analysis: the sub-title of the book is 'Prelude to a Critique of Economic Theory', and Sraffa in his preface expresses the hope that someone will eventually attempt the job of basing a critique of the marginal analysis on his foundations. Or, finally, it can be regarded as a sort of magnificent rehabilitation of the Classical (and up to a point Marxian) approach to certain crucial problems relating to value

and distribution. It is upon this third aspect of the book that I wish
to concentrate ... In doing so, I do not of course want to suggest
that the *essence* of Sraffa's book lies in this rehabilitation of the
Classical approach: Sraffa's primary aim is to build a twentieth-
century model to deal with twentieth-century problems. I am
approaching his book in this particular way largely because I think
it affords the best method of understanding his basic argument.
(p. 161.)

Meek begins by making three general points about the relation
between Sraffa's model and the old Classical models, only the first of
which need concern us here.

Both Sraffa's model and the Classical models are concerned with the
investigation of one and the same set of properties of an economic
system – those properties as Sraffa puts it, which 'do not depend
on changes in the scale of production or in the proportions of
"factors" '. The Classical economists, at any rate in their basic
analysis of the economy as such, were usually *in effect* concerned
with these properties alone, since they often tended to assume that
under given technological conditions returns to scale for the
industry as a whole would be constant, and that the proportions in
which the different means of production were used in an industry
would be technically fixed. Sraffa, by way of distinction, makes no
assumption whatever about the variability or constancy of returns.
Rather, he simply selects for analysis a particular kind of economic
system in which the question of whether returns are variable or
constant is irrelevant. This system is one in which production goes
on from day to day and from year to year in exactly the same way,
without any changes in scale or factor proportions at all. By this
means Sraffa is able *deliberately* to concern himself with the
investigation of the same properties of an economic system
which the Classical economists *objectively* concerned themselves
with, while at the same time avoiding the necessity of making any
(possibly objectionable) assumptions about the nature of returns.
(p. 162.)

'Prices' or 'values' in an economy which is merely *capable of* repro-
ducing itself reflect the exchange ratios which would restore the original
distribution of the means of production and such prices 'spring directly
from the methods of production' (p. 3). For instance, assuming the
means of subsistence to be included among the means of production, we
may express the conditions of production of k industries producing k

products (each industry producing a separate product $a, \ldots, k$) as follows

$$A_a p_a + \ldots + K_a p_k = A p_a = [A_a + \ldots + A_k] p_a$$
$$\cdots\cdots\cdots\cdots\cdots\cdots\cdots\cdots\cdots\cdots\cdots\cdots\cdots\cdots \qquad (A.1)$$
$$A_k p_a + \ldots + K_k p_k = K p_k = [K_a + \ldots + K_k] p_k$$

where $A_a, \ldots, K_a$ represent the quantities of $a, \ldots, k$ employed in the production of quantity A of a; $A_k, \ldots, K_k$ represent the quantities of $a, \ldots, k$ employed in the production of quantity K of k; and where $p_a, \ldots, p_k$ represent prices.

Since we are able to infer any one equation from the sum of the remaining equations, setting the price of one commodity as unity leaves us with $k-1$ independent linear equations and $k-1$ prices. It should be noted that in this case each commodity enters either directly or indirectly into the production of itself and every other commodity. Such commodities are defined as 'basic commodities' and are distinguished from 'non-basics' (commodities which enter neither directly nor indirectly into the production of all commodities) which appear with the production of a surplus.

An economic system with a surplus is one whose equations have the property of *permitting* repetition of the productive process for each industry with the gross product exceeding the means of production. That is, it is possible to replace, item by item, the means of production employed and still have some products remaining. As we can no longer infer any one equation from the sum of those remaining, we are now left with k equations and $k-1$ unknowns.

At this point Sraffa introduces the notion of a uniform rate of profits and notes that, since the surplus and the means of production consist of different goods, we cannot determine the rate of profits without prices. Nor, however, can we have prices without having a rate of profits. Thus, Sraffa concludes, prices and the rate of profits must be determined *simultaneously* and through the same mechanism. We may regard the uniform rate of profits, r, as a simplifying assumption or we may view it as the result towards which an actual economic system tends through the operation of long-run competitive forces, which push r to a level determined by the underlying rate of growth and the saving (and borrowing) propensities of its capitalist class, see chapter 5 below.

Assuming a surplus of commodity a (designated by A_s) and introducing r as another unknown, we again have a determinate system which may be expressed as follows

$$(1+r)(A_a p_a + \ldots + K_a p_k) = (A_a + \ldots + A_k)p_a + A_s p_a$$
$$\cdots\cdots\cdots\cdots\cdots\cdots\cdots\cdots\cdots\cdots\cdots\cdots\cdots\cdots\cdots\cdots \quad (A.2)$$
$$(1+r)(A_k p_a + \ldots + K_k p_k) = (K_a + \ldots + K_k)p_k$$

Non-basics play no active role in the determination of the prices and the rate of profits. Their 'prices' merely reflect the rate of profits and the 'prices' of the various means of production used to produce them. Basics, on the other hand, play an active role since they enter (directly or indirectly) into the production of one another and hence their 'prices' influence (and are simultaneously determined with) the 'prices' of their means of production. This is one of the key distinctions of Sraffa's book.

Rather than regarding part of the wages as necessities and another part as surplus, Sraffa regards the whole as variable. Also, wages are no longer viewed as 'advanced', and the means of subsistence are now 'replaced' by the quantities of homogeneous labour appropriate for each industry. Our system is therefore altered as follows

$$(1+r)(A_a p_a + \ldots + K_a p_k) + L_a w = A p_a$$
$$\cdots\cdots\cdots\cdots\cdots\cdots\cdots\cdots\cdots\cdots\cdots\cdots\cdots \quad (A.3)$$
$$(1+r)(A_k p_a + \ldots + K_k p_k) + L_k w = K p_k$$

where $L_a, \ldots, L_k$ represent the appropriate quantities of labour employed in the production of $a, \ldots, k$; w equals total wages; $L_a + \ldots + L_k = 1$; and where $A \geqslant A_a + \ldots + A_k$; $K \geqslant K_a + \ldots + K_k$. The national income (equals the net product) of the system consists of $[A - (A_a + \ldots + A_k)]$ $+ \ldots + [K - (K_a + \ldots + K_k)]$. Sraffa sets the value of the national income equal to unity, that is, $[A - (A_a + \ldots + A_k)]p_a + \ldots + [K - (K_a + \ldots + K_k)]p_k = 1$, and adopts this as the new standard in which to express the k prices and w (r is a pure number). We now have $k+1$ equations and $k+2$ unknowns.

He then examines the effect on r and relative prices of letting w vary from 1 to 0. At first glance, permitting w to vary without altering the composition of output may not seem permissible. This objection vanishes, however, when it is realized that Sraffa is examining, in a situation of unchanged technical conditions, the effects of changes in the distribution of income on relative prices. He wishes to isolate those changes in relative prices which are due to changes in income distribution from those associated with changing technical conditions.

Under the given assumptions, when $w = 1$, the commodities exchange in proportion to their direct and indirect labour requirements. The device of sub-systems – rearrangements of the equations of the actual system such that only one commodity is contained in the net product of each sub-system – is used to show this proposition. We discuss this device in detail in section II below, see also Harcourt and Massaro [1964a]. Here the important point to note is that it is the *equations* of the conditions of production in each industry, and not the *proportions* in which the product of each industry appears in the actual system, which are relevant to the determination of relative prices and *r*; from which it follows that the given *w*, relative prices and *r* of the main economic system and each sub-system are identical.

When *w* is given a value less than unity, the entire national income no longer goes to wages, and exchange ratios are now influenced by a uniform rate of profits. Prices then vary according to the different ratios of labour to the means of production, with the modification that we must take into account the different ratios producing the means of production at each remove. For instance, in comparing the relative price movements of commodities *a* and *b*, where *a* is apparently more labour-intensive than *b*, we cannot immediately conclude that the price of *a* will increase relative to that of *b* (following a rise in *w*) since the means of production producing commodity *a* (and the means of production producing those means of production, and so on) may be highly commodity-intensive; whereas the means of production producing commodity *b* (and again the various means of production producing those means of production, and so on) may be of such a labour-intensive nature as to offset or reverse the price movements initially expected.

We may imagine a commodity produced by an industry employing labour and means of production in a 'balancing' ratio such that, were *w* to rise by a total of $50, total profits (paid at the uniform rate) would decrease by exactly the same amount. We may suppose further that the means of production employed by this industry were produced by the same balancing ratio of labour to means of production and likewise those means of production, and so on. Then, under the given assumptions, we would have found a commodity whose 'price' would not vary in relation to its own means of production when wages rise. Any variation in the prices of other commodities relative to its own would therefore originate in the conditions of production of these other commodities. A commodity with this property would be an ideal standard of value.

In order to discover the 'balancing' ratio, Sraffa adopts the ratio of the value of the net product to the value of the means of production and finds that, when $w = 0$, this ratio is the same for each industry and coincides with the 'maximum rate of profits', R. This is the ratio which, if found, would not vary with changes in w and it is also the 'balancing' ratio.

We now come to the standard commodity, the commodity which is to serve as the standard of value of the system. From an economic system containing only basics, Sraffa constructs a standard system, multiplying each equation of the actual system by unique, positive multipliers such that the commodities of the derived standard system enter and are produced in the same proportion. And a collection of commodities in these proportions *is* the standard commodity. The 'standard national income', the amount of standard commodity which would form the net product of a standard system if it employed the same total labour as the actual system, becomes the new unit in which to measure the prices and wages of the actual economic system. It should be noted that the quantity-ratio of the net product to the means of production of the standard system, that is, the standard ratio, R', would not be affected by changes in distribution, since both numerator and denominator are quantities of the same standard commodity. (It is also equal to R, the maximum rate of profits of the system.) We have thus found a ratio which would not be affected by variations in w (or by the corresponding changes in the rate of profits and prices).[1] Given the share of wages in the standard net product, the ratio of the rate of profits to the standard ratio, R, equals the ratio of the share of profits to the standard net product, that is

$$\frac{r}{R} = \frac{1-w}{1} \quad \text{or} \quad r = R(1-w) \qquad (A.4)$$

This is, of course, Sraffa's version of the *FpF* or wage-rate–rate-of-profits trade-off relation. Notice that Sraffa's straight-line w–r relationship depends upon all values being measured in terms of the standard commodity of *one* technique (or economy). There is, therefore, no *common* unit whereby an envelope consisting of segments of each straight-line w–r relationship could be formed.[2] Since the actual system differs from the standard system only in the proportions in which the

---

[1] Formally, there are k sets of multipliers which would transform the actual system into k standard systems, each with different values of R and different sets of prices. Sraffa shows, however, that there is only one set which will give all positive prices, namely, that associated with the minimum value of R. This is the only solution which has economic relevance.

[2] I am indebted to Nobuo Okishio for this point.

same equations enter, the above relation extends to the actual economic system as well. Provided that the wage is measured in terms of standard product, the rate of profits of the actual system, which is a ratio of values, will then be the same as the rate of profits of the standard system, which is a ratio of quantities.

Sraffa shows that if w and r of the actual economic system vary according to the relation $r = R'(1-w)$, relative prices and w are expressed in terms of a standard net product whose composition is unknown. We can then find R' by calculating the maximum rate of profits of the actual system. But, given r, we can replace the standard net product by a quantity of labour which will serve equally well as a standard of value which is independent of price movements. The quantity of labour which becomes the new absolute measure of value is the labour that can be purchased by the standard net product at any given level of r.

Wages were previously taken as given because they were regarded as subsistence, determined exogenously to that part of the system being examined. This view becomes less satisfactory once we discuss the division of the net product between wage-earners and profit-receivers. Sraffa therefore takes the rate of profits as exogenous to the system, because it is a ratio independent of prices and may be determined by, say, 'the level of the money rates of interest' (p. 33).

Sraffa concludes part I by examining reduction to 'dated' labour. This operation consists of reducing a given quantity of a commodity into the direct and indirect labour necessary for its production. The commodity is first split into its direct labour and means of production components; the means of production are themselves similarly split into their two components; and so on. This process can, of course, continue without limit. But (provided that $r \neq R$) we may approximate the total labour component of the commodity by making the residue of commodities[1] as small as we like and summing the labour components, each one of which has been accumulated at the appropriate rate of profits up to the 'present' period. Reduction does not occur in historical time (as we saw in chapter 4, pp. 152–4 above). Rather, it shows the

---

[1] In appendix D, Sraffa speaks of Marx's attack on Smith's assertion that the price of a commodity resolves itself entirely into wages, profits and rent, without a commodity residue. Sraffa's view of the economic system, as expressed in this book, reminds us that while macro-economic theory concentrates on the consolidated national accounts where final expenditures equal total values added and incomes, and intermediate goods cancel, price theory cannot ignore the large stock of commodities which is in existence before the year's production starts.

labour component of a commodity, given the current technical conditions, wage rate and rate of profits.

This technique is used to compare the 'dated' labour components of the same commodity at different rates of profits; and the labour components of different commodities at the same rates of profits. This allows Sraffa to dismiss once and for all the notion of a quantity of capital which is independent of distribution and prices (p. 38).[1]

(The reduction to dated labour terms has some bearing on the attempts that have been made to find in the 'period of production' an independent measure of the quantity of capital which could be used, without arguing in a circle, for the determination of prices and of the shares in distribution. But the case just considered seems conclusive in showing the impossibility of aggregating the 'periods' belonging to the several quantities of labour into a single magnitude which could be regarded as representing the quantity of capital. The reversals in the direction of the movement of relative prices, in the face of unchanged methods of production, cannot be reconciled with *any* notion of capital as a measurable quantity independent of distribution and prices.)

It follows that it is a fruitless task to construct a theory of distribution for the economy as a whole which depends upon the concept of an aggregate production function in which the quantity of capital is one of the factors of production, and the returns to labour and capital are related to the slope of the production function.

In parts II and III Sraffa adapts the analysis of part I to include further important characteristics of actual economic systems. He discusses in part II the implications of joint production for the construction of the standard system and commodity, the definitions of basics and non-basics, and the determination of relative prices and wages for given rates of profits. The main purpose of the discussion is to enable the prices of fixed assets (durable instruments of production) and the rent of land to be included among the unknowns of the main economic system. Thus fixed assets are regarded as joint products, one of the components of total outputs now being fixed assets one year older than those included in the means of production at the beginning of the year. Land is regarded as a non-produced commodity, a non-basic which is included in

---

[1] Readers of the first printing should note that the two expressions on p. 37 should read:

$$n = \frac{1+r}{R-r} \quad \text{and} \quad r = \frac{nR-1}{1+n}$$

the means of production of the actual system but not in its products. Part III contains a discussion of different methods of producing single commodities, and the principles underlying switches from one to the other as the rate of profits changes.

The introduction of joint production requires that the concept of an industry which produces one commodity, and for which there is one equation of production, be replaced by the concept of processes in which *all* commodities may be included both as means of production and as products. One process is distinguished from another by the proportions in which the different commodities appear in the means of production and the total outputs. (Of course, the amount of a commodity in any process may be zero, and single-commodity systems are those in which all but one commodity are zero in the total outputs of each process.)

The inclusion of joint production in the analysis explains why Sraffa did not use the more familiar input per unit of output notation in the single-commodity system (which, however, *is* used in chapter 4 above and in section II of this appendix below). This notation has no meaning once there is joint production; on the other hand, joint production is easily accommodated by Sraffa's notation. We write

$$A_1 + \ldots + K_1 + L_1 \rightarrow A_{(1)} + \ldots + K_{(1)}$$
$$\ldots\ldots\ldots\ldots\ldots\ldots\ldots\ldots\ldots\ldots\ldots\ldots\ldots\ldots\ldots\ldots \qquad (A.5)$$
$$A_k + \ldots + K_k + L_k \rightarrow A_{(k)} + \ldots + K_{(k)}$$

Quantities of commodities in the means of production of each process have unbracketed subscripts, those in the total outputs have subscripts in parentheses.

The standard system is again defined in terms of the equality of the ratios of the output of each basic commodity to its use as a means of production. The standard commodity, however, becomes an abstract concept instead of one which has a clear economic meaning. With joint production, negative multipliers may be needed to transform the actual system into the standard system. There is a limit to the proportions in which individual commodities can be produced *vis-à-vis* other commodities; for any two commodities and processes, the possible proportions lie between the proportion of one process and that of the other. If the two commodities are used as a means of production in proportions which lie outside this range, negative multipliers must be used in the transformation process. Furthermore, because non-basics may be produced jointly with basics but may not enter the standard system or commodity, negative multipliers are needed to remove them.

The inclusion of negative as well as positive commodities in the standard system is likened by Sraffa to an individual share in a company which contains a fraction of each asset and liability.

With joint production, the intuitively satisfying definition of non-basics as those commodities which do not enter directly or indirectly the production of all commodities disappears. Basics and non-basics can now enter the means of production and emerge as products side by side in the same processes. However, the key distinction between basics and non-basics is that the former are *price-determining*. Sraffa now defines non-basics (for a system of k processes and k commodities) as 'a group of n linked commodities' ($n < k$) where 'of the k rows (formed by the $2n$ quantities in which they appear in each process) not more than n rows are independent, the others being linear combinations of these' (p. 51). It is a property of this definition that a set of multipliers (some positive, some negative) can always be found which when applied to the k equations allows a new system of equations to be formed, equal to the number of basics, and from which non-basics have been eliminated. These equations are called 'Basic' equations. They have the property that the maximum rate of profits and the relative prices at each rate of profits derivable from them are the same as those derivable from the actual system.

The Basic equations are changed into the standard system by applying the appropriate set of multipliers. If there are j basic commodities there will be j Rs and j sets of multipliers. However, as with the single-commodity system, it can be shown that only the smallest of these Rs is meaningful – meaningful in the sense that only the standard commodity with which it is associated will give finite prices of commodities as r passes from R to 0 (and w from 0 to 1) in terms of the standard commodity.

The device of sub-systems can again be used to show that, when $r = 0$, the value of any commodity is equal to the value of the labour which directly and indirectly produced it. If we compare two systems, one of which contains in its *net product* more of one commodity than the other does, and the same amount of all other commodities, the extra labour of the first system is naturally associated with the extra amount of the commodity. This is so even if the quantities of the means of production also differ, because indirect labour is as relevant as direct labour. It is as if we were to add to the second system a sub-system which contains all these commodities in its means of production and total outputs, but only the additional amount of the relevant commodity in its net product.

It follows that, when $r = 0$, the value of the commodity will equal its direct and indirect labour components.

While the sub-system approach may be used to show the above proposition, the alternative approach used in the single-products system – the reduction to 'dated' labour – cannot be used. To attempt reduction means introducing negative quantities of labour, which have no meaning; moreover, there is no guarantee that the series will converge towards a zero residue of commodities. There are two further modifications of propositions derived from the single-products system. First, it is now possible to have negative prices. With joint production, the prices of some commodities may be raised sufficiently to offset negative prices of other commodities and allow the uniform rate of profits to be earned in the process as a whole. Secondly, and again because of offsetting movements in other prices, the price of any one jointly-produced commodity may fall faster than the wage rate. (This was not possible in the single-products system.) The second modification implies that more than one rate of profits may correspond to one level of wages measured in terms of a commodity, the price of which, measured in terms of the standard commodity, falls faster than the wage, similarly measured.

As we noted above, the interest in joint production lies 'in its being the genus of which Fixed Capital is the leading species' (p. 63). Treating fixed assets as joint products one year older than when they are counted in the means of production introduces as many extra unknowns (that is, prices of fixed assets) as there are years in the economic lifetimes of the fixed assets concerned. (Sraffa does not make clear what determines these lifetimes.) Each industry is therefore divided into processes which are distinguished one from another by the ages of the fixed assets in their means of production and total outputs. The equations of these processes provide the additional equations needed to solve for the prices of the fixed assets.

The fixed assets do not have to be sold for their prices to be effective; the imputed prices of the fixed assets to the process must be such that they correctly allocate profits and allow for depreciation. 'Correctly' means that the annual charge for the use of fixed capital is such that replacement of the means of production is possible, together with payment of the uniform rate of profits on the value of the fixed assets.

Sraffa shows that in the case of 'one-hoss shays', that is, machines of equal productive efficiency over their lifetimes, the annual charge for the use of fixed capital obtained by solving this system of equations equals the expression obtained by using the annuity method to calculate equal annual payments of depreciation and interest combined. The expression is

$$Pm_0 \frac{r(1+r)^n}{(1+r)^n - 1} \qquad (A.6)$$

where Pm_0 = the original price of the machine
           r = the rate of profits
and n = the life of the machine

The Sraffa formulation, unlike the annuity method, is quite general; regardless of the pattern of productive efficiency over the life of the machine, the prices which emerge allow the correct depreciation to be calculated year by year (depreciation is defined as the decline in the value of the machine over the course of the year). Depreciation plus profit, reckoned as the uniform rate of profits on the value of the machine at the start of the year, give the annual charge for capital, that is, the capital component of the price of the commodity which it helps to produce.

Reverting to the example of machines of constant productive efficiency, it is clear that the price of the commodity which they produce must be the same, irrespective of their ages. It follows that, because the annual charge for capital is the same each year but the prices of machines fall as they age, the profit component of the charge must fall and the depreciation component must rise as they age. Hudson and Mathews [1963] have shown that straight-line depreciation is 'correct' only when the expected net services associated with a machine decline at a particular rate. Sraffa's formulation brings out clearly why this should be so. Suppose that the prices of the commodities which the machine produces are expected to remain constant for its lifetime. The profit component of the annual net service must decline from year to year for the reason given above. Therefore, the depreciation components will rise unless the net services decline at just that rate which will keep them constant.

The proposition that, when $r = 0$, the value of commodities equals the value of the labour which directly and indirectly is used to produce them, can be extended, Sraffa argues, to the cases of new and ageing machines. In the case of a new machine, it is the amount of direct and indirect labour which produces it; in the case of an older machine, it is this quantity less such quantities as have passed in previous 'years' into its product.

Sraffa gives an example on pp. 68–9 which illustrates the proposition. Assume that four units of labour, indirect and direct, are needed to make a tractor of constant productive efficiency which lasts for four years. Suppose that we compare two systems which use the same techniques and which are in self-replacing states; one has 1,000 units of wheat in its *net product*, while the other has two two-year-old tractors as well. When $r = 0$, the total labour of the first system is equal in value to 1,000 units of wheat, so that the labour value of wheat in *both* systems can be calculated. The aim of the comparison is to show that the second system has four extra units of labour in it, from which it follows that each two-year-old tractor in the net product embodies two units of labour.

In the first system, twenty tractors are spread evenly, according to age, among four processes which jointly produce wheat and tractors. There are five new tractors in the means of production of the first process, five one-year-old tractors in those of the second, and so on. (The total outputs similarly contain five tractors, one year older.) In a further process five new tractors are produced each year. In the second system, six new tractors are produced each year. Twenty tractors are again employed in the wheat processes, and are distributed among the means of production as follows: six brand new ones, six one-year-old ones, four two-year-old ones and four three-year-old ones. Sraffa argues that, when the total means of production are subtracted from the gross product of the second system, two two-year-old tractors appear in the net product, as well as 1,000 units of wheat; and that the two tractors are found to be associated with four extra units of labour.

This example is wrong as it stands unless it is assumed, first, that tractors are made from labour alone; in which case, the result is trivial and, moreover, introduces a process in which, when $r \neq 0$, the uniform rate of profits cannot be earned. Secondly, it could be assumed that wheat is a non-basic which may be used to make itself but not tractors or other commodities. The example could then be interpreted as what we would see if a spotlight were to light up only those processes, of a much larger economic system, in which the components of the net product, one of which is a non-basic, were produced. But, to regard wheat, a wage good, as a non-basic is most unsatisfactory, as Sraffa himself says, see p. 10, where he discusses treating the whole wage, including the 'necessaries of consumption' as part of the surplus, i.e. the net product, to be distributed.

However, the example can be easily adapted to handle the case of two basic commodities, wheat and tractors. There are still only twenty tractors at work in the wheat processes, so that the total output of wheat in the two systems is the same. But there is one more new tractor produced in the tractor process of the second system. It follows either that the tractor process of the second system is at the moment short of the wheat needed to make one tractor; or, alternatively, that the wheat component of the net product as it stands at the moment is this amount short of 1,000 units of wheat. We therefore have to introduce, as it were, a further system which is in a self-replacing state and which has, as its net product, the present short-fall of wheat. This system is easily obtained by scaling down (or up) all the processes of the first system by the ratio of the short-fall of wheat to 1,000 units of wheat. When $r = 0$, the labour value of the short-fall of wheat plus the direct labour content of one tractor is four units of labour. And the labour of the second system, when the two parts are combined, exceeds that of the first system by exactly this amount. We have therefore the desired components in the net product and the desired increase in labour; so the proposition concerning the labour content of the two two-year-old tractors can be established.

Sraffa next discusses depreciation and the value of capital within the context of a balanced stock of machines. He shows that the value of a balanced stock rises as r increases, the limit to the rise being the aggregate value of all the machines in the stock when new. This is, of course, the Kahn–Champernowne formula: see Robinson [1953–4]. In view of the prominence given to this formula in recent years, it is an intriguing question to ask just when among the thirty-to-forty-year gestation period of the present work this proposition was established and in what condition capital theory and economic theory generally would be today if this and other propositions had been published twenty years earlier.

The proposition that the value of capital increases when r *increases is regarded by Sraffa as a 'remarkable' result, because it appears to imply that it is impossible to have a measure of the quantity of capital which is invariant to changes in distribution.* The proposition here must be seen within the context of given technical conditions, equilibrium prices of commodities and machines, and the appropriate wage rate for each given rate of profits, that is, within the context of the economic system as a whole which is, of course, the relevant context for this proposition.

Durable instruments are easily fitted into the standard system. Machines in the means of production are given such multipliers that machines *of the same age* in the total output of the standard system exceed them by R', the standard ratio. Thus, if m machines are $(n-1)$ years old (where n is the length of life of the machine) in the means of production of the actual system, there will be $m(n-1)$-year-old machines, $m(1+R')$ $(n-2)$-year-old machines, up to $m(1+R')^{n-1}$ new machines in the means of production of the standard system. However, reduction to 'dated' labour is impossible with durable instruments which are, as we have seen, joint products.

Part II closes with a discussion of the implications of treating land as a non-basic and includes an account of rent's role in the system. Part III[1] discusses the implication for single-products systems of different ways of producing one commodity. It is concerned with the question: which method will be the most profitable at different levels of the rate of profits? If the commodities are basics, a common unit of value in which prices can be measured must be found; this is a difficulty because each method implies a different economic system and maximum rate of profits. The problem is solved by supposing that, while the commodity can be regarded as identical for all basic uses, so that the choice between methods is entirely on the grounds of cheapness, in its use in the production of non-basics, some uses require one method rather than another. Any system therefore will contain all methods.

In conclusion we may distinguish at least two essential points which constitute the foundation for Sraffa's proposed critique of marginal theory. In an economy in which commodities are mainly produced by other commodities:

(1) prices are determined by the methods of production, given the constraints of a uniform rate of profits and the possibility of self-replacement;

(2) commodities can be classified into basics and non-basics, with the former playing a vital role in the determination of prices for the system as a whole.

Sraffa prices are therefore based on a labour theory of value. When $r = 0$, the position of the price of any commodity on a scale of relative prices is determined simply by its direct and indirect labour components. Once $r \gtrdot 0$, the simple relationship no longer holds. Nevertheless, it is always possible *in principle*, provided only that we know r and the direct and indirect labour components of the commodity, to say what its new position will be (even though, in practice, this may be a difficult task). Moreover, by concentrating on technical conditions and *industries* it is unnecessary, in order to explain prices, to make *any* assumptions about the motives and behaviour of individual economic units, in parti-

---

[1] I have left the account of part III substantially as it was written in 1964 in order to show how completely we missed its significance.

cular, whether they are maximizers or not and, if they are, *what* it is
that they maximize.

Meek makes this point very strongly. Thus he postulates:
as Marx himself did, an industry in which the ratio of used-up means
of production to wages is equal to the ratio of these quantities when
they are aggregated over the economy as a whole, . . . an industry
in which, to use Marx's terminology, the 'organic composition of
capital' is equal to the 'social average'. In such an industry, . . . the
ratio of surplus value to means of production . . . is equal to the
ratio of these quantities over the economy as a whole. . . . We can
thus say, as Marx did, that the average rate of profits over the
economy as a whole is determined by the ratio of surplus value to
means of production *in this industry*, whose conditions of production represent a sort of 'social average'. Or, to put the same proposition in another way, the average rate of profits over the
economy as a whole is given by the following expression:

$$\frac{\text{labour embodied in net product of [this] industry}}{\text{labour embodied in its means of production}} \left(1 - \begin{array}{l}\text{proportion of net} \\ \text{product of [this]} \\ \text{industry going to} \\ \text{wages}\end{array}\right)$$

The similarity between this Marxian relation and that expressed in
Sraffa's $r = R(1-w)$ is surely very striking. For, in the first place,
let us note that Sraffa's R, although usually expressed as the ratio of
the *value* of the net product of the 'standard' industry to the *value*
of its means of production, is in fact equal to the ratio of the *labour*
embodied in the net product of the 'standard' industry to the *labour*
embodied in its means of production. In other words, Sraffa is postulating precisely the same relation between the average rate of profits
and the conditions of production in his 'standard' industry as Marx
was postulating between the average rate of profits *and the condi-*
tions of production in his industry of 'average organic composition of
capital'. What both economists are trying to show, in effect, is that
(when wages are given) the average rate of profits, and therefore
the deviations of price ratios from embodied labour ratios, are
governed by the ratio of direct to indirect labour in the industry
whose conditions of production represent a sort of 'average' of
those prevailing over the economy as a whole. Marx reached this
result by postulating as his 'average' industry one whose 'organic
composition of capital' was equal to the 'social average'. But his

result could only be a provisional and approximate one, since in reaching it he had abstracted from the effect which a change in the wage would have on the prices of the means of production employed in the 'average' industry. Sraffa shows that the same result can be achieved, without abstracting from this effect at all, if we substitute his 'standard' industry for Marx's industry of 'average organic composition of capital'. (Meek [1967], pp. 176–8.)

Finally, it remains to be shown that Sraffa prices are more fundamental than any other system of prices which can be deduced in a 'period' of time. The answer may be found in the view that the distribution of income can, within wide ranges, be regarded as independent of the technical conditions of production. These technical conditions may in turn be influenced by prices and the distribution of income through their impact on the choice of technique – Sraffa analyses this aspect in part III – and resource allocation generally, but this influence may be tenuous and, anyway, is of a long-run nature. Therefore, as a first approximation, it may be reasonable to assume that technical conditions are unrelated to, or at least unaffected by, the distribution of income; and to have relative prices determined by an historically given rate of profits (itself related to the rate of interest, an exogeneous monetary phenomenon, or to the other factors analysed in chapter 5 below) and existing technical conditions. Such an answer would in turn imply that the elements of the actual economic system which Sraffa has included in his analysis are more important (as far as price-formation is concerned) than those left out, in particular, demand and change. The exclusion of change is crucial. In an actual economic system in which change is occurring, it would not be possible, in the absence of constant returns to scale, to determine prices independently of the level and composition of output.

By way of contrast with our assessment, we quote in full Blaug's [1968], pp. 143–4, whose view that theory has a life of its own is cogently argued in *Economic Theory in Retrospect*.

P. Sraffa, the editor of Ricardo's works, has recently published a puzzling book, entitled *Production of Commodities by Means of Commodities. Prelude to a Critique of Economic Theory* (1960). It is a kind of 'Ricardo in modern dress', containing all the characteristic Ricardian touches: the search for a standard of value independent of demand and unaffected by changes in the distribution of the total product between wages and profits; the neglect of factor substitution and changes in the scale of operations; the division of commodities into two classes – 'basic' commodities that do and 'non-basic' commodities that do not enter into the production of all commodities including themselves; the emphasis on a 'standard commodity' as the yardstick of value, defined as a commodity produced only by basic commodities in a 'standard ratio', that is, in the same proportion as they enter into the production of total output; culminating, of course, in the demonstration that relative prices depend only on the technical conditions of producing the 'standard commodity' and on nothing else. The argument is intimately related to some 20th-century linear-programming models of the economy, and yet no reference is made to any work more recent than Marx. It is the sort of book Ricardo might have written if only he had gone straight to the point without ifs and buts: the reasoning is terse and condensed, no concessions are made to the reader, and it is not clear, even when we reach the end, just how this could constitute a 'Prelude to a Critique of Economic Theory'. Without first struggling through Ricardo, one might find Sraffa incomprehensible; but after Ricardo, he is plain sailing, and we can almost see on the first page where we are going.

II

We now use the concept of sub-systems in order to discuss Joan Robinson and Naqvi's example: see chapter 4, pp. 132–5 above. As we have seen, the relative prices of commodities are determined by the input–output relationships, together with one of either r or w (one of which is given exogenously). They are therefore independent of the proportions in which the commodities themselves appear in the net product of a self-replacing system, or indeed of whether they appear there at all, see Harcourt and Massaro [1964a], p. 721. A sub-system is therefore a device by which we may construct a mini-self-replacing economic system which, while it has only one commodity in its net product, yet nevertheless has relative prices that correspond *exactly* to those of the actual economic system from which it is taken.

Joan Robinson and Naqvi's arithmetical example shows that if the means of production to labour ratios of *all* commodities are the same when $r = 0$, relative prices are independent of r, constant, and in fact equal to the ratios of their direct labour inputs per unit of output. To provide a simple backdrop to Sraffa's intuitive explanation (see chapter 4, p. 135 above), we first form the sub-systems for commodities 1 and 2 and find their respective *total* labour requirements.[1] When $r = 0$, the ratio of these *is* their relative price – this is *always* true (see, for example, Harcourt and Massaro [1964a]) – for the whole of the sub-system's 'national income' (= net product) goes to the direct and indirect labour which produced it.

Sub-system 1 is

$$x_{11}X_1 + x_{21}X_1 + l_{01}X_1 \to X_1 \qquad (A.7)$$

$$x_{12}X_2 + x_{22}X_2 + l_{02}X_2 \to X_2$$

subject to

$$x_{11}X_1 + x_{12}X_2 = X_1 - 1 \qquad (A.8)$$

$$x_{21}X_1 + x_{22}X_2 = X_2$$

so that the net product is *one* unit of X_1. (All but one unit of X_1 and all of X_2 are absorbed when we allow for the replacement of what has been used up in production, so that none of X_2 and one unit of X_1 remain for the net product.)

Solving expression $(A.8)$ for X_1 and X_2, we obtain

$$X_1 = \frac{1 - x_{22}}{A} \quad \text{and} \quad X_2 = \frac{x_{21}}{A} \qquad (A.9)$$

where $A = (1 - x_{11})(1 - x_{22}) - x_{12}x_{21}$.

The total labour requirement of sub-system 1 is therefore

$$l_{01}X_1 + l_{02}X_2 = \frac{l_{01}(1 - x_{22}) + l_{02}x_{21}}{A} \qquad (A.10)$$

Similarly, we may show that the total labour requirement of sub-system 2 is

$$\frac{l_{01}x_{12} + l_{02}(1 - x_{11})}{A} \qquad (A.11)$$

When $r = 0$, these are their labour values and the relative price (B), if commodity 1 is the *numéraire*, is

$$B = \frac{l_{01}x_{12} + l_{02}(1 - x_{11})}{l_{01}(1 - x_{22}) + l_{02}x_{21}} \qquad (A.12)$$

[1] It might be a useful exercise for the reader to regard commodity 1 as wheat and commodity 2 as copper and to parallel the steps that follow by using the values of the coefficients, *etc.*, of Joan Robinson and Naqvi's example. Those who are lucky enough to be skilled in the techniques of matrix algebra will find this section a bore and are urged either to skip it or to skim it lightly. Those who, like the author, are not so equipped may find it insightful to work through the analysis.

We obtain the ratio of the labour value of their means of production to their direct labour contents by estimating

$$\frac{x_{11}+x_{21}B}{l_{01}} \quad \text{and} \quad \frac{x_{12}+x_{22}B}{l_{02}}$$

Of course, in general, these two ratios are *not* equal to one another. However, in the special case where they are

$$\frac{x_{11}+x_{21}B}{l_{01}} = \frac{x_{12}+x_{22}B}{l_{02}} = \lambda \qquad (A.13)$$

When $r = 0$, we have the following price equations

$$x_{11}+Bx_{21}+wl_{01} = 1$$
$$x_{12}+Bx_{22}+wl_{02} = B \qquad (A.14)$$

From expression $(A.13)$ we get

$$x_{11}+x_{21}B = \lambda l_{01}$$
$$x_{12}+x_{22}B = \lambda l_{02} \qquad (A.15)$$

Substituting expression $(A.15)$ in expression $(A.14)$, we get

$$(\lambda+w)l_{01} = 1$$
$$(\lambda+w)l_{02} = B \qquad (A.16)$$

Now $l_{01} = 1/(\lambda+w)$ so that, when $r = 0$,

$$\frac{l_{02}}{l_{01}} = B \qquad (A.17)$$

(which is exactly what Joan Robinson and Naqvi's example shows).

We now show that, when $r \neq 0$, $B = l_{02}/l_{01}$ so establishing, *for this special case*, that relative prices are constant and independent of r (which last we have just shown for $r = 0$). We write the price equations

$$(1+r)(x_{11}+p_{21}x_{21})+wl_{01} = 1$$
$$(1+r)(x_{12}+p_{21}x_{22})+wl_{02} = p_{21} \qquad (A.18)$$

where p_{21} is the price of 2 in terms of 1.

Expressions $(A.18)$ hold for *all* economically meaningful values of r. We eliminate r by multiplying the first equation of expressions $(A.18)$ by l_{02}, the second, by l_{01} to get

$$(1+r)\{x_{11}l_{02}-x_{12}l_{01}+p_{21}(x_{21}l_{02}-x_{22}l_{01})\} = l_{02}-p_{21}l_{01}$$

Now we know that

$$B = \frac{l_{02}}{l_{01}} = \frac{l_{01}x_{12} + l_{02}(1-x_{11})}{l_{01}(1-x_{22}) + l_{02}x_{21}}$$

which (because, for example, $\frac{a}{b} = \frac{c}{d} = \frac{a+c}{b+d}$) implies that:

$$B = \frac{l_{01}x_{12} - l_{02}x_{11}}{l_{02}x_{21} - l_{01}x_{22}} (= B') \qquad (A.19)$$

It follows that

$$-(l_{01}x_{12} - l_{02}x_{11}) = -B(l_{02}x_{21} - l_{01}x_{22}) \qquad (A.20)$$

and $$l_{02} = Bl_{01}$$

We substitute expression $(A.20)$ in expression $(A.19)$ and, after some manipulation, obtain

$$(B - p_{21})\{l_{01} + (1+r)(x_{21}l_{02} - x_{22}l_{01})\} = 0 \qquad (A.21)$$

For this equality to hold for *all* values of r (*not just one*)

$$B = p_{21} \qquad (A.22)$$

the result we were looking for.[1]

Finally we may convert x_{21} and x_{22} into the same units as x_{11} and x_{12} by multiplying them by B and show that the w–r relationship is now a straight line. We may use either price equation. Thus

$$(1+r)(x_{11} + Bx_{21}) + wl_{01} = 1$$

so that

$$w = \left\{\frac{1}{l_{01}} - \frac{x_{11} + Bx_{21}}{l_{01}}\right\} - \left\{\frac{x_{11} + Bx_{21}}{l_{01}}\right\}r \qquad (A.23)$$

which is obviously a straight line. Similarly, we may show, using the price equation of commodity 2, that

$$w = \left\{\frac{B}{l_{02}} - \frac{x_{12} + Bx_{22}}{l_{02}}\right\} - \left\{\frac{x_{12} + Bx_{22}}{l_{02}}\right\}r \qquad (A.24)$$

---

[1] I am indebted to Denzo Kamiya for this derivation, the mathematics of which are as simple as the economic sense shown is profound. This example of maths as the handmaid of economics could perhaps be contrasted with Burmeister's derivation of the same result, in Burmeister [1968], in which, to my untutored mind anyway, economics acts as the handmaid of maths.

Because, in this special case, $B/l_{02} = 1/l_{01}$ for all meaningful values of r, and because

$$\frac{x_{12} + Bx_{22}}{l_{02}} = \frac{x_{11} + Bx_{21}}{l_{01}} = \lambda \qquad \text{(see } A.13)$$

expressions $(A.24)$ and $(A.23)$ are the same equation. Thus, though commodities are produced by commodities right enough, with these special assumptions and from the point of view of relative prices and $w-r$ relationships, we are, in effect, in a one-commodity (jelly) world in which neoclassical parables may be told, but only as comparisons. We are *not* in a world of 'leets': see Robinson [1970a, 1970b].

III

Nell's article [1967b], 'Theories of Growth and Theories of Value', is one of the most challenging, relevant and insightful articles to have been written in recent years. It examines a number of themes that we have already met in this book. The first concerns Meek's view that while Sraffa's arguments can best be understood 'as a sort of magnificent rehabilitation of the Classical (and up to a point Marxian) approach to certain crucial problems relating to value and distribution', his 'primary aim is to build a twentieth-century model to deal with twentieth-century problems'. Nell is concerned to show how a theory of value based on Ricardian–Sraffa prices both illuminates and points the way to the solutions of puzzles associated with the most vital of all twentieth-century economic problems, those of economic growth and the distribution of the net product.

His starting point is to argue that growth models contain either a Walrasian, i.e. neoclassical, theory of value or a Ricardian–Sraffa one (in fact, most contain the former) and that it makes an enormous difference to our approaches to certain vital aspects of growth – capital measurement, the composition, distribution and disposal of surplus, population growth and technical progress – which theory of value is adopted. He is, of course, a partisan of the latter approach:

> The purpose of this paper will be to contrast Walrasian and Ricardian general equilibrium theories, and in doing so to suggest that providing a Ricardian value theory as the context for growth models eliminates the difficulties outlined above. (p. 16.)

Secondly, Nell returns, in a context of growth, to the basic puzzle of the measurement of capital and the theory of distribution where neo-classical theory, because it tries to 'determine relative shares along with prices and the rate of profits, given the *quantities* of capital . . . can only work with a very simple concept of capital which is inappropriate for the study of growth' (p. 23) – and distribution. The Ricardian–Sraffa approach, by contrast, 'can more easily examine the effects of growth on the labour market and thus on distribution' because it introduces either a real-wage rate or a rate of profits from *outside* the production system. One of these in turn is determined by relative shares which are, them-selves, related to Marx's degree of exploitation and which are a direct outcome of the conflict between capital and labour.

Nell is quite explicit on this point: if we *know* the share of profits, we may determine relative prices, the wage rate and the rate of profits. He suggests that the share of profits may be determined by collective bar-gaining, see Nell [1967b], p. 17. Following Joan Robinson [1965b], pp. 177–8, and using a result from Hahn and Matthews [1964], p. 798, the argument could perhaps be put as follows.

Collective bargaining, the outcome of which reflects the relative strengths of capital and labour in the economy, has, over the years, established a relatively constant share of profits (Π) in income (Y), one that has come to be accepted – call it $\bar{E}(=\Pi/Y)$. Joan Robinson quotes values of $\bar{E}$ in the manufacturing industries of various countries which show a superb (negative) correlation between the unionization and militancy of wage-earners, on the one hand, and the share of profits in value added, on the other.[1] Suppose that the *mps* (= *aps*) of profit-receivers is s_π, and that of wage-earners is s_w, where $s_\pi > s_w$. Then, in Keynesian short-run equilibrium, $S = I$,

i.e. $$\{\bar{E}(s_\pi - s_w) + s_w\}Y = I \qquad (A.25)$$

where I is the (autonomous) level of planned investment.

Now go over to the long run and suppose that the long-run rate of growth of the economy, g, is given autonomously (either as a 'natural' rate or by 'animal spirits' – either way, the level of I will now be deter-mined each short period). Suppose, further, that the economy has in fact been growing at a rate of growth of g for a long time so that expecta-tions are realized (or, at least, are a surrogate for realized ones) and, therefore, r and K, where K is the value of capital, may be given

[1] In 1953, and on this basis anyway, Australian workers were the least exploited and the most militant – in the world!

meanings. Finally, suppose that K/Y is a constant, i.e. that Y and K grow at the same rate, g. Then[1]

$$r = \frac{\Pi}{K} = \frac{\bar{E}Y}{K} = \frac{\bar{I}}{s_\pi K} - \frac{s_w(1-\bar{E})}{s_\pi}\frac{Y}{K}$$

i.e.
$$r = \frac{g}{s_\pi} - \frac{s_w(1-\bar{E})}{s_\pi}\frac{Y}{K} \tag{A.26}$$

as $\bar{I}/K = g$ under the assumed conditions. Now all terms on the right-hand side of expression $(A.26)$ are 'givens' so that if we know the value of $\bar{E}$, for the reasons which Nell gives, we also know r and so may determine w and the Sraffa prices of the system. The inference is that these will correspond more closely to observed prices than those which would be deduced by a neoclassical approach.

We should point out now that there is a flaw in the argument, as it stands, for it assumes that wage-earners save but get no return on their savings: see Pasinetti [1962], and chapter 5, pp. 216–17 below. Another approach is to proceed again via a theory of the simultaneous determination of the short-run level of activity and the distribution of income. If we further assume that the money-wage level is given in the short run, the real wage may be calculated either in terms of any one of the prices implied by the level of profits and technical conditions or by Sraffa's method, whereby employment is measured as unity and the *numéraire* of the system is the national income itself, and the Sraffa prices may again be calculated, see Robinson [1971]. The same inference as above follows. These themes are taken up again in chapter 5.

Even more important in the context of growth and changing technical possibilities, because Sraffa's system allows technology to be displayed in detail, it can easily handle the minutiae of technical change. Moreover, *because* the rate of profits (or real wage) and prices are determined simultaneously, it can also handle, at one and the same time, a disaggregated view of capital in its production aspects, to any degree of disaggregation required, and an aggregated view which is concerned with capital as property and the capitalists' share of the surplus. 'Factors of production' become 'income-bearing property', i.e. *collections* of inputs held for such a purpose and so separable from the inputs themselves, rather than actual productive agents. 'Goods' and 'skills'

---

[1] From expression $(A.25)$, $s_\pi \bar{E}Y = I - s_w(1-\bar{E})Y$.

i.e.
$$\bar{E}Y = \Pi = \frac{I}{s_\pi} - \frac{s_w(1-\bar{E})Y}{s_\pi}$$

enter into production, for specific goods and skills are required in each activity, all of which get prominence in Sraffa's system.

On the other hand, when we consider the receipt of income these distinctions are irrelevant: '... in equilibrium the same amount of capital receives the same profit income (making due allowance for risk) and whatever the particular job, labour of the same degree of skill and training receives the same wage', Nell [1967b], p. 21. Moreover, what they receive is not related to their contribution to production but to their relative ownership of property which allows them to share in the distribution of the surplus. Thus the Sraffa system neatly handles, at one and the same time, the two aspects of capital (and labour), both faithfully reflecting the technical conditions of production and the crucial role that they play in price formation and, simultaneously, allowing the institutions of the society concerned, in this instance, capitalism, to influence the distributive process.

Related to this theme is another contrast whereby intermediate products and the productive processes themselves are brought to the fore in Sraffa's system. With the Walrasian approach, however, intermediate goods often disappear from view, interdependence of the markets for 'final products' and 'factors', in which maximizing and minimizing individuals are the principal actors, takes the centre of the stage, and the more fundamental interdependence of production is neglected. Furthermore, because the Walrasian approach concentrates on individuals and their behaviour, we become committed to *particular* views on behaviour in order to obtain solutions for equilibrium prices and distributive shares.

The Ricardian–Sraffa view does not require *any* assumption about individual behaviour, for it concentrates on industries and their technological attributes – 'prices are determined without anything being maximized.' 'A Ricardian system shows the interlocking of possibilities and necessities, rather than of motives, plans and information.' (p. 18.) This has the further implication that the concept of equilibrium differs as between the two theories of value. One involves choice among alternatives and maximization; the other has to satisfy the condition of self-replacement (whether or not this occurs in fact), with the additional proviso that the surplus (net product) be entirely distributed in proportions given from outside.

The important thing to see ... is that the two concepts of exchange have different logical forms. 'Equilibrium in exchange' in one case means trading a set of outputs in such a way as to allocate them so that they can function as inputs; here exchange is an operation designed to eliminate the difference between the matrix of outputs and the matrix of inputs. In the other case, 'equilibrium in exchange' means that the set of quantities associated with the prices (or the two sets taken together) will maximize some index. These two notions have nothing in common. (p. 23.)

Finally we may note an important implication which arises from considering a Sraffa system in the context of national accounting procedures, a point to which Nell refers and which is analysed more fully in Harcourt and Massaro [1964a]. This context serves to highlight the distinction between the income shares associated with the annual production of a surplus or net product in a capitalist economy and the composition of that surplus in terms of the commodities of which it is composed, that is, the quantities of commodities that 'remain' when account is taken of the amounts which have been 'used up' in production. When planning is considered, it is, of course, the second aspect that is relevant, especially if plans concerning accumulation are allied with detailed examinations of the technical possibilities that are revealed in Sraffa systems. On the other hand, it is the *income* aspects of the surplus, and especially its profit component, that are of interest to the decision-makers in the private sectors of a capitalist economy. Thus it is obvious that *total* values added and the value of the net product must be equal to each other, as both equal the incomes created by the year's production. But the *commodities* associated with the calculation of values added are not in general the same as those that make up the net product of the economic system. This point is most easily seen in a sub-system where the net product consists of only one product even though each activity in which a product is produced has a positive value added, its means of production earn the same rate of profits as elsewhere and its direct labour is paid the same wage rate as that paid elsewhere.

This appendix has touched on some fundamental issues. The treatment, of necessity, has been sketchy, but it is hoped that enough vistas have been opened up to encourage the reader to go further, both in his reading and his thinking.

5 The rate of profits in capitalist society: whose finest hour?

Kaldor sets the pace

In order to determine the rate of profits in capitalist society it is necessary, as we saw in chapter 4, to introduce further factors from outside the production system itself. Certain economists – Kaldor, Joan Robinson, Pasinetti[1] – have argued that the factors are the saving propensities associated with different classes of income receivers in the community and the rate of growth of the economic system as given *either* by the rate of growth of the labour force and Harrod neutral technical progress *or* by the capitalists themselves, depending upon the author concerned. (This is an avenue that, it must be said, not all or even most economists would wish to tread, or, at least, not for the same reasons.) These views have been discussed in a series of articles which appeared, principally, in the *Review of Economic Studies* and the *Economic Journal*: Kaldor [1955–6, 1957, 1959a, 1959b], Pasinetti [1962], Meade [1963], Pasinetti [1964], Chang [1964], Meade and Hahn [1965], Pasinetti [1966b], Meade [1966], Samuelson and Modigliani [1966a], Pasinetti [1966c], Kaldor [1966], Robinson [1966], Samuelson and Modigliani [1966b], Sato [1966], Britto [1968], Davidson [1968b], Morishima [1969], chapter II, Nell [1970], Robinson [1970c].[2]

It should be stressed at the outset that some of the writers concentrate on the characteristics of equilibrium when the economy is constrained by some means or other to be growing at the above rate of growth; others, though, are concerned also to show that there are forces which will take the economy to such an equilibrium rate of growth and keep it there, as well as to examine the characteristics of the equilibrium itself.

[1] Pasinetti adds Champernowne [1958], Kahn [1959] and von Neumann [1945–6]. All would, I am sure, acknowledge the prior inspiration of Kalecki's work on the distribution of income: see Kalecki [1939], pp. 76–7 and the comments by Dobb [1960], p. 91.

[2] An alternative view which 'closes' the system in a more traditional manner by using time preference will be found in an article by Hirshleifer [1967].

They ask: *are* there forces which will both put the economy on to this rate of growth *and* bring the economy back to it, whether nudges off be great or small? We shall, however, concentrate in this chapter on existence and properties, especially those that relate to the expression for the equilibrium value of the rate of profits.

We should also stress that the rate of profits that we are now discussing should not be confused with the rate of interest, a monetary phenomenon (even when, as is sometimes argued, see Pasinetti [1962] and p. 217 below, it equals it). The rate of interest is the rate of return on rentier wealth, not on productive capital assets, and is determined in financial markets. Modern stock exchange facilities are such that what Joan Robinson calls 'marketable placements' are much less risky than productive assets; this implies that, usually, the level of interest rates is normally well below the expected rate of profits that is required to attract investment in productive assets. The rate of interest, or, rather, the patterns of rates, settle at any moment of time at levels where the large existing stocks of placements and trickles of new ones match the demands to hold them, including in those demands those new savings which seek placements: see Davidson [1968b].

Kaldor's statement of the problem in 1959, as set out in Kaldor [1959a, 1959b], contains, in essence, the principal features.[1] He shows that the rate of profits in a growing economy which has attained long-run, steady-state equilibrium at full employment equals the rate of growth of the economy divided by the profit-receivers' marginal propensity to save. He links this result to an earlier one of his own (in an analysis of a slave state), proceeding via his well-known 'Keynesian' widow's cruse theory of distribution, Kaldor [1955–6], and to von Neumann's famous model of an expanding economy, in which the rate of interest is equal to the net productivity of the whole system, see p. 207 below.[2] He develops it further to obtain the same expression for the marginal efficiency of investment in order to explain investment demand in an expanding capitalist economy. (This was before he worked for H.M. Treasury.)

Champernowne [1945–6] has written a magnificent literary exposition

[1] It should be clear from the dates at which these and the other relevant papers were published that the account in this chapter of the manner in which the various strands of the argument fit together is more an *ex post* hindsight view than a literal description of how the participants necessarily saw the points at issue when they made their contributions.

[2] See also Nell [1967a] in which Wicksell's *natural* rate of interest is interpreted in these terms.

of von Neumann's model. One possible interpretation of the model is that it is a growing classical system in which wages are kept to the minimum level needed to keep labourers alive, and in elastic supply, constant returns to scale rule in all activities, land is not scarce and demand plays no role in the determination of prices (or of overall activity, because it is assumed, sometimes implicitly, that the income-elasticity of demand for all products is the same and unity). Labour does not share in the surplus which is all profits and all of which is saved and reinvested. The production processes consist of goods producing goods, where some of the goods are the wage goods fed to, or otherwise used by, the workers. Prices are determined by the technical conditions of production and the rate of profits.

It is clear, intuitively, that with these assumptions, the rate of profits is equal to the rate of growth of the economy. This in turn depends on the rate of expansion of those goods, the supply of which can be expanded least rapidly (because all goods help to produce all goods, i.e. are basics in Sraffa, part I, terminology). Champernowne suggests as examples, whales or Mathematical Wranglers, which in the case of Keynes, if we may go as low as Twelfth Wrangler, would have brought the system to a halt in one generation, euthanasia of the rentier indeed. Like Ricardo and Sraffa – indeed, the classicals generally and, also, at times and places, Marshall–von Neumann's model stresses the primacy of methods of production in the determination of prices.[1]

An integral part of Kaldor's result is his view that the share of profits in *full-employment* national income may be explained by the *share* of investment in national output, provided only that investment itself is determined by long-run growth forces, that the saving propensities of profit-receivers are greater than those of wage-earners and that industrial market structures are sufficiently competitive to allow prices to respond to changes in demand. Especially must it be supposed that prices are *more* flexible than *money* wages at any moment of time. For simplicity the latter are usually taken as momentarily fixed and given.

Suppose that the long-run equilibrium position of a growing capitalist economy is a full-employment one.[2] The full-employment level of

---

[1] Joan Robinson [1971] has suggested some modifications to his model which allow capitalists' consumption to play a role, and has likened the system to Marx's analysis of capitalism in vol. I in which, however, the realization of the surplus is not a puzzle. See also, Kemeny, Morgenstern and Thompson [1956], Morishima [1964, 1969].

[2] Sometimes Kaldor assumes this, sometimes he attempts to demonstrate that it must be so. See, for example, Kaldor [1959a], Kaldor and Mirrlees [1962], Kaldor

income is Y_f. Assume simple proportional saving functions so that the *mps* of profit-receivers is s_π and that of wage-earners is s_w, with $s_\pi > s_w$. Let Π be total profits, W be total wages. Then the Keynesian saving–investment equilibrium condition may be shown in these circumstances to determine the distribution of income rather than the level of activity, Y_f, which is assumed to be given from outside.

Thus

$$S = s_\pi \Pi + s_w W = \bar{I} \tag{5.1}$$

where $\bar{I}$ is autonomous.

i.e.

$$s_\pi \Pi + s_w (Y_f - \Pi) = \bar{I}$$

i.e.

$$\Pi = \frac{\bar{I}}{s_\pi - s_w} - \frac{s_w}{s_\pi - s_w} Y_f$$

and

$$\frac{\Pi}{Y_f} = \left\{ \frac{1}{s_\pi - s_w} \right\} \frac{\bar{I}}{Y_f} - \frac{s_w}{s_\pi - s_w} \tag{5.2a}$$

Notice that as $s_w \to 0$, $\dfrac{\Pi}{Y_f} \to \dfrac{1}{s_\pi} \dfrac{\bar{I}}{Y_f}$ 　　　　(5.2b)

The expressions (5.2) express the equilibrium value of the share of profits in full-employment income as a function of $\bar{I}/Y_f$, provided that the latter is given from elsewhere. Consider fig. 5.1 which shows S/Y_f and $\bar{I}/Y_f$ plotted against Π/Y_f. $\bar{I}/Y_f$ is a horizontal straight line, S/Y_f rises as Π/Y_f rises, reflecting the higher level of planned saving associated with the shift to profits because $s_\pi > s_w$. (If $s_w = 0$, S/Y_f starts at the origin; if $s_\pi = 1$, it is a 45° line.) If the value of Π/Y_f were not, initially, at the intersection of the two lines, the arrows indicate that planned saving would stand in such a relationship to planned investment that, via the impact of excess demand or excess supply pressures on flexible prices, Π/Y_f would change until S/Y_f *were* equal to $\bar{I}/Y_f$. We assume that the value of Π/Y_f settles within a range, beyond the upper bound of which workers either starve or revolt, and below the lower bound of which capitalists are so browned off as to cease to invest. The latter reflects the Keynesian view that the direction of causation

---

[1970], though none of his attempts appears to me to be convincing: see Harcourt [1963b] for my reasons why. Sometimes the theory of distribution is said to be a long-run one (see Kaldor [1955–6]), sometimes a short-run one (see Kaldor [1957, 1959a] and Harcourt [1963b] for a further discussion of this point). There are some weaknesses in the arguments of my 1963 paper (which are pointed out in a later paper, Harcourt [1965b]). Nevertheless, I feel that the basic criticisms still stand.

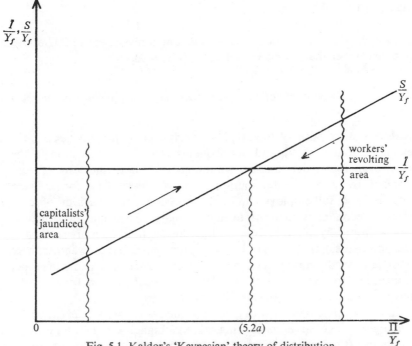

Fig. 5.1. Kaldor's 'Keynesian' theory of distribution

always runs from investment (which is done by profit-seeking business-men exercising their 'animal spirits') to saving and not the other way round.

Now we enter the world of long-run steady growth in which capital and output grow at the same rate. Until now, $\bar{I}/Y_f$ has been taken as given; now it is shown to depend on g_n (the rate of growth) and K/Y_f, the capital–output ratio. Thus

$$\frac{\bar{I}}{Y_f} = \frac{\Delta K}{K}\frac{K}{Y_f} = g_n\frac{K}{Y_f} \tag{5.3}$$

remembering that $\Delta Y_f/Y_f = \Delta K/K = g_n$ in steady-state growth.

$$r = \frac{\Pi}{K} = \frac{\Pi}{Y_f}\frac{Y_f}{K} = \left\{\frac{1}{s_\pi - s_w}\left(g_n\frac{K}{Y_f}\right) - \frac{s_w}{s_\pi - s_w}\right\}\frac{Y_f}{K}$$

i.e.

$$r = \frac{\Pi}{K} = \frac{g_n}{s_\pi - s_w} - \left(\frac{s_w}{s_\pi - s_w}\right)\frac{Y_f}{K} \tag{5.4}$$

As $s_w \to 0$ $$r \to \frac{g_n}{s_\pi}$$ (5.5)

(and as $s_\pi \to 1$, $r \to g_n$, which is von Neumann's result: see p. 207 above and remember that, in his model, $s_w = 0$, $s_\pi = 1$).

Digression: the level of activity and the distribution of income in the short run

Kaldor's assumption of full employment has puzzled many people, for example, Riach [1969], and one wonders what *is* his objection to the Keynesian forces determining, simultaneously, both the level of economic activity and the distribution of income (even if the former were not to be a full-employment one). Indeed Japanese critics of neo-classical economics concentrate not on marginalism and maximizing, which, ironically in their custom-ridden society (and no more so than in the universities), they seem to be quite happy with, but on whether there is or is not full employment, regarding the latter as a neo-Keynesian stance: see, for example, Fukuoka [1969]. Joan Robinson, for example, has sketched such a process as follows:

> In any given situation, with given productive capacity in existence, a higher rate of investment brings about a higher level of total gross income (through a higher level of employment of labour and utilization of plant) and a higher share of gross profit in gross income (by pushing up prices relatively to money-wage rates). Thus, within reason, investment generates the saving that it requires. (Robinson [1965b], p. 177.)

The following simple model illustrates these ideas, arrives at Kaldor's results as well (and may also suggest *why* Kaldor took the stance that he did).[1]

There is a very simple utilization function

$$Y = \frac{L}{l}$$ (5.6)

where Y is some measure of *real* output, L is *employment* (see expression (5.7) below) and l is the (constant) labour input per unit of output. (This is the simplest compromise between the diminishing short-run

[1] We should mention here two excellent articles, one by Riach [1969], the other by Sen [1963]. They present a framework for tackling these puzzles and provide a synthesis of the various strands of distribution theory to be found in the literature.

marginal productivity of theory and the increasing one of fact.) Because this is a Keynesian model in which the direction of causation is $Y{\to}L$, we write expression (5.6) as

$$L = lY \tag{5.7}$$

The money wage rate, w_m, may be taken as given in any short period. (It will, of course, change from short period to short period, the outcome of collective bargaining or compulsory arbitration in which experienced rates of price inflation and overall productivity growth and levels of economic activity will play key roles.)

i.e.
$$w_m = \bar{w}_m \tag{5.8}$$

The general price level we take to be a simple function of the level of planned investment expenditure, say

$$p = \lambda \bar{I} \tag{5.9}$$

where p is a price index, the base of which corresponds to the prices in which Y is measured, and λ is a constant.

This is the simplest way to express the rise in prices relative to money wages associated with a rise in investment expenditures.

Our assumption might perhaps be rationalized as follows. The businessmen who make the investment decisions, i.e. set the level of $\bar{I}$, may also be the principal price-makers, via price leadership, in the economy. (We may suppose their numbers to be relatively constant and that the bulk of the sum of the separate investments which constitute $\bar{I}$, even if not the bulk of the decision-makers, are associated with those who are also price-leaders.) If, then, the level of $\bar{I}$ is, in part, an index of the current state of their confidence, it may also be a proxy for the profit-margins that they wish to set and feel that they can get away with. This view seems all the more reasonable if we posit as well a longer-run link between profits arrived at and investment plans which are *internally* financed.[1] *Money* profits (Π_m) are

$$\Pi_m = pY - \bar{w}_m L = pY - \bar{w}_m lY = (\lambda\bar{I} - \bar{w}_m l)Y \tag{5.10}$$

As we end up assuming that $s_w = 0$, i.e. that the *net* saving of wage-earners is zero, we may as well start with this assumption. (It is often justified by saying that after we abstract from net personal investment,

---

[1] This assumption is consistent with Kaldor's 'kind of oligopoly-cum-price-leadership theory', see Kaldor [1970], p. 3.

for example, in housing, s_w is zero for wage-earners as a whole: see Kaldor [1966], p. 316.) The saving function therefore is

$$S_m = s_\pi \Pi_m = s_\pi (\lambda \bar{I} - \bar{w}_m l) \, Y \qquad (5.11)$$

where all values are in money terms.

The equilibrium condition is

$$S_m = p\bar{I} \qquad (5.12a)$$

i.e.

$$s_\pi (\lambda \bar{I} - \bar{w}_m l) Y = \lambda \bar{I}^2 \qquad (5.12b)$$

from which it follows that the equilibrium value of Y, Y_e (*which is not necessarily the full-employment one*), is

$$Y_e = \frac{\lambda \bar{I}^2}{s_\pi (\lambda \bar{I} - \bar{w}_m l)} \ (\leqslant Y_f) \qquad (5.13)$$

Expression (5.13) *may* be the reason why Kaldor assumed full employment. The response of the value of Y_e to a change in planned real investment expenditures is not, necessarily, the orthodox one of changing in the *same* direction, i.e. acting in a manner to which the Kahn–Keynes multiplier has become accustomed, as $\delta Y_e / \delta \bar{I} \gtrless 0$, so that real income may in fact *fall*. The reason why is a simple one. We are analysing a model in which when real investment plans change so, too, will their money value per unit, the distribution of income and so the level of real and money saving planned at any *given* level of real income. The accompanying change in planned consumption expenditures may be so great as to more than wipe out the impact on activity of the change in planned investment expenditures.

Can we say when orthodoxy will reign and when it won't? Corresponding to each value of $\bar{I}$ is a given value of $p\bar{I}$ ($= \lambda \bar{I}^2$). The distance between each value of $p\bar{I}$ gets greater and greater as $\bar{I}$ rises ($\delta p\bar{I}/\delta \bar{I} = 2\lambda \bar{I}$ and $\Delta(p\bar{I}) = 2\lambda \bar{I} \Delta \bar{I}$): see fig. 5.2, where the values of $p\bar{I}$ corresponding to four different values of $\bar{I}$ are shown. (The distance between each $p\bar{I}$ line is: $\Delta(p\bar{I}) = 2\lambda \bar{I} \Delta \bar{I}$.) Corresponding to any *given* value of $\bar{I}$, say $\bar{I}_i$, will be a saving function with a slope of $s_\pi (\lambda \bar{I}_i - \bar{w}_m l)$, i.e. the saving coefficient weighted by the share of profits in the national income, itself influenced by the value of $\bar{I}_i$: see expression (5.11) above and fig. 5.2. Planned money saving changes as $\bar{I}$ changes but, for given *values* of Y the distance between each level of money saving remains the same ($\delta S_m / \delta \bar{I} = s_\pi \lambda Y$ and $\Delta S_m = s_\pi \lambda Y \Delta \bar{I}$).

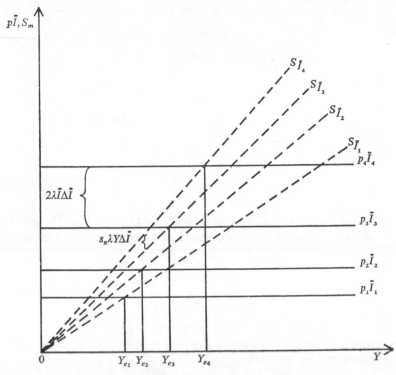

Fig. 5.2. The orthodox case

Whether Y (and Y_e) rise or not when $\bar{I}$ rises depends, then, upon whether

$$\frac{\delta p\bar{I}}{\delta \bar{I}} \gtreqless \frac{\delta S_m}{\delta \bar{I}} \quad [\text{or } \Delta(p\bar{I}) \gtreqless \Delta S_m],$$

i.e. it depends upon whether

$$2\lambda\bar{I} \gtreqless s_\pi \lambda Y \quad (\text{or } 2\lambda\bar{I}\Delta\bar{I} \gtreqless s_\pi \lambda Y \Delta\bar{I})$$

i.e. upon whether $2(\bar{I}/Y) \gtreqless s_\pi$.

(In fig. 5.2 we show the case corresponding to the top inequality.) It may be convenient to suppose that we *are* in this range, say $\bar{I}/Y \geqslant 0.2$, $s_\pi \leqslant 0.4$, for it is clear from fig. 5.2 that, *eventually*, there will be levels of $\bar{I}$ which will ensure it. But there is nothing inevitable about the result and, in general, $\delta Y_e/\delta\bar{I}$ may be positive, zero or negative. Mercifully, the signs of $\delta Y/\delta\lambda$ and $\delta Y/\delta s_\pi$ are unambiguous, both being <0, which makes good economic sense.

The equilibrium value of money profits is therefore

$$\Pi_{me} = \frac{(\lambda \bar{I} - \bar{w}_m I)\lambda \bar{I}^2}{s_\pi(\lambda \bar{I} - \bar{w}_m I)} = \frac{\lambda \bar{I}^2}{s_\pi} \qquad (5.14a)$$

and of *real* profits

$$\frac{\Pi_{me}}{p} = \frac{\bar{I}}{s_\pi} \qquad (5.14b)$$

The *equilibrium* distribution of income is thus

$$\frac{\Pi_{me}}{pY_e} = \frac{1}{s_\pi}\frac{\bar{I}}{Y_e} \qquad (5.15)$$

which corresponds to Kaldor's if $s_w = 0$, see expression (5.2b) above, but with the important difference that $Y_e \neq Y_f$. In the long run, given much the same assumptions as we made in Kaldor's case,

$$r = \frac{\Pi_m}{pK} = \frac{\bar{I}}{s_\pi Y_e}\frac{Y_e}{K} = \frac{g}{s_\pi} \qquad (5.16)$$

K must be supposed to be an equilibrium *money* value deflated by p and g need *not* necessarily equal g_n, i.e. it could be Harrod's warranted rate, as determined by realized 'animal spirits'.

Asimakopulos [1969, 1970] has an excellent exposition of Joan Robinson's model of growth and distribution. His second paper [1970] tackles puzzles similar to those discussed above. He distinguishes between direct and indirect labour, see Robinson [1969c]. Direct labour varies (proportionately) with output, indirect does not, so that labour productivity *rises* as output rises. This implies that there is a considerable range of short-run levels of output within which prices, money and real wages remain constant, and profit margins lengthen, as investment rises. The model above ignores the distinction between the two types of labour. It could perhaps be argued that the Robinson–Asimakopulos mechanism applies to ranges of output within which, *in the model above*, $\partial Y_e/\partial \bar{I}$ <0. Then the mechanism described above, possibly modified by introducing the direct–indirect labour distinction, may be thought of as taking over at higher levels of output. At these, it would not be unreasonable to assume that increases in planned demand would have an impact on price levels.[1]

---

[1] We discuss further Asimakopulos' model on pp. 232–40 below.

'*Excuse me, Professor Kaldor, but your slip is showing,*' *L.L.P.,* *1962*

Pasinetti's 1962 paper, which arose partly as a critique of one aspect of Kaldor's theory of distribution and partly from his own work on a multi-sector growth model, Pasinetti [1965], precipitated the remaining papers. Though the discussion centres around key parameters and broad aggregates, there lies behind them the disaggregated view of the economy that we discussed in chapter 4, with its myriads of commodities produced by commodities and maze of relative prices.

The debate is intricate and fierce and one despairs of giving its full flavour. It is not really possible to describe the full blast of the escaped steam associated with the boiling over into print of what Solow [1962a], p. 218, has dubbed 'conversational economics'. The debate centres on the characteristics and values of certain key economic variables and ratios associated with long-run, steady-state equilibria, *if the latter exist.* Meade [1966] especially has dealt with the existence problem and shown the limits outside of which the various steady-state equilibria cannot exist. Much of Samuelson and Modigliani's two papers [1966a, 1966b] is concerned with the existence and stability of the various equilibria. The simplest statement of the issues in the controversy is to be found in Meade's taxonomic note which uses one diagram (see below, pp. 221–6) to show how the key economic variables of the analysis – Π/K, Y_f/K, Π/Y_f, I/Y_f, s_w, s_c and g_n – interact.

The level of analysis is highly abstract, though when it suits them, each side dips happily into the statistics in order to obtain 'explicit realism'. Nevertheless, the debate is concerned with important empirical characteristics of capitalist economies, in particular, with the role of the class that accumulates capital, both by making investment decisions and by organizing the saving (their own or borrowed) to finance investment. We call this class 'pure' capitalists; they are defined as those whose only source of income is profits, which derive from their ownership of capital (see Pasinetti [1964], p. 489). It is in the spirit of the analysis to regard the class as profit-retaining companies organized by, say, Dr Marris's managers (Marris [1964]), as Kaldor [1966] does in his reply to Samuelson and Modigliani (see pp. 227–30 below.) The managers might well have the saving behaviour of workers in their private lives (this is not *all* that fanciful when the consumption and other perks of expense account living are added to managerial incomes – as reported to the Inland Revenue – in order to obtain their *mps*s = *aps*s), yet, simultaneously, organize the savings of companies in their role of good organization men.

The other group in the community – Pasinetti's 'workers' – may receive two classes of income, wages and profits on the *financial* capital which they own. It is financial capital because it results from lending their savings, as they accrue, to the 'pure' capitalists, who invest them in real, productive assets. Both classes are assumed to have simple proportional saving functions – $S_w = s_w(W + \Pi_w)$ and $S_c = s_c\Pi_c$. Stiglitz [1968] has suggested that if workers think they're capitalists when they consider the disposal of their income from profits, Π_w may be subsumed along with Π_c in an all-embracing Π. But this would drive a wedge between classes and income classes and only allow the determination of the income distribution of the latter. It does solve Nell's puzzle, though, see the appendix to chapter 4, p. 202, above and Kaldor's problem, see pp. 216–17 below. It is, of course, an empirical issue.

Be that as it may, the two classes are permanent classes of income-receivers – once there, always there – otherwise the respective property holdings of each will *not* grow at the rates assumed in the model. This is easier to accept for the 'pure' capitalists, where companies as going concerns immediately spring to mind, than for workers. This takes *some* sting out of Meade's comment [1963], pp. 671–2, that: 'For Mr. Pasinetti's results to have practical use we must assume a self-perpetuating class of property-owners who do no work and who, even after allowing for death duties, save a proportion of their income greater than $1/1 - T$ times the saving proportion of the rest of the community.' (*T* is the *proportional* marginal product of labour, i.e. labour's exponent in the neoclassical model which Meade uses partly to go over the same ground as Pasinetti.) If $T = \frac{3}{5} - \frac{3}{4}$, the ratio is $2\frac{1}{2} - 4$ and the requirement is $s_c > 2\frac{1}{2}s_w - 4s_w$. If $s_w = 0.05 - 0.10$, we get $s_c > 0.125 - 0.40$, which, *for companies*, does not seem unreasonable. The debate may be seen, therefore, to relate to an integral part of the theory whereby 'the rate of growth ... is determined in a modern economy by the investment decisions (of business firms) which can be actually financed and carried out within the monetary and resource constraints of society' (Davidson [1968b], p. 268).

Pasinetti first got into the act by pointing out that Kaldor, in his Keynesian theory of distribution, see pp. 207–10 above, either did a Stiglitz or forgot that workers' saving would also lead to their accumulating financial capital and receiving profits – or interest – on it. (Pasinetti could, perhaps, have asked whether workers' savings typically go into financial assets which earn profits or interest instead of being used to reduce hire-purchase indebtedness associated with the purchase of durable consumer goods and/or, possibly, to acquire equity in houses.) In any event, by allowing for this and by assuming that in long-run, steady-state equilibrium, the rate of interest will be equal to the rate of profits, so that all classes receive the same return on their savings, Pasinetti shows that

$$\frac{\Pi}{K} = \frac{1}{s_c}\frac{\dot I}{K} = \frac{g_n}{s_c} \qquad (5.17)$$

and

$$\frac{\Pi}{Y_f} = \frac{1}{s_c}\frac{\dot I}{Y_f} \qquad (5.18)$$

Pasinetti's assumption that all classes receive the same rate of return on their savings has not been much commented on in the literature (but see Chang [1964], Laing [1969a]). All Pasinetti [1962] says is 'that, in order to say anything about share and rate of profits, one needs first *a theory of the rate of interest*. In a long-run equilibrium model, the obvious hypothesis to make is that of a rate of interest equal to the rate of profits' (pp. 271–2), no doubt a reflection of the properties of a competitive equilibrium in which risk and uncertainty are absent and expectations are fulfilled. It *may* be a clue to the meaning of Sraffa's throw-away remark that the rate of profits is related to the money rate of interest, in which case there may be little conflict between Pasinetti, Kaldor and Joan Robinson, on the one hand, and Sraffa, on the other. Joan Robinson's analysis [1965b], pp. 176–81, of this point is not really conducive to this viewpoint, however. Nuti [1970a] regards Sraffa's suggestion as a false lead because, unless the money-price level is constant, the level of *money* rates of interest cannot determine technical choice.

Expressions (5.17) and (5.18), which on the surface are similar to those of Kaldor, see expressions (5.2), (5.4) and (5.5), are also 'remarkable', because they assert that the *steady-state* values of Π/K and Π/Y_f are *independent* of the workers' saving propensities and of any factors connected with a (the) production function, other than those associated with g_n. They are moreover, general results, not specific cases as were Kaldor's expressions (5.2b) and (5.5). Well might Meade [1963], p. 666, remark: 'How can this be so?' Furthermore, Pasinetti explains income *shares*, i.e. Π/Y_f, which now differ from the distribution of income between persons (which, however, is also explained in his paper).

His results are derived within the context of a theory of *long-run equilibrium*, a full-employment system 'where the possibilities of economic growth are externally given by population increase and technical progress' and 'the amount of investment – in physical terms – necessary in order to keep full employment through time, is also externally given'. (p. 268.) The possibilities of growth are assumed to be exponential, so that all relevant ratios remain constant. This context differs, of course, from the one that, up until now, we have been discussing. In his conclusion Pasinetti writes:

> I should look ... at the ... analysis simply and more generally as a logical framework to answer interesting questions about what *ought* to happen if full employment is to be kept over time, more than as a behavioural theory expressing what actually happens. (p. 279.)

A crucial assumption on the way to his results is that $s_w < \bar{I}/Y_f$ (and, by implication, $s_c > \bar{I}/Y_f$) which, when written in its equivalent saving terms, is: $s_w < g_n K/Y_f = s_c r K/Y_f$. (Thus, in Golden Age equilibrium, $\bar{I}/K = g_n$ and $r = g_n/s_c$ so that $rs_c = g_n$. Now $\bar{I}/Y_f = g_n K/Y_f$, so that the equivalent Pasinetti–Kaldor–Robinson saving condition is $s_w < g_n K/Y_f$ or $s_w Y_f < g_n K = s_c r K$: see Meade and Hahn [1965], p. 447, and Robinson [1966], p. 307.)

Pasinetti justifies his assumption on empirical grounds, namely, that $s_w < \bar{I}/Y_f$ is the economically relevant range of s_w to investigate in advanced capitalist economies. (The typical order of magnitude of $\bar{I}/Y$ is, after all, 15–20 per cent.) A subsidiary justification is that the share of profits in national income, as given by Kaldor's theory of distribution, would be ≤ 0 if $s_w \geq \bar{I}/Y_f$ (and ≥ 1, if $s_c \leq \bar{I}/Y_f$).[1] This second justification is of value to Kaldor but not necessarily so to Pasinetti who is, as we have seen, investigating the characteristics which are associated with full employment which itself has been attained by having the correct value of $\bar{I}/Y_f$. That is to say, for Pasinetti the level of $\bar{I}$ is what is dictated by g_n, not because there are forces making it so (as Kaldor argues) but because he wishes to investigate the characteristics of long-period equilibrium when it has been *made* so.

If we accept that Kaldor made a slip, it follows that, in expressions (5.2*a*) and (5.4) above, he has found the equilibrium values of Π_c/Y_f and Π_c/K, not those of Π/Y_f and Π/K, respectively. We therefore need

[1] Suppose $s_w = \bar{I}/Y_f$; then, via (5:2*a*)

$$\frac{\Pi}{Y_f} = \left(\frac{1}{s_\pi - (\bar{I}/Y_f)}\right)\frac{\bar{I}}{Y_f} - \frac{\bar{I}/Y_f}{s_\pi - (\bar{I}/Y_f)} = 0$$

expressions for $\Pi/Y_f\{=\Pi_c/Y_f+\Pi_w/Y_f\}$ and $\Pi/K\{=\Pi_c/K+\Pi_w/K\}$. We start with Π/K.

We already know Π_c/K, see expression (5.4) above and note that s_π must now be interpreted as s_c. Let K_w be the amount of capital which workers own indirectly and which they lend to the capitalists who pay them a rate of interest of i (which, we know, will soon become Π/K itself). Thus, we have

$$\frac{\Pi}{K} = \frac{1}{s_c-s_w}\frac{I}{K} - \frac{s_w}{s_c-s_w}\frac{Y_f}{K} + i\frac{K_w}{K} \tag{5.19}$$

Now, in dynamic equilibrium

$$\frac{K_w}{K} = \frac{S_w}{S} = \frac{s_w(Y_f-\Pi_c)}{I} \tag{5.20}$$

i.e. the proportion of total property owned by the workers remains constant and, of course, therefore, equal to the marginal proportion.

Substituting Π/K for i, and expression (5.20) for K_w/K, in expression (5.19), we have

$$\frac{\Pi}{K}\left(1 - \frac{s_w s_c}{s_c-s_w}\frac{Y_f}{I} + \frac{s_w}{s_c-s_w}\right) = \frac{1}{s_c-s_w}\frac{I}{K} - \frac{s_w}{s_c-s_w}\frac{Y_f}{K}$$

i.e.

$$\frac{\Pi}{K}\frac{s_c(I-s_w Y_f)}{I} = \frac{I-s_w Y_f}{K}$$

and, provided that $I>s_w Y_f$ (i.e. the key condition, $s_w<I/Y_f$, which also implies $I \neq s_w Y_f$),[1]

$$\frac{\Pi}{K} = \frac{1}{s_c}\frac{I}{K} = \frac{g_n}{s_c} \tag{5.21}$$

By similar reasoning we may show that

$$\frac{\Pi}{Y_f} = \frac{1}{s_c}\frac{I}{Y_f} \tag{5.22}$$

In long-run, steady-state equilibrium, the ratio of saving to profits of *all* classes must be the same – otherwise the proportions of financial property owned by each class would be changing. The actual value of the ratio is determined by the ratio of the 'pure' capitalists who directly

---

[1] $I-s_w Y_f = 0$ implies $0/0$, an indeterminate ratio, 'a whisper rather than a shout' that, according to Samuelson and Modigliani [1966a], p. 279, n1, there was a 'dual' awaiting to be found. But what of $s_w>I/Y_f$ – wait for it!

control their own accumulation, both saving and investing, i.e. $s_c\Pi_c/\Pi_c$ is a key, independent ratio and $s_w(W+\Pi_w)/\Pi_w$ $(=S_w/\Pi_w)$ adapts to it. This in turn implies that if workers save they must receive enough profits to make *their* savings be what they would have been had capitalists received the workers' profits and saved them at the capitalists' rate!

i.e.
$$s_w(W+\Pi_w) = s_c\Pi_w \qquad (5.23a)$$

Or, to put the same proposition in a different form, workers' saving from wages equals workers' extra consumption out of profits, i.e. over and above what capitalists would have spent, had they received the workers' profits. Thus

$$s_wW = \{(1-s_w)-(1-s_c)\}\Pi_w \qquad (5.23b)$$

Kaldor's neo-Pasinetti theorem allows this assumption to be dropped and introduces roles for companies' borrowing behaviour and that 'with it' statistic, the valuation ratio: see Kaldor [1966], pp. 316–19 and pp. 227–30 below. Unfortunately, according to Davidson [1968b], p. 259, it also takes Kaldor unwittingly into the neo-neoclassical camp as his analysis implies that 'the *deus ex machina* of the neoclassical system – the rate of interest –' not only serves to maintain equilibrium in the securities market but also ensures a level of effective demand consistent with full employment.

Samuelson and Modigliani try to show that s_w must be less than a 'modest [their words] 0.05' in order that $s_w < \bar{I}/Y_f$ and the Pasinetti result holds. However, this value depends upon the choice of un-realistically low values of s_c and $\bar{I}/Y_f$ (see Pasinetti [1966c], p. 304, and Samuelson and Modigliani [1966b], p. 329). It further implies that outside the Pasinetti range and using Samuelson and Modigliani's value of s_w, $\bar{I}/Y$ equals 5 per cent. s_w cannot *exceed* $\bar{I}/Y$ without there being a lack of effective demand and therefore continuing unemployment, which is inconsistent with the assumption of full employment that underlies the present analysis (see p. 227 below). If $s_w = \bar{I}/Y_f$, which it must if a steady-state solution *outside* the Pasinetti range is to exist (see pp. 221–7 below), 'there corresponds a particular growth path on which the proportion of the total stock owned by workers tends to unity, and the proportion owned by the capitalists tends to zero: the economic system ends up with only one category of savers; the workers' (Pasinetti [1966c], p. 304). Samuelson and Modigliani's order of magnitude of s_w in turn implies an absurdly low value of the capital–output ratio in steady-state equilibrium. For example, with a rate of growth of 4 per cent per annum it would be 1.25.

There is, of course, the puzzle about the relevance of values taken from the 'real world' in order to obtain orders of magnitude which are to apply within a steady state; but no one is really in a position to cast the first stone here. Nevertheless, much of the critics' space is devoted to analysing what happens when s_w is *outside* the Pasinetti–Kaldor range, where the steady-state output–capital ratio, $Y_f/K, = g_n/s_w$, the 'dual' of Pasinetti's result, $r = g_n/s_c$, and the steady-state value of Π/K *does* depend upon the production function. Of course, s_w is only just outside the Pasinetti–Kaldor range – indeed, it is right on the margin – because $Y_f/K = g_n/s_w$ *implies* that $s_w = I/Y_f$ in steady-state equilibrium.

Meade [1963, 1966] and Samuelson and Modigliani [1966a, 1966b] have exhaustively investigated these possibilities (at a ratio of words of 1 : 5) and we reproduce Meade's version below, see pp. 221–6. As I see it, they are examining the characteristics of a world where workers' saving dominates the accumulation process (capitalists' property relative to workers' approaches zero), a world of bloodless revolution in which socialism in the guise of a workers' state has been painlessly ushered in and the characteristics of which, though fascinating in their own right, are irrelevant for a debate about what determines the rate of profits in capitalist societies. One attraction of this case is supposed to be that there is in effect only one saving coefficient and no classes, or anyway none of significance for economic analysis, see Stiglitz [1967], Lecture 4. This is regarded as more 'realistic', which prompts the question whether (or how) labour economics is taught at either Cambridge. Of course, if there is an asymptotic approach to a single saving propensity, s_w, and if we are in a world where the natural (g_n) and warranted rates of growth (g_w) coincide, and if, in addition, we suppose that capital is malleable, we get the Hahn–Matthews version of Solow's neoclassical solution of Harrod's puzzle: see Hahn and Matthews [1964], pp. 788–9. It is that $g_n = s/v$, where $v = K/Y_f$, from which it follows that, for $s = s_w$, $Y_f/K = g_n/s_w$ – the 'dual' of Pasinetti's result: see Samuelson and Modigliani [1966a], p. 278, and p. 227 below.

Meade's analysis

As we have seen, the Pasinetti process is concerned with the values of key variables in steady-state equilibrium when the ratio of property ownership of the two classes has tended to its final value. Three possibilities present themselves:

(1) no steady state exists

(2) the distribution settles at a value where

$$\frac{\Pi}{K} = \frac{g_n}{s_c} \quad \text{(Pasinetti Land)}$$

(3) the distribution settles at a value where

$$\frac{Y_f}{K} = \frac{g_n}{s_w} \quad \text{(MSM Land)}$$

Where we are (or will be) depends upon the interplay of g_n, s_c and s_w *and the technical characteristics of the production function*. Pasinetti would deny this last, arguing that *his* world is as independent, as MSM's is not, of these characteristics. Indeed he once claimed that while his result may be associated with any world, theirs can only be associated with either a neoclassical world in which substitution possibilities may need to be infinite (so that Y_f/K can take on its required value) or with a Harrod knife edge in which the output–capital ratio takes the required value: see Pasinetti [1964]. Pasinetti's view is, perhaps, more explicable now, in the light of the arguments of his 1969 and 1970 papers, than when it was propounded initially.

In any event, consider fig. 5.3. On the vertical axis we measure Y_f/K, on the horizontal one, Π/K. OA is a 45° line (that priceless, malleable tool of our trade). OC measures g_n/s_w, OB measures g_n/s_c. Because $s_c > s_w$, $OC > OB$. We are only concerned with areas between OA and the vertical axis (below OA, $\Pi/K > Y_f/K$, i.e. $\Pi/Y_f > 1$).

The long-run, steady-state values of Y_f/K and Π/K, *if they exist*, must lie on DE or CD. Why? Consider any point to the right of BG so that $\Pi/K > g_n/s_c$, i.e. $s_c \Pi/K > g_n$, i.e. the property of the capitalists is growing faster than the steady-state value (remember that $\Pi_c/K_c = \Pi_w/K_w = \Pi/K$). This implies that sooner or later *total* K will grow faster than g_n, which is *not* compatible with steady-state equilibrium. At any point above CF, $Y_f/K > g_n/s_w$, i.e. $s_w Y_f/K > g_n$. But total K must grow at least as fast as $s_w Y_f/K$ so, again, no steady-state.

Finally, consider any point within $OCDE$ where $s_c \Pi/K < g_n$ and $s_w Y_f/K < g_n$. Capitalists' property will be growing at a rate less than g_n in a steady-state (if it exists) so that the ratio of capitalists' to workers' property approaches zero. But if this were so, as $s_w Y_f/K < g_n$, K would be growing at less than g_n – again no steady state exists. On CD,

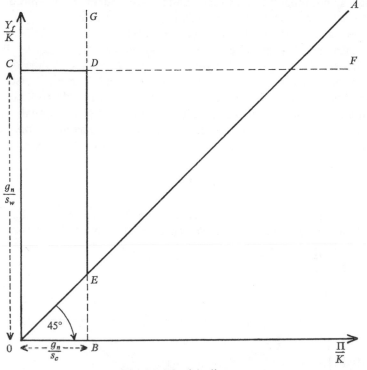

Fig. 5.3. Meade's diagram

$s_w Y_f/K = g_n$ and $s_c \Pi/K < g_n$, i.e. we have a long-run steady-state where workers' property comes to dominate capitalists', i.e. where

$$Y_f/K = g_n/s_w \text{ (MSM Land)}$$

On *DE*, $s_w Y_f/K < g_n$, $s_c \Pi/K = g_n$ and the distribution of property between workers and capitalists adjusts until

$$\Pi/K = g_n/s_c \text{ (Pasinetti Land)}$$

Notice that $s_w Y_f/K < g_n$ may be written as

$$s_w < (K/Y_f)(\dot{I}/K) = \dot{I}/Y_f \text{ (the Pasinetti–Kaldor range)}$$

Notice also that the relative sizes of *CD* and *DE* depend upon the relative sizes of s_w and s_c. If we think of s_w as being one-quarter to one-eighth of s_c, *DE* is large relative to *CD*. Sometimes, though, the diagrams are drawn so that *CD* is large relative to *DE*. This may mislead the unwary traveller into believing that it is easier to find his way into

MSM Land than into Pasinetti Land. The orders of magnitude of Π/Y_f are also such that he should expect to find himself – if he ever arrives – at a point on DE that is much nearer to D than to E. In Meade's diagrams (see Meade [1966], pp. 162–4), however, judging by their implied shares, the profit-receivers seemingly do very well indeed.

How do we bring in the production function? Consider, first, the Swan–Solow–Cobb–Douglas production function with (Harrod) neutral technical progress (see chapters 1 and 2 above). We *know* that Π/Y_f will equal the capital exponent of the function (see chapter 1, pp. 35–6 n1, above). Suppose its value $\{(\Pi/K)/(Y_f/K)\}$ is such that it is *less* than

$$\frac{g_n}{s_c} \bigg/ \frac{g_n}{s_w} \left(= \frac{OB}{OC} \right)$$

so that, in fig. 5.4, it lies on OH (which has a slope *greater* than that of a line from the origin and through OD). We thus get MSM's case (the

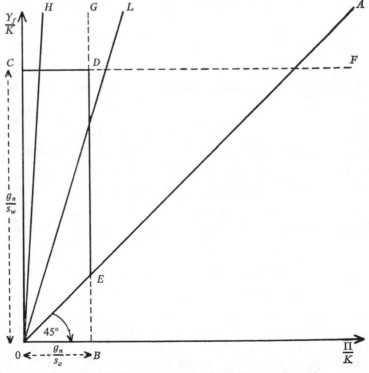

Fig. 5.4. Pasinetti and *MSM* Lands, Cobb–Douglas-style

'dual' of Pasinetti's case) in which $Y_f/K = g_n/s_w$. With Π/Y_f such that it lies on OL, we get Pasinetti's case, where $\Pi/K = g_n/s_c$.

Now consider a fixed coefficients case so that Y_f/K is given. Three possibilities – $Y_f/K = OM$, ON, OJ – only one of which (ON) gives a steady-state solution (Pasinetti's) – are shown in fig. 5.5. Thus for a steady state to exist, $g_n/s_w > Y_f/K > g_n/s_c$, i.e. $s_w < g_n K/Y_f < s_c$, i.e. $s_w < \bar{I}/Y_f < s_c$, Pasinetti's condition. In general, whether CD, or DE, or neither is cut depends upon the production function which determines the relationship between Y_f/K and Π/K, if $\Pi/K = \partial Y_f/\partial K$. In a neo-classical world Y_f/K and Π/K relate in a well-behaved manner, as determined by the production function. In general, the smaller is Π/K ($= \partial Y_f/\partial K$), the smaller is Y_f/K, so that the Y_f/K, Π/K curve either cuts DE (Pasinetti Land), or CD (MSM Land), or not at all. In a neo-Keynesian world, there is *no* production function, as we saw in

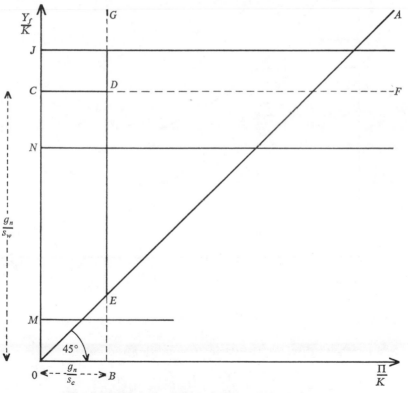

Fig. 5.5. With (vulgar) Harrod–Domar in Pasinetti Land

chapter 4, and the Y_f/K, Π/K relationship can be all over the place. Meade's note, though, fulfils admirably its purpose of providing clarity while not adding to (indeed, it greatly substracts from) controversy.

Samuelson and Modigliani also supply a neat diagram which illustrates the two regimes – Pasinetti and MSM or anti-Pasinetti – *for the neoclassical case*. In fig. 5.6 we show (well-behaved) average and marginal product of capital curves; k, the capital–labour ratio, is shown

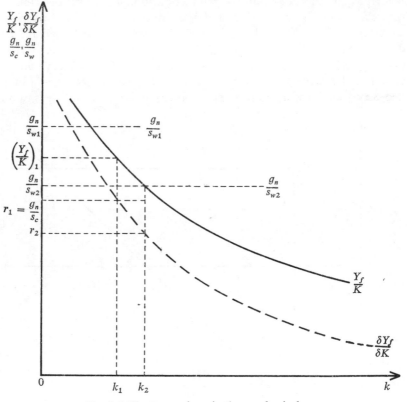

Fig. 5.6. The two regimes in the neoclassical case

on the horizontal axis and the average and marginal products of capital, together with the values of g_n/s_c and g_n/s_w, are shown on the vertical axis. In a neoclassical world, the Pasinetti condition is

$$r = \frac{\Pi}{k} = \frac{\partial Y_f}{\partial K} = \frac{g_n}{s_c} \quad \left(\text{and } s_w < \frac{I}{Y_f}\right) \tag{5.24}$$

The anti-Pasinetti case is

$$\frac{Y_f}{K} = \frac{g_n}{s_w} \quad \left(\text{and } s_w > \frac{\bar{I}}{Y_f} \right) \tag{5.25}$$

Now consider fig. 5.6 in which one value of g_n/s_c and two values of g_n/s_w are shown. Where the line, g_n/s_c, cuts the $\partial Y_f/\partial K$ curve is the Pasinetti condition, to which there corresponds a capital–labour ratio of k_1. If we consider g_n/s_{w1}, i.e. a 'small' value of s_w, we can see that $\{Y_f/K\}_1$, the value of the average product of capital which corresponds to k_1, *is less than* g_n/s_{w1}, i.e. $s_{w1} < g_n(K/Y_f) \, (= \bar{I}/Y_f)$ – Pasinetti Land. However, if s_w is 'large' so that $g_n/s_{w2} < \{Y_f/K\}_1$, $s_{w2} > \bar{I}/Y_f$ at k_1, and we are in MSM Land in which k_2 is the long-run, steady-state value of k and $Y_f/K = g_n/s_{w2}$ (and, as ever, $r_2 = \Pi/K = \partial Y_f/\partial K$).

But, the neo-Keynesian critics argue, MSM Land may only be entered if we accept that it is also a land of butter, i.e. of malleable capital. We may put the point most simply as follows. Suppose that we *are* in a land of butter and that saving determines investment. Assume, initially, that s_w is greater than $\bar{I}/Y_f$. Then, in terms of fig. 5.1 above (see p. 209), the S/Y_f line starts *above* the $\bar{I}/Y_f$ line *even when* Π/Y_f *is zero*. (It is, of course, always above it at any other income distribution.) However, *if* $\bar{I}/Y_f$ responds to changes in r in a neoclassical way, that is to say, if any tendency to excess saving lowers r and so raises K/Y_f and, thus, $\bar{I}/Y_f$, then the $\bar{I}/Y_f$ line will rise until it meets the S/Y_f line at the point where the latter intercepts the vertical axis. (If it rose any higher, we would be back in Pasinetti Land.) We thus have a possible steady-state equilibrium position at the point where Π/Y_f is zero, i.e. where all of the national income goes to wage-earners (who also own property) so that only *their* saving propensity is relevant for accumulation. Of course, if we are *not* in a butter world, K/Y_f and $\bar{I}/Y_f$ may *not* respond in the desired manner to changes in r.

Destry Kaldor rides again

In a fascinating appendix entitled 'A Neo-Pasinetti Theorem', Kaldor [1966] expounds a model which has many of the features that have been hinted at as either desirable or reasonable interpretations of Pasinetti Land and its inhabitants. The starting point is Pasinetti's result that the additional consumption by workers out of their property income (relative to what capitalists would have done) offsets their saving out of wage income, i.e. s_w is applied to their total income regardless of its source, an anti-Stiglitz view. This runs into a puzzle when property income is dividends distributed by companies that retain profits, ostensibly on behalf of their (worker and other) shareholders. For we must suppose that workers overspend their dividend income by the exact proportion required to make their consumption from *their* profits equal $(1 - s_w)\Pi_w$, even though they do not now get *all* of Π_w as personal disposable income.

Thus, suppose companies retain a proportion, ∂, of all profits. Then workers get an amount, $(1-\partial)\Pi_w$, to dispose of. Had they got the lot, they would have spent $(1-s_w)\Pi_w$; now they spend $(1-s_w)/(1-\partial)\Pi_w$.

$$\left\{(1 - s_w)\Pi_w = x(1-\partial)\Pi_w \quad \text{i.e.} \quad x = \frac{1-s_w}{1-\partial}\right\}$$

$$\frac{1-s_w}{1-\partial} > 1, \quad \text{or } \partial(= s_c) > s_w$$

But if workers can have an extra-dividend orgy, so, too, can capitalists, by spending their capital gains (or even their capital, in this post-Forsyte age).

We may picture a world, then, when at any time there are shareholders overspending their dividend income, retired workers dissaving the savings accumulated over their working lives, and active workers saving for *their* retirement. Net dissaving out of income (equivalent to net consumption from capital gains or capital) provides a *supply* of securities just as net saving out of income provides a *demand* for them. In addition companies add to the supply of securities by their (net) issues of new ones. As the price of securities settles where the total (non-speculative) supply and demand for them are equal (a debatable proposition with which Kaldor himself has not always agreed, see Davidson [1968b], p. 258 n7), we need a mechanism whereby spending from capital gains or capital just balances saving out of income *less* net new issues of securities by companies, i.e. a mechanism whereby *old* securities voluntarily change hands from dissavers to savers.

Kaldor considers a community of wage- and salary-earners with income of W, who save via pension funds and insurance companies during their working lives, and dissave in retirement, to be nil savers over their lifetimes. With a growing population, *total* saving from this group will be positive, let it be a proportion, s_w, of their current wage and salary incomes (and ignore personal investment in housing, *et al.*). Let the net consumption from capital gains (G) by shareholders be $\bar{c}G$ and let companies retain s_c of their profits and issue new securities equal to an exogenously given proportion, z, of their current investment expenditure, gK, where g is the rate of growth (not, necessarily, g_n) and K is capital.

Equilibrium in the securities market is then

$$s_w W - zgK = \bar{c}G \tag{5.26}$$

For equilibrium to be attained one at least of the variables must respond to changes in the market prices of shares. Obviously it is G, for G *is the* change in the market prices of shares. The latter varies not only with changes in dividends and earnings per share but also with changes in the 'valuation' ratio, V^*, where V^* is defined as

$$\frac{\text{market value of shares}}{\text{capital employed by companies}}$$

If P = price of shares, N = number of shares, and V^* = constant,

$$G = N\Delta P = V^*\Delta K - P\Delta N \tag{5.27a}$$

i.e. the increase in the companies' assets multiplied by V^* *less* the value of new shares issued. As $\Delta K = gK$ and $P\Delta N = zgK$, expression (5.27a) becomes

$$G = V^*gK - zgK \tag{5.27b}$$

and expression (5.26) becomes

$$s_w W - \bar{c}(V^*gK - zgK) = zgK \tag{5.28}$$

Now we impose the further equilibrium condition, $S = I$, to obtain

$$s_w W - \bar{c}(V^*gK - zgK) + s_c\Pi = gK \tag{5.29}$$

[From expression (5.26)

$$s_c W - \bar{c}G = zgK$$

By definition

$$s_c\Pi = (1-z)gK$$

so that $\quad s_c W - \bar{c}G + s_c\Pi = zgK + (1-z)gK = gK$]

Now write $W = Y - \Pi$, where $\Pi = rK$, and substitute these expressions in expressions (5.28) and (5.29), rearrange terms and divide by gK to obtain

$$\frac{s_w}{g}\frac{Y}{K} - \frac{s_w r}{g} - \bar{c}V^* + \bar{c}z = z$$

$$\frac{s_w}{g}\frac{Y}{K} + \frac{(s_c - s_w)r}{g} - \bar{c}V^* + \bar{c}z = 1 \tag{5.30}$$

The expressions (5.30) may be solved for V^* and r to give

$$V^* = \frac{1}{\bar{c}}\left[\frac{s_w}{g}\frac{Y}{K} - \frac{s_w}{s_c}(1-z) - z(1-\bar{c})\right]$$

$$r = \frac{g(1-z)}{s_c} \tag{5.31}$$

Thus given the saving coefficient, s_w, and the capital gains coefficient, $\bar{c}$, there is a certain valuation ratio which will secure just enough saving by the personal sector to take up the securities issued by companies (saving is a function of its return – it is at this point that Davidson raised objections: see p. 220 above). Thus the personal sector's net saving depends not only on its saving propensity but also on the policy of companies towards new issues. In a Golden-Age equilibrium, given constant values of g and K/Y_f, *however determined*, V^* will be a constant $\geqq 1$, according to the values of key parameters. r will depend only on g, s_c and z, so is *independent* of the personal saving propensities, s_w and $\bar{c}$. When $z = 0$, $r = g/s_c$, Pasinetti's expression, but reached by a different route.

Kaldor [1966], p. 318, says of his neo-Pasinetti theorem that it is similar because of these independencies but that 'it will hold in any steady growth state, and not only in a "long-run" Golden Age; it does not postulate a class of hereditary capitalists with a special high-saving propensity'. The appendix closes with an ingenious argument to suggest that the split up of total assets between workers and capitalists will approach a constant equilibrium value, so avoiding leaving, even in the very long run, Neo-Pasinetti Land. Down with 'duals'. This appendix may be counted a mighty performance by anyone's standards – even James Stewart's – but all the more so as it was written while Kaldor was simultaneously busily revolutionizing H.M. Inland Revenue. The unresolved questions of this approach relate to the nature of price formation in the market for placements, for example, the time period in which the stocks or the flows dominate the determination of prices, and the lack of analysis of any links between, say, current changes in the prices of financial assets and the values of the various saving and investment coefficients.

We close the discussion of the Pasinetti, *et al.*, controversy by sketching the approach to distributive shares in the short and long run via the degree of exploitation as set out by Joan Robinson in, for example, Robinson [1965b], pp. 173–81, and Robinson [1971]. As we saw above, see p. 210 and the appendix to chapter 4, Joan Robinson has placed considerable emphasis on the rate of exploitation – the ratio of net profits to wages – in her explanations of distributive shares in the short run and the rate of profits in the long run. The latest statement of her views is in Robinson [1971], also Robinson [1970b], p. 315 and Robinson [1970c]. Thus, in a modern capitalist economy with strongly unionized workers, oligopolistic industries and near full-employment conditions (for *Report from Iron Mountain* reasons rather than for neo-neoclassical or Kaldorian ones though), mark-ups in different trades tend to become conventionalized.[1] This occurs both because stable mark-ups allow firms to have certain retention ratios and because, in a rough-and-ready way, firms find from experience that their conventional mark-ups earn them certain realized rates of profits.

Wages overall therefore tend to rise as fast as overall productivity (sometimes lagging for a while as, for example, in the United States over 1961–5, when the workers were conned into doing *their* bit to cure inflation while the profit-receivers took advantage of this to lengthen their profit margins: see Evans [1969], pp. 540–1, Robinson [1969e]). *Relative* prices may then be treated *as if* they were determined by technical conditions (which change over time with technical progress, 'deepening' and scales of operation) and a uniform structure of rates of profits (or, alternatively, a given real wage at any moment of time).

If, finally, the rate of profits, whether determining or determined, fluctuates around a level of g/s_c, because these parameters are related to *why* the rate of exploitation (which in turn reflects the businessmen's ability to realize their investment plans) is what it is in the first place, g being related (via the expected rate of profits) to investment expenditure, s_c being related to saving levels from company profits, we have, in outline, a short-run and a long-run theory of distributive shares and prices. The rate of profits would, of course, be considerably greater than the rate of interest, because we have brought back risk and uncertainty.

---

[1] Clearly, this hypothesis is related to Kalecki's degree of monopoly theories. Riach [1971] has written an excellent paper in which he shows that the charge that Kalecki's statements are tautological is unfounded and that, in fact, Kalecki has provided a behavioural relationship which leads to a testable set of hypotheses.

However, with Davidson's and Joan Robinson's help, plus references to Marshall, Wicksell, Fisher and Keynes, the determination of the rate of interest could also be sketched in.

That this may seem slimming fare after the rich diets to which we have become accustomed is unquestioned; but that it is also healthy fare, fitting us for developments in the right direction, seems to me at least a working hypothesis. For

Presumably, no one would deny that there is more hope of under-standing what is going on in the world when we recognize that the wage bargain is made in terms of money; that the level of prices is influenced by effective demand and the degree of imperfection of competition; that accumulation is controlled by the policy of firms and governments, not by the propensity to consume of private citizens, and that today is an ever moving break in time between an irrevocable past and an uncertain future.

To understand is not easy, but at least we could try. (Robinson [1965b], p. 68.)

Harcourt on Asimakopulos on Robinson

Using simple algebra and diagrams, Asimakopulos [1969, 1970] has given a very clear exposition, in terms of a one-commodity, putty-clay model, of Joan Robinson's vision of the growth process. He draws especially on her 1962 book, Robinson [1962a]. In what follows we give the simplest version of his version! The first characteristic of Joan Robinson's approach is that the analysis concentrates on the short period where, of necessity, the action is, though, of course, many decisions have longer-run consequences. Secondly, as we have seen, the different saving behaviour of wage-earners and profit-receivers (in this instance, the firms in the economy) is emphasized. We shall assume that $s_\pi = 1$ and $s_w = 0$ (and ignore rentiers' consumption), simplifications that do not alter significantly the argument in any way. Thirdly, the driving force of the economies considered is the 'animal spirits' of the businessmen, these being expressed formally as a relationship between expected rates of profits and desired rates of accumulation (see p. 236 below). This is, as we shall see, a positive relationship, because the higher is the rate of profits, the more are the appetites of businessmen whetted and the more do gambles seem worth taking, and because the ability to self-finance is enhanced.

The businessmen are also price-makers, though, in one sort of economy, profit margins and prices are nevertheless regarded as flexible enough to allow normal-capacity working of the capital stock, but not necessarily full employment of the labour force, to be established. In another sort of economy, profit margins are inflexible in the short run, so that the short-run level of activity that is established may imply some unemployment of both the existing capital stock and labour force. (The employed portion of the labour force is then allocated arbitrarily among the plants and firms in the economy.) The level of the money wage rate is given in the short run and, indeed, is exogenous to the model, but it would be easy to introduce a process which made it endogenous: see p. 211 above.

Expectations with regard to prices and (real) wage levels are formed on the basis of recent experiences and they consist of projections of these into the future. (This assumption is not meant to be realistic; it is merely illustrative of how expectations about the future courses of the relevant variables are both formed and may be introduced into the analysis.) The capital stock is a datum for each short period. It consists of the vintages inherited from previous short periods. These are associated with a unique capacity level of output and overall labour productivity, as we assume, for simplicity, a constant labour productivity *for each vintage*, this being the outcome of the choice of technique made in the light of businessmen's expectations at the time.

The equilibrium condition in the short run is that saving equals investment, the level of investment being given exogenously in the short run. This condition implies a distributive mechanism which, in the case of the first type of economy, the one with flexible margins, is akin to Kaldor's (see pp. 207–10 above). In the case of the second type of economy (fixed margins), it is an inflexible-margins version of the model described on pp. 210–14 above: see also Harcourt [1965b, 1969b].

We start the analysis by considering the choice of technique for the economy as a whole. The assumption of one commodity – putty-clay – implies that, at any moment of time, there is a series of 'best-practice' techniques, the engineering possibilities whereby a unit of putty may be produced by differing amounts of itself (*when clay*) per unit of output and the complementary amounts of labour per unit of output. We suppose that putty may take its various clay forms instantaneously and costlessly, and that these are then held for the rest of their lives. Thus all methods of production, either existing or potential, produce a homogeneous output of putty. However, the use to which the output subsequently is to be put determines the form that it ultimately takes. As it is a one-commodity model we may write the technical possibilities as

$$l = f(c) \tag{5.32}$$

where $f'(c)<0, f''(c)>0$ and

l = labour input per unit of output of putty

c = putty (clay) input per unit of output of putty

To introduce the economic aspect of the choice of technique, we note first that the money-wage rate, $\bar{w}_m$, and the expected price of the future output of putty, p^*, are known. Following Joan Robinson we assume that businessmen will choose the technique that offers the highest *expected* rate of profits, r^*_{max}. This may now be found since in any period the 'best-practice' techniques are known (technical progress consists of changes in the input–output coefficients from period to period), as is the *expected* value of the *real*-wage rate, $w^* = \bar{w}_m/p^*$. Thus we write

$$p^*c = \frac{p^* - \bar{w}_m l}{r^*} = \frac{p^* - \bar{w}_m f(c)}{r^*} \tag{5.33a}$$

or
$$c = \frac{1 - w^* f(c)}{r^*} \tag{5.33b}$$

(We ignore depreciation, scale puzzles, and expected lifetimes.) As we know from chapter 2, see p. 62 above, the technique for which r^* is a maximum is that for which[1]

$$-f'(c) = \frac{r^*_{max}}{w^*} \tag{5.34}$$

The constraint of a one-commodity model precludes us from using the more satisfying *ex ante* production function whereby we may consider the time patterns of inputs of labour over the construction periods of the 'best-practice' techniques as well as those over their productive lifetimes. Even if we assume that clay machines are made from labour alone, we still run into the puzzle of identifying both the physical output and the value of the output of a period, when some of the output of

---

[1] If the reader objects to choosing the technique with the highest rate of profits (when this is not equal to the rate of interest), he may substitute in its place, the decision rule of choosing the technique with the highest present value, using a *required* rate of profits, r_r, as the discount factor. (Its value presumably is determined by g/s_c.) A different technique will, of course, be chosen unless the maximum rate of profits coincides with r_r. This value of r_r may then be used in all the subsequent calculations.

putty is made by labour co-operating with (inherited) clay machines, while other outputs are putty made by labour alone which has to become clay at the end of the various gestation periods, whence it is added to the stock of clay machines. Part of the physical accumulation of the period is therefore an addition to the stock of clay machines; another part is that portion of the current output of putty which is made by clay machines and men, and which is used to pay the wages of those making putty which eventually will become clay. With the present model, *all* output, i.e. putty, is made by labour co-operating with existing clay machines and, then, as we shall see below, it is either consumed or hardened, instantaneously and costlessly, into clay inputs per unit of output of the currently *chosen* 'best-practice' technique.

If we were to ignore this puzzle, we could write

$$\bar{w}_m l_{gi}(1+r^*)^{t_i} = \frac{p^* - \bar{w}_m l_i}{r^*} \qquad (5.35a)$$

or

$$w^* l_{gi}(1+r^*)^{t_i} = \frac{1 - w^* l_i}{r^*} \qquad (5.35b)$$

where l_{gi} is labour input required at the start of the gestation period, t_i, in order to produce technique i, $i = 1, \ldots, m$, and l_i is labour input per unit of output of putty (and we again ignore depreciation, expected lifetimes, and problems of scale).

Corresponding to the expressions (5.35) of each technique is its own w–r trade-off relationship

$$w^* = \frac{1}{l_i + r^* l_{gi}(1+r^*)^{t_i}} \qquad (5.36)$$

which holds for all feasible values of w^*.[1] A w–r trade-off envelope may therefore be formed from the expressions (5.36) of the various techniques, that is to say, our engineering data have again been transformed into the *ex ante* production function for the economy as a whole. (The envelope in this case may, of course, exhibit both capital-reversing and double-switching.) As we know w^*, both the technique to be chosen and r^*_{max} itself may be found.

Knowing the value of the expected rate of profits, r^*_{max}, we may now show how the planned level of (net) investment, $\bar{I}$, is determined in any

---

[1] Expressions (5.35b) and (5.36) have as analogues, expressions (1.1) and (1.4), see chapter 1, pp. 24–5 above. The model itself is a simplified version of Nuti [1970b], see pp. 244–8 below. See also, Hicks [1970].

short period. It is here that the 'animal spirits' function, the relationship between the planned rate of accumulation, g^*, and the expected rate of profits, r^*, which was referred to on p. 232 above, first enters the analysis. We write it as

$$g^* = g^*(r^*) \qquad (5.37)$$

where $g^{*\prime}(r^*) > 0$, $g^{*\prime\prime}(r^*) \gtreqless 0$. If we use r^*_{max} as a discount factor with which to capitalize the realized profits of the preceding period (their value will be discussed below, see p. 236), we obtain the *current* value of the existing capital stock, K_{-1}, that is, all the vintages that recently have been in use. (This implies in turn, a level of output, either that for the normal capacity, Y_f, of all existing vintages in the flexible margin economy or the level determined by effective demand, Y_e, in the fixed margin one.) Then

$$\bar{I} = g^* K_{-1} \qquad (5.38)$$

($\bar{I}/p^*$ is the putty value of planned investment; the chosen technique determines its clay form.)

With planned investment, $\bar{w}_m$, and the saving propensities, s_w and s_π, all now known, the short-run equilibrium condition that $S = \bar{I}/p^*$ implies that, in the flexible margin economy, there is a unique profit margin and therefore price level, p. These both establish the normal capacity level of output of the existing vintages – Y_f – and, of course, a distribution of income such that $\Pi = S = \bar{I}/p^*$, together with a real wage, w, all measured in terms of putty. (We assume that the value of $\bar{I}/p^*$ is such that w is not pushed so low as to run the economy into what Joan Robinson [1956] calls the 'inflation barrier', whereby wage-earners take militant action in order to protect themselves against an intolerable cut in their current living standards.) In the fixed margin case, $\Pi = S = \bar{I}/p^*$ and $Y_e \leqslant Y_f$.[1]

Now $$\Pi_m = Y_f - \bar{w}_m L \qquad (5.39)$$

where L is the labour force employed on the existing vintages in use. This relationship may be used to obtain a short-period relationship between possible values of $\bar{I}$, the actual rate of growth of the capital stock, g, and r. Thus we use r^*_{max} to capitalize the current value of profits (Π_m) in order to obtain (anew) the current value of the existing capital stock, K. Thus

---

[1] We ignore this case in our exposition from here on but the reader may easily fill in the details for himself.

$$K = \frac{Y_f - \bar{w}_m L}{r^*_{max}} \qquad (5.40)$$

and

$$g = \frac{\bar{I}}{K} \qquad (5.41)$$

all valued in terms of p, the current price level.

We digress now to consider the possible form of the relationship between r^*_{max} and g, i.e. we consider the comparative statics of a given short period. From the choice of technique decision (either $l = f(c)$ or the w–r trade-off version) we know that the lower is the value of w^*, the higher is the value of r^*_{max} and, thus, $\bar{I}/p^*$ and the lower also is the subsequent value of w *itself.* If the value of K in expression (5.40) were invariant to changes in the value of r^*_{max}, i.e. if there were a *neutral price Wicksell effect*, Asimakopulos [1969], p. 51, argues that the g, r^*_{max} relationship would be a straight line. It is instructive to derive the conditions associated with the various Wicksell effects that may be generated by expression (5.40). We meet some old friends, as is only to be expected. Thus, differentiating K/p, the current value of K in terms of putty, with respect to r^*_{max}, we find that

$$\frac{\partial K/p}{\partial r^*_{max}} \gtreqless 0 \quad \text{if} \quad \frac{dw}{dr^*_{max}} \gtreqless \frac{K/p}{L} \qquad (5.42)$$

[Thus,

$$K/p = \frac{Y_f/p - wL}{r^*_{max}} \qquad (5.43)$$

where

$$w = f(r^*_{max}) \quad \text{and} \quad \frac{dw}{dr^*_{max}}\{= f'(r^*_{max})\} < 0$$

$$\frac{\partial K/p}{\partial r^*_{max}} = \frac{1}{(r^*_{max})^2}\{-r^*_{max}f'(r^*_{max})L - (Y_f/p - wL)\}$$

i.e.

$$\frac{\partial K/p}{\partial r^*_{max}} \gtreqless 0 \quad \text{if} \quad -f'(r^*_{max}) \gtreqless \frac{Y_f/p - wL}{r^*_{max}L} = \frac{K/p}{L} \qquad (5.42)]$$

The first inequality of expression (5.42) is a *negative* price Wicksell effect. The equality, of course, is a near relative, if not the son of the surrogate production function result, and the second inequality is a *positive* price Wicksell effect.

We now come to the two-sided relationship between g and r which is the lynch-pin of Joan Robinson's analysis of economic growth. Expression (5.41), $g = \bar{I}/K$, establishes a point such as P in the g, r^* space of fig. 5.7. P is the relationship between the *realized* rate of accumulation in one short period, g_1, and its accompanying rate of profits, r_1^*. (The analysis of the two preceding paragraphs was concerned with the nature of the comparative statics curve through P.) We also show in fig. 5.7 the g^*, r^* relationship or 'animal spirits' function, expression (5.37) above, which reflects the current state of 'animal spirits' of the business-men in the economy.

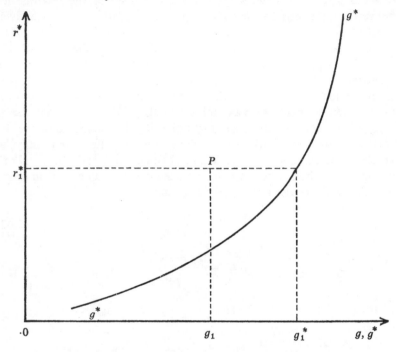

Fig. 5.7. The two faces of the g–r^* relationship

It will be seen that the actual rate of growth associated with P, i.e. g_1, is less than the desired rate of growth, g_1^*, corresponding to r_1^*. In the real world, with non-tranquil conditions, varying proportions of vintages in the capital stock, biased technical progress and with no reason to suppose that the g^*, r^* relationship is a stable one from period to period, there is no reason to suppose that over time P will move towards the g^*g^* curve. Thus realized rates of growth may fluctuate considerably from short period to short period – a not unexpected but certainly reassuring result.

However, suppose that we *are* in a steady state such that Harrod neutral technical progress is occurring (this implies that the coefficients of the *ex ante* production function change in a particular manner, see Read [1968], Rymes [1968, 1971]) and that the expected rate of profits is both constant and realized from period to period, with 'normal' prices being charged. Then, *in these circumstances*, we get the special case of the neo-Keynesian relationship, $r = g/s_\pi$, namely $r = g$. Moreover, this relationship is *on* the g^*g^* relationship, i.e. it is to be found at the point where the 45° line cuts g^*g^*, see the point g_e, r_e in fig. 5.8. This requires that 'the propensity to accumulate' – g^*g^* – be fairly inelastic. 'If accumulation were more sensitive to the expected rate of profits than the actual rate of profits is to the rate of accumulation,

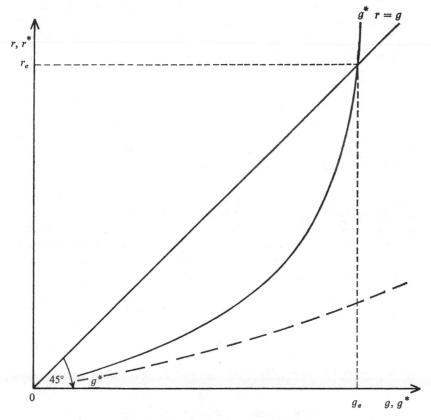

Fig. 5.8. The two faces in a steady state

there would exist no path capable of being steadily maintained' (Robinson [1965b], p. 54). (The latter case is shown by the dotted line in fig. 5.8.)

Notice finally, though, that the intersection is *not* the solution to either Harrod's or Domar's problem, for g_e is the rate of *accumulation* and there is no reason why it should correspond with the natural rate of growth, '. . . nor is there any mechanism in the model to cause it to seek such a path when it does exist'. (Robinson [1965b], p. 54.) Joan Robinson uses these particular pieces of apparatus to analyse other puzzles in the theory of economic growth, a study of which we have not the space to go into here.

Quo Vadis?

We close the chapter and the book by examining another 'dual', a relationship between maintainable rates of maximum consumption per head and steady-state rates of growth, a relationship which is the exact analogue of the wage-rate–rate-of-profits trade-off relationship (or the neoclassical *FpF*). Its origins lie in the neo-neoclassical theorem or Golden Rule of Accumulation, see chapter 4, p. 149 above. The context in which we eventually examine it is that of the choice of technique in a textbook capitalist economy and two types of socialist economy, one centralized, the other decentralized, our discussion being based on a brilliant paper by Nuti [1970b]. Heterogeneous capital goods, no substitution *ex post* and double-switching make fleeting farewell appearances.

Our point of departure, though, is strictly neoclassical; it draws on a neat paper by K. Sato [1966] in which he links the Golden Rule with Pasinetti Land in order to say things about the distributions of income and property, and the values of s_c and s_w that are implied by them. The Golden Rule of Accumulation states that per capita consumption is maximized in a state of balanced growth when $r = g$ (and $S/Y_f = \Pi/Y_f$).[1]

We write the well-behaved, constant-returns-to-scale production function as

$$Q = F(K, L) \qquad (5.44a)$$

(where all quantities are measured *net* of depreciation), i.e.

$$q = f(k) \qquad (5.44b)$$

---

[1] The main purpose of Sato's paper is to show that this requires either that $s_c = 1$ or that $s_w = \Pi/Y_f$, but these results are not our immediate concern here.

where $f'(k)>0, f''(k)<0$ and all quantities are now measured per capita. Ignore technical progress and let labour grow exponentially at g; in balanced growth, K grows at the same rate as L, k is constant and net investment is gK. Per capita consumption, c, is

$$c = q - gk = f(k) - gk \qquad (5.45)$$

c is at a maximum, c_{max}, when

$$\frac{dc}{dk}(= f'(k) - g) = 0$$

i.e. when
$$r = f'(k^*) = g \qquad (5.46)$$

where k^* is the capital–labour ratio that lets c_{max} do its thing.

(Moreover
$$\frac{S}{Y_f} = \frac{I}{Y_f} = \frac{gk^*}{q} = \frac{rk^*}{q} = \frac{\Pi}{Y_f})$$

All these results are for a *given* value of g. We now show, by means of a simple diagram (see fig. 5.9)[1], that c_{max} is a simple decreasing

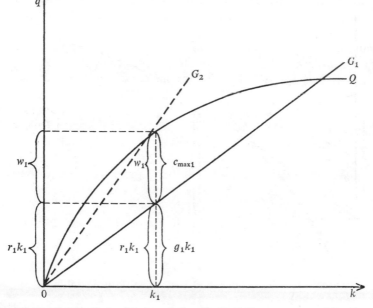

Fig. 5.9. The Golden Rule of Accumulation (By T. C. Koopmans, as told to the Pope)

[1] Koopmans [1965] was, I am told, the first to use this diagram, when he was thinking up simple things to tell the Pope. See, also, Pearce [1962].

function of g which coincides exactly with the *FpF* corresponding to expression (5.44*b*) which is, after all, the jelly world. We measure q on the vertical axis and k on the horizontal axis; OQ is the production function. Consider any growth rate, g_1. Then the net investment per capita associated with g_1 and any value of k lies on the straight line from the origin, OG_1, which has a slope of g_1. The vertical distances between OG_1 and the k axis are values of $g_1 k$; the vertical distances between OG_1 and OQ are the values of c corresponding to each value of k. Clearly, for a given value of g, c_{max} occurs where OQ is parallel to OG_1, i.e. where $r_1 = f'(k_1) = g_1$.

Now it is obvious that as we consider larger values of g, OG_1 swivels on O to the left (see OG_2 in fig. 5.9), $g = r = f'(k)$ rises, c_{max} gets smaller, and k gets smaller. (If the reader suspects people who use words like 'obvious', he may think of OQ as a monopolist's total revenue curve, of OG as his total cost curve and ask what happens to maximum profits when (constant) costs per unit rise. Alternatively, he could think

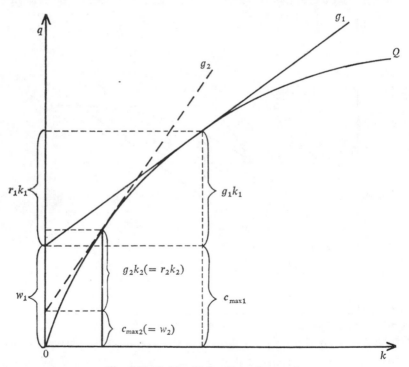

Fig. 5.10. Golden Rule, alternative version

of parallel lines of slope g_1 covering the diagram and pick out the one which is tangential to OQ. Then g_1k_1 and c_{max1} are as shown in fig. 5.10. Now change the value of g and pick out the new tangent, *et al.*)

Thus we may draw the relationship between c_{max} and g as in fig. 5.11. But now suppose that the rate of profits were r_1 ($= g_1$). Then profit per capita would be r_1k_1 ($= g_1k_1$) and wages per capita would be $w_1 = c_{max1}$, i.e. we may label the vertical axis w as well as c_{max} and the horizontal one r as well as g, and our curve is interchangeably the *FpF* and the c_{max}–g relationship.

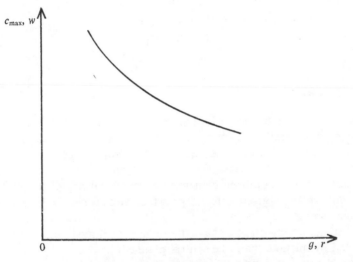

Fig. 5.11. 'And the two shall be as one': *FpF* and c_{max}–g

I now assert (and it may be proved rigorously) that the correspondence between the two carries over to a world of heterogeneous capital goods in which there are no substitution possibilities *ex post*, with these differences, that double-switching possibilities arise and in Nuti's world there is the possibility of bumps in the w–r trade-off, c_{max}–g relationships. An extremely rigorous analysis of these relationships, beautifully done and replete with the regulation remarkable results, will be found in a recent paper by Bruno [1969]. We may make the same point with Samuelson's model, before it was jellified, so that $k_c \neq k_k$ and $l_c \neq l_k$: see chapter 4, p. 137 above.

Assume a steady state with a rate of growth of g, a total (physical) capital stock at any moment of time of K, i.e. so many machines, and measure all quantities, etc., per capita. The quantity equations which are the 'dual' of the price equations (4.10) are

$$l_k g k + l_c c = 1$$
$$k_k g k + k_c c = k \tag{5.47}$$

Solve equations (5.47) by eliminating k to obtain the c_{max}–g relationship

$$c_{max} = \frac{1 - g k_k}{g(k_c l_k - k_k l_c) + l_c} \tag{5.48}$$

Then expression (5.48), with c_{max} substituted for w and g for r (and depreciation ignored), is identical with the FpF^1

$$w = \frac{1 - r k_k}{r(k_c l_k - k_k l_c) + l_c} \tag{4.11}$$

Nuti to the fore!

The aim of Nuti's paper [1970b] is to contrast the choice of technique made by a capitalist businessman (or manager) who maximizes the present value of his firm's assets at a given rate of interest (in a textbook capitalist economy experiencing full employment), with that of a socialist planner who is maximizing consumption per head associated with the maintenance of a given rate of growth. (Sometimes he is a central planner, sometimes decentralization rules. In the latter case, though, socialist managers often behave more like capitalist ones who have defected by mistake than like central planners.)

Nuti uses a putty-clay, i.e. vintage model in which, however, labour *is* needed to mould and bake putty into clay and there *are* gestation lags in investment – putty cannot be turned into clay machines instantaneously. Both of these modifications take him away from orthodox putty-clay models; the first takes him out of a one-commodity world and allows him to grapple with a fundamental issue of capital theory where, to quote Kaldor of the vintage that Solow [1963a], p. 9, prefers, '... the inputs of different dates jointly produce the outputs of different dates; and it is impossible to separate out the contribution to the output of different dates of the input of a single date' (Kaldor [1960], p. 159). 'Output per head – whether gross or net – associated with a given technique would then depend both on the rate of interest – determining the price of each machine in terms of putty – and the growth rate, deter-

---

[1] Spaventa [1970] provides an excellent exposition of these and related relationships.

mining the relative proportion of putty and machines of all kind in total output' (Nuti [1970b], p. 33). The second assumption allows a discussion of 'the possibility of a trade-off between the length of the gestation period and the durability of fixed equipment' (p. 33).

We have homogeneous labour and a versatile commodity, putty, which must be used within one period if it is consumption, but lasts longer if it is made into clay. Putty is produced by labour and machines but it can only be used in given proportions with labour thereafter to make given amounts of putty. A technique of production is represented by a time flow of putty output, in which the part to be moulded and baked into machines appears with a negative sign, and a time flow of labour inputs. Once the machine is made, the output resulting from using it with labour is positive and total output over its whole life is positive. (A simple version of the model has been described on pp. 234–5 above.) Full employment is assumed, the labour supply is given and grows at a steady rate (and is therefore the *relevant* rate for the c_{max}–g relationship) and production is organized in firms by managers of equal efficiency. Wages are paid at the end of the period.

The economic systems differ as to their property relations, market conditions and criteria for technical choice. The central planner chooses the technique which maximizes consumption per head, subject to the maintenance of full-employment steady growth. With decentralization, the managers borrow at a rate, r, and choose the technique which maximizes the present value of their assets at this rate. In capitalism, r is the perfectly elastic supply price of loans (shades of Phelps Brown?) and managers choose the technique which maximizes the present value of their assets.

Nuti then derives the w–r relationships – his 'wage–interest' frontiers – under the assumption that present values will be forced to zero in order to attain (full-employment) equilibrium in the labour market, and forms an envelope which may exhibit bumps and double-switching both. This is shown to coincide with the c_{max}–g relationship – his 'consumption-growth' frontier (pp. 41–2). The main purposes of his paper are, first, to derive simple rules for investment choice and, secondly, to analyse what happens when $r \neq g$ and decision-makers are guided by the former as in capitalism and decentralized socialism. Equilibrium comparisons alone are being made but hopefully (and faithfully, if not charitably) it is thought that the results have some application and throw some light on real-world possibilities. Especially is this true of the socialist economies.

The basic philosophy which underlies Nuti's analysis of the choice of techniques in society as a whole is well expressed in an article by Kurz [1965], pp. 42–3. Thus there are

... two main differences between preferences of individuals and society as a whole ...

(1) society, as opposed to the individual, has an infinite horizon, and (2) society should not discriminate among generations; hence, it should not have a discount factor ... In order to accommodate requirements·(1) and (2) ... consider the following point of view ... Society should seek the highest technologically feasible level of consumption per capita for its citizens. The need not to discriminate among generations imposes a restriction upon such a goal [namely] that the maximum level ... should be a *sustainable* level. A sustainable rate of consumption per capita is a rate that the economy can attain and maintain for ever with the appropriate investment policy. Social goals may, therefore, be defined in terms of such sustainable rates of consumption per capita.

If we are in Sato's world, $r = g$ is a sufficient and necessary condition for consumption maximization. But once $r \neq g$ and reswitching is occurring, 'the difference between g and r ... cannot be taken as a measure of inefficiency' (pp. 44–5); for if c is maximized at a given value of g, the technique with which it is associated may constitute the 'wage–interest' frontier over a range of very low values of r and very high ones. Nuti also considers the case where r, for some reason, is constrained from being within the range of values at which the c_{max} corresponding to the given rate of growth is chosen. Thus, suppose that $\bar{g}$ is the rate of growth so that d is the technique which, ideally, ought to be chosen (see fig. 5.12). r, however, is constrained not to enter the range $r_{db} < \bar{g} < r_{bd1}$ (or $0 - r_{bd2}$). Suppose r were the value, r_b. Then b would be chosen *even though* there is a 'second best' technique, e, in the sense that with a growth rate of $\bar{g}$, it would give the second highest c_{max}, though it will never be on the envelope at *any* rate of interest. In this case there is an argument for abandoning the present value rule.

If we are in Phelps Brown's world (see chapter 2, pp. 87–8 above and Phelps Brown [1968], Phelps Brown with Browne [1968]), where the supply of capital is perfectly elastic at $r = \partial Q / \partial K$, but r is *not* equal to g, are we to say *on the basis of these results* that his vision of the merits of liberal capitalism may be faulty in at least this respect? And if $r = g/s_c$ and $s_c \neq 1$, have we driven yet another nail into the (theoretical) coffin of the 'right and proper' functioning of the perfectly

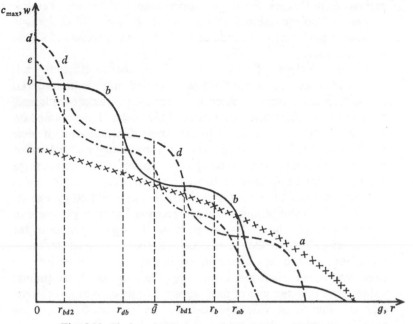

Fig. 5.12. Choice of technique with constrained values of *r*

competitive model of capitalism? And, finally, if a country has a slow rate of growth, but, because its currency is also an international reserve currency, *r* is required to be considerably greater than *g*, have we uncovered additional social costs of 'the City' which were undreamt of even in the most bitter *Tribune* editorial? The answer to all three questions is probably 'Yes' – but probably not for the reasons above.

Nuti covers a wide range of topics with his model – technical progress, the formation of relative prices, valuation – all in all, a fascinating pot-pourri which includes most of the ingredients that go to make up this book, albeit with some special flavours added of his own. To further prolonged tastings I leave the interested reader. In order, though, to go out where, as it were, we came in, I should like to end by quoting his closing paragraphs. They seem to me to sum up excellently and with more than a touch of spice, many of the issues that we have touched on in these pages.[1]

In a capitalist as in a socialist economy, the notion of 'value of

[1] This quote is from the manuscript version of his paper. In the published version he was persuaded, unfortunately in my view, to tone it down slightly.

capital' is not necessary to determine technical choice. Yet this concept is indispensable to the political economy of capitalism, because it performs two fundamental roles, one practical and one ideological.

At a practical level, the evaluation of machines of different kinds and different ages in terms of output is needed to settle transactions among capitalist firms, to determine the value of the exclusive legal right to use machinery, and the value of the pieces of paper embodying such rights. It is necessary to determine distribution of income not between the haves and the have-nots, but among the haves.

The ideological role of 'the value of capital' is that of breaking the actual direct link between the *time pattern* of labour inputs and the time pattern of output [into] which any technology can be resolved, and establishing instead a relation between *current* output and *current* labour. To this purpose the *current* 'value of the capital stock' is needed; a mythical conceptual construction in which the past and the future of the economy are telescoped into the present. Attention is focused not on past labour but on the present value of the embodiment of past labour, and its current productiveness is taken to provide a justification for the attribution of the surplus of current output over the wage bill to those who have appropriated the embodiment of past labour, thereby providing the current basis of future appropriation.

In a planned socialist economy, the only relevant parameters are consumption per head – and its behaviour in time if there is technical change or the economy is out of a steady state – and the growth rate of employment. The concept of the value of capital would not be needed to guide technical choice, nor to determine income distribution among individuals. 'Capital' can be removed altogether from the box of tools of the socialist planner, and, indeed, from his economic vocabulary.

There are those who think it could and should be removed from the box of tools of economists in non-socialist economies as well; that too much time of the best brains in the trade has been (and is) whittled away on fruitless disputes associated with its meaning and measurement. Some, perhaps many, have suggested that the issues which are discussed in this book are of no practical consequence or importance; that they add little of note to our theoretical knowledge. To them, the controversies are more of a game, or, rather, a film (not a silent one) which has already been seen too many times. The moral which is drawn is to give up going to the cinema, in order that some real work may be done and some real problems settled.

For others, including myself (though, like any rational believer, I often have doubts) there *are* fundamental issues at stake, not least of which is the need to redeploy onto problems and issues which are of vital political and social concern, the heavy guns from the schools that have installed the latest 'best-practice' techniques, a view which echoes some strong words of Kaldor's:

> It is the hallmark of the neoclassical economist to believe that, however severe the abstractions from which he is forced to start, he will 'win through' by the end of the day – bit by bit, if he only carries the analysis far enough, the scaffolding can be removed, leaving the basic structure intact. In fact, these props are never removed; the removal of any one of a number of them – as for example, allowing for increasing returns or learning-by-doing – is sufficient to cause the whole structure to collapse like a pack of cards. It is high time that the brilliant minds of M.I.T. were set to evolve a system of non-Euclidean economics which starts from a non-perfect, non-profit maximizing economy where such abstractions are initially unnecessary. (Kaldor [1966], p. 310.)

So as to avoid charges of being both a techniques Luddite and unfair, we should mention that the dynamic models of, for example, Hahn [1965, 1966], Cass and Stiglitz [1969], Shell and Stiglitz [1967], Solow and Stiglitz [1968], and Burmeister, Dobell and Kuga [1967, 1968], are intended as steps in these directions, steps which unfortunately take us to such rare heights that many of us become too dizzy to comprehend properly. Stiglitz [1968] has suggested that the simpler models, even the neoclassical parables, are an aid to research strategy, teaching us not about the real world as such, but, rather, about how we might tackle the puzzles thrown up by these – to him anyway – more realistic but devilishly difficult models. He, himself, has done yeoman work in examining the effects of uncertainty and sophisticated expectations hypotheses on the stability of growth paths. In similar vein, Hahn [1971], pp. vii–viii, in reviewing a selection of the 'most important contributions to the modern theory of economic growth' which were first published in the *Review of Economic Studies*, comments:

> It was right for economists to investigate these simple and more abstract questions first . . . by no means always an easy task. If the answers we have are not made to bear a weight much larger than that intended by the original questions, they will be found useful in

disposing of certain claims and of silly theories. Whether they can be used as part of the foundations for much more complex (and realistic) undertakings, remains to be seen; certainly there is no evidence to date to suggest that they cannot.

Davidson [1968b] has made a plea – and a start himself, for example, Davidson [1968a] – for more concentration on money in growth models, as, of course, has Tobin. But none of these movements comes to grips with criticisms associated with either, for example, non-maximizing behaviour or capitalist economies behaving in a *long-run* Keynesian manner, maybe because, to these authors, they are as yet non-criticisms (but see Solow [1968], Ferguson [1969]). Moreover, when we consider, on the one hand, Hahn's modest, if rather complacent claim above, and, on the other, the genuine – and pressing – economic problems of the real world, it is hard not to entertain the suspicion that an intellectual smokescreen of seemingly sophisticated and important dimensions has been used to obscure the latter for far too long.

Finally, we should state values explicitly and either reject or defend them, instead of pretending that they do not exist or matter: see Myrdal [1970], p. 61 – Myrdal's all, if you like. When I reread Dobb's *Political Economy and Capitalism* [1940] in the process of preparing my survey article, I became convinced that not only was it as fresh and relevant now as when it was first published in 1937, but also that divergent views concerning the nature of economic analysis and its relationship to the existing stages, classes and institutions of society *are* still central to the controversies. One should mention also, in this context, the various wise asides in the recent magnificent – and witty – survey of microeconomics by Shubik [1970].

I said at the end of my survey article that we broke off in midstream with little really settled and with virtue unlikely to triumph this side of the grave. Since then the arguments have been carried further and the issues – and their reconciliation – are now far more clear cut. I suspect, though, that both vested interests and a natural reluctance to scrap past accumulations of knowledge may delay considerably the full implications of the debates being realized and acted upon. Therefore, if, in this book, I have succeeded in setting out some of the issues in a simple and straightforward manner and in restoring, at least a little, senses of proportion, balance and good humour, the book will have achieved all that could have been hoped of it – and more.

References

BOOKS

Allen, R. G. D. [1938] *Mathematical Analysis for Economists* (London: Macmillan).

Bensusan-Butt, D. M. [1960] *On Economic Growth: An Essay in Pure Theory* (Oxford: Clarendon Press).

Blaug, M. [1968] *Economic Theory in Retrospect* (London: Heinemann, 2nd ed.).

Carr, E. H. [1961] *What is History?* (London: Pelican Books).

Cockburn, Alexander and Blackburn, Robin (eds.) [1969] *Student Power* (London: Penguin Books in association with New Left Review).

Dewey, Donald [1965] *Modern Capital Theory* (New York: Columbia University Press).

Dobb, M. H. [1940] *Political Economy and Capitalism* (London: Routledge).
  [1960] *An Essay on Economic Growth and Planning* (London: Routledge and Kegan Paul).
  [1967] *Papers on Capitalism, Development and Planning* (London: Routledge and Kegan Paul).

Evans, Michael K. [1969] *Macroeconomic Activity. Theory, Forecasting, and Control. An Econometric Approach* (New York: Harper and Row).

Ferguson, C. E. [1969] *The Neoclassical Theory of Production and Distribution* (Cambridge: Cambridge University Press).

Fisher, Irving [1930] *The Theory of Interest* (New York: Macmillan).

Gårlund, Torsten [1958] (translated from the Swedish by Nancy Adler) *The Life of Knut Wicksell* (Stockholm: Almqvist and Wiksell).

Hahn, F. H. (ed.) [1971] *Readings in the Theory of Growth* (London: Macmillan).

Harcourt, G. C., Karmel, P. H. and Wallace, R. H. [1967] *Economic Activity* (Cambridge: Cambridge University Press).

Harcourt, G. C. and Laing, N. F. (eds.) [1971] *Capital and Growth. Selected Readings* (London: Penguin Books).

Harrod, R. F. [1948] *Towards a Dynamic Economics: Some Recent Developments of Economic Theory and their Application to Policy* (London:Macmillan).

Hicks, J. R. [1932] *The Theory of Wages* (London: Macmillan).
  [1965] *Capital and Growth* (Oxford: Clarendon Press).

Holroyd, Michael [1968] *Lytton Strachey: a Critical Biography. Vol. II The Years of Achievement (1910–1932)* (London: Heinemann).

Kalecki, Michal [1939] *Essays in the Theory of Economic Fluctuations* (London: Allen and Unwin).

Kaldor, N. [1960] *Essays on Value and Distribution* (London: Duckworth).

Keynes, J. M. [1919] *The Economic Consequences of the Peace* (London: Macmillan).
  [1930] *A Treatise on Money* (2 vols.) (London: Macmillan).
  [1933] *Essays in Biography* (London: Macmillan).
  [1936] *The General Theory of Employment, Interest and Money* (London: Macmillan).

Leijonhufvud, Axel [1968] *On Keynesian Economics and the Economics of Keynes. A Study in Monetary Theory* (New York: Oxford University Press).

Lewin, Leonard C. (ed.) [1967] *Report from Iron Mountain* (Great Britain: Penguin Books).

Marris, Robin [1964] *The Economic Theory of 'Managerial' Capitalism* (London: Macmillan).

Meade, J. E. [1961] *A Neoclassical Theory of Economic Growth* (London: Allen and Unwin).

Meek, R. L. [1967] *Economics and Ideology and Other Essays. Studies in the Development of Economic Thought* (London: Chapman and Hall).

Minhas, B. S. [1963] *An International Comparison of Factor Costs and Factor Use* (Amsterdam: North-Holland).

Morishima, Michio [1964] *Equilibrium, Stability and Growth. A Multi-sectoral Analysis* (Oxford: Clarendon Press).

[1969] *Theory of Economic Growth* (Oxford: Clarendon Press).

Myrdal, Gunnar [1970] *Objectivity in Social Research* (London: Duckworth).

Phelps Brown, E. H. [1968] *Pay and Profits* (Manchester: Manchester University Press).

Phelps Brown, E. H. with Browne, Margaret H. [1968] *A Century of Pay* (London: Macmillan).

Robinson, Joan [1933] *The Economics of Imperfect Competition* (London: Macmillan).

[1969a] *The Economics of Imperfect Competition* (London: Macmillan, 2nd ed.).

[1937] *Introduction to the Theory of Employment* (London: Macmillan).

[1969b] *Introduction to the Theory of Employment* (London: Macmillan, 2nd ed.).

[1956] *The Accumulation of Capital* (London: Macmillan).

[1960] *Exercises in Economic Analysis* (London: Macmillan).

[1962a] *Essays in the Theory of Economic Growth* (London: Macmillan).

[1965b] *Collected Economic Papers*, Vol. III (Oxford: Basil Blackwell).

[1971] *Economic Heresies: Some Old-fashioned Questions in Economic Theory* (New York: Basic Books).

Rymes, T. K. [1971] *On Concepts of Capital and Technical Change* (Cambridge: Cambridge University Press).

Salter, W. E. G. [1960] *Productivity and Technical Change* (Cambridge: Cambridge University Press).

[1966] (With addendum by Reddaway, W. B.) *Productivity and Technical Change* (Cambridge: Cambridge University Press, 2nd ed.).

Samuelson, Paul A. [1947] *Foundations of Economic Analysis* (Cambridge: Harvard University Press).

Solow, Robert M. [1963a] (Professor Dr. F. De Vries Lectures, 1963) *Capital Theory and the Rate of Return* (Amsterdam: North-Holland).

Sraffa, Piero (ed.) with the collaboration of Dobb, M. H. [1951–5] *The Works and Correspondence of David Ricardo*, 10 volumes (Cambridge: Cambridge University Press).

[1960] *Production of Commodities by Means of Commodities. Prelude to a Critique of Economic Theory* (Cambridge: Cambridge University Press).

Stigler, George J. [1941] *Production and Distribution Theories: The Formative Period* (New York: Macmillan).

Stiglitz, Joseph E. (ed.) [1966] *The Collected Scientific Papers of Paul A. Samuelson*, Vol. I (Cambridge: M.I.T. Press).

Wicksell, Knut [1934] *Lectures on Political Economy*, Vol. I (London: Routledge).

Wicksteed, P. H. [1933] *The Commonsense of Political Economy and Selected Papers and Reviews of Economic Theory* (London: Routledge).

ARTICLES AND CHAPTERS FROM BOOKS

Arrow, Kenneth J., Chenery, Hollis B., Minhas, Bagicha S., and Solow, Robert M. [1961] 'Capital-Labor Substitution and Economic Efficiency', *Review of Economics and Statistics*, XLIII, pp. 225–50.

Arrow, K. J. [1962] 'The Economic Implications of Learning by Doing', *Review of Economic Studies*, XXIX, pp. 155–73.

Asimakopulos, A. [1969] 'A Robinsonian Growth Model in One-sector Notation', *Australian Economic Papers*, VIII, pp. 41–58.

[1970] 'A Robinsonian Growth Model in One-sector Notation – An Amendment', *Australian Economic Papers*, IX, pp. 171–6.

Atkinson, A. B. and Stiglitz, J. E. [1969] 'A New View of Technological Change', *Economic Journal*, LXXIX, pp. 573–8.

Bardhan, P. K. [1967] 'On Estimation of Production Functions from International Cross-Section Data', *Economic Journal*, LXXVII, pp. 328–37.

[1969] 'Equilibrium Growth in a Model with Economic Obsolescence of Machines', *Quarterly Journal of Economics*, LXXXIII, pp. 312-23.

Bhaduri, A. [1966] 'The Concept of the Marginal Productivity of Capital and the Wicksell Effect', *Oxford Economic Papers*, XVIII, pp. 284–8.

[1969] 'On the Significance of Recent Controversies on Capital Theory: A Marxian View', *Economic Journal*, LXXIX, pp. 532–9.

Bharadwaj, K. R. [1963] 'Value Through Exogenous Distribution', *Economic Weekly*, XV, pp. 1450–4.

Black, J. [1962] 'The Technical Progress Function and the Production Function', *Economica*, XXIX, pp. 166–70.

Bliss, C. J. [1968a] 'On Putty–Clay', *Review of Economic Studies*, XXXV, pp. 105–32.

[1970] 'Comment on Garegnani', *Review of Economic Studies*, XXXVII (2), pp. 437–8.

Britto, R. [1968] 'A Study in Equilibrium Dynamics in Two Types of Growing Economies', *Economic Journal*, LXXVIII, pp. 624–40.

Brown, Murray [1966] 'A Measure of the Change in Relative Exploitation of Capital and Labor', *Review of Economics and Statistics*, XLVIII, pp. 182–92.

[1969] 'Substitution–Composition Effects, Capital Intensity Uniqueness and Growth', *Economic Journal*, LXXIX, pp. 334–47.

Bruno, M., Burmeister, E. and Sheshinski, E. [1966] 'Nature and Implications of the Reswitching of Techniques', *Quarterly Journal of Economics*, LXXX, pp. 526–53.

[1968] 'The Badly Behaved Production Function: Comment', *Quarterly Journal of Economics*, LXXXII, pp. 524–5.

Bruno, M. [1969] 'Fundamental Duality Relations in the Pure Theory of Capital and Growth', *Review of Economic Studies*, XXXVI, pp. 39–53.

Burmeister, E. [1968] 'On a Theorem of Sraffa', *Economica*, XXXV, pp. 83–7.

Burmeister, E., Dobell, R. and Kuga, K. [1968] 'A Note on the Global Stability of a Simple Growth Model with Many Capital Goods', *Quarterly Journal of Economics*, LXXXII, pp. 657–65.

Cass, D. and Stiglitz, J. E. [1969] 'The implications of Alternative Saving and Expectations Hypotheses for Choices of Technique and Patterns of Growth', *Journal of Political Economy*, LXXVII, pp. 586–627.

Champernowne, D. G. [1945–6] 'A Note on J. v. Neumann's Article on "A Model of Economic Equilibrium" ', *Review of Economic Studies*, XIII, pp. 10-18.

[1953–4] 'The Production Function and the Theory of Capital: A Comment', *Review of Economic Studies*, XXI, pp. 112–35.

[1958] 'Capital Accumulation and the Maintenance of Full Employment'. *Economic Journal*, LXVIII, pp. 211–44.

[1963] 'Review of D. M. Bensusan-Butt, *On Economic Growth: an Essay in Pure Theory*, 1960', *Economic Journal*, LXXIII, pp. 703–5.

Chang, P. [1964] 'Rate of Profit and Income Distribution in Relation to the Rate of Economic Growth: A Comment', *Review of Economic Studies*, XXXI, pp. 103–5.

Clark, J. B. [1889] 'The Possibility of a Scientific Law of Wages', *Publication of the American Economic Association*, IV, pp. 39–63.

[1891] 'Distribution as Determined by a Law of Rent', *Quarterly Journal of Economics*, V, pp. 289–318.

Davidson, Paul [1968a] 'Money, Portfolio Balance, Capital Accumulation, and Economic Growth', *Econometrica*, XXXVI, pp. 291–321.

[1968b] 'The Demand and Supply of Securities and Economic Growth and Its Implications for the Kaldor–Pasinetti Versus Samuelson–Modigliani Controversy', *American Economic Review*, Papers and Proceedings, LVIII, pp. 252–69.

Denison, E. F. [1966] 'Capital Theory: A Discussion', *American Economic Review*, Papers and Proceedings, LVI, pp. 76–8.

Diamond, P. A. [1965] 'Technical Change and the Measurement of Capital and Output', *Review of Economic Studies*, XXXII, pp. 289–98.

Dobb, Maurice [1970] 'The Sraffa System and Critique of the Neo-Classical Theory of Distribution', *De Economist*, 4, pp. 347–62.

Eltis, W. A. [1965] 'A Theory of Investment, Distribution, and Employment,' *Oxford Economic Papers*, XVII, pp. 1–23.

Ferguson, C. E. and Allen, Robert F. [1970] 'Factor Prices, Commodity Prices, and the Switches of Technique', *Western Economic Journal*, VIII, pp. 95–109.

Fisher, F. M. [1965] 'Embodied Technical Change and the Existence of an Aggregate Capital Stock', *Review of Economic Studies*, XXXII, pp. 263–88.

[1969] 'The Existence of Aggregate Production Functions', *Econometrica*, XXXVII, pp. 553–77.

Fukuoka, Masao [1969] 'Monetary Growth à la Keynes', *Keio Economic Studies*, VI, pp. 1–9.

Garegnani, P. [1966] 'Switching of Techniques', *Quarterly Journal of Economics*, LXXX, pp. 554–67.

[1970a] 'Heterogeneous Capital, the Production Function and the Theory of Distribution', *Review of Economic Studies*, XXXVII (3), pp. 407–36.

[1970b] 'A Reply', *Review of Economic Studies*, XXXVII (3), p. 439.

Griliches, Z. and Jorgenson, D. W. [1966] 'Sources of Measured Productivity Change: Capital Input', *American Economic Review*, Papers and Proceedings, LVI, pp. 50–61.

Hahn, F. H. and Matthews, R. C. O. [1964] 'The Theory of Economic Growth: A Survey', *Economic Journal*, LXXIV, pp. 779–902.

Hahn, F. H. [1965] 'On Two Sector Growth Models', *Review of Economic Studies*, XXXII, pp. 339–46.

[1966] 'Equilibrium Dynamics with Heterogeneous Capital Goods', *Quarterly Journal of Economics*, LXXX, pp. 633–46.

[1970] 'Some adjustment Processes', *Econometrica*, XXXVIII, pp. 1–17.

Harcourt, G. C. [1963a] 'A simple Joan Robinson Model of Accumulation with One Technique: A Comment', *Osaka Economic Papers*, XI, pp. 24–8.

[1963b] 'A Critique of Mr Kaldor's Model of Income Distribution and Economic Growth', *Australian Economic Papers*, II, pp. 20–36.

[1964] 'Review of B. S. Minhas, *An International Comparison of Factor Costs and Factor Use*, 1963', *Economic Journal*, LXXIV, pp. 443–5.

Harcourt, G. C. and Massaro, Vincent G. [1964a] 'A Note on Mr Sraffa's Subsystems', *Economic Journal*, LXXIV, pp. 715–22.

[1964b] 'Mr Sraffa's Production of Commodities', *Economic Record*, XL, pp. 442–54.

Harcourt, G. C. (1965a) 'The Accountant in a Golden Age', *Oxford Economic Papers*, XVII, pp. 66–80.

[1965b] 'A Two-Sector Model of the Distribution of Income and the Level of Employment in the Short Run', *Economic Record*, XLI, pp. 103–17.

[1966] 'Biases in Empirical Estimates of the Elasticities of Substitution of C.E.S. Production Functions', *Review of Economic Studies*, XXXIII, pp. 227–33.

[1967] 'Review of D. Dewey, *Modern Capital Theory*, 1965', *Economic Journal*, LXXVII, pp. 359–61.

[1968a] 'Investment-Decision Criteria, Capital-Intensity and the Choice of Techniques', *Czechoslovak Economic Papers*, IX, pp. 65–91.

[1968b] 'Investment-Decision Criteria, Investment Incentives and the Choice of Technique', *Economic Journal*, LXXVIII, pp. 77–95.

[1969a] 'Some Cambridge Controversies in the Theory of Capital', *Journal of Economic Literature*, VII, pp. 369–405.

[1969b] 'A Teaching Model of the "Keynesian" System', *Keio Economic Studies*, VI, pp. 23–46.

[1970a] 'G. C. Harcourt's Reply to Nell', *Journal of Economic Literature*, VIII, pp. 44–5.

[1970b] 'Review of C. E. Ferguson, *The Neoclassical Theory of Production and Distribution*, 1969', *Journal of Economic Literature*, VIII, pp. 809–11.

Harrod, R. F. [1939] 'An Essay in Dynamic Theory', *Economic Journal*, XLIX, pp. 14–33.

[1961] 'Review of P. Sraffa, *Production of Commodities by Means of Commodities. Prelude to a Critique of Economic Theory*, 1960', *Economic Journal*, LXXI, pp. 783–7.

Hicks, J. R. [1960] 'Thoughts on the Theory of Capital – The Corfu Conference', *Oxford Economic Papers*, XII, pp. 123–32.

[1970] 'A Neo-Austrian Growth Theory', *Economic Journal*, LXXX, pp. 257–81.

Hirshleifer, J. [1958] 'On the Theory of Optimal Investment Decision', *Journal of Political Economy*, LXVI, pp. 329–52.

[1967] 'A Note on the Böhm-Bawerk/Wicksell Theory of Interest', *Review of Economic Studies*, XXXIV, pp. 191–9.

Hogan, W. P. [1958] 'Technical Progress and Production Functions', *Review of Economics and Statistics*, XL, pp. 407–11.

Hudson, H. R. and Mathews, R. L. [1963] 'An Aspect of Depreciation', *Economic Record*, XXXIX, pp. 232–6.

Johansen, L. [1959] 'Substitution versus Fixed Production Coefficients in the Theory of Economic Growth: A Synthesis', *Econometrica*, XXVII, pp. 157–76.

[1961] 'A Method for Separating the Effects of Capital Accumulation and Shifts in Production Functions upon Growth in Labour Productivity', *Economic Journal*, LXXI, pp. 775–82.

Johnson, H. G. [1962] 'A Simple Joan Robinson Model of Accumulation with One Technique', *Osaka Economic Papers*, X, pp. 28–33.

Jorgenson, D. W. and Griliches, Z. [1967] 'The Explanation of Productivity Change', *Review of Economic Studies*, XXXIV, pp. 249–83.

Kahn, R. F. [1959] 'Exercises in the Analysis of Growth', *Oxford Economic Papers*, XI, pp. 143–56.

Kaldor, N. [1955–6] 'Alternative Theories of Distribution', *Review of Economic Studies*, XXIII, pp. 83–100.

[1957] 'A Model of Economic Growth', *Economic Journal*, LXVII, pp. 591–624.

[1959a] 'Economic Growth and the Problem of Inflation – Part I', *Economica*, XXVI, pp. 212–26.

[1959b] 'Economic Growth and the Problem of Inflation – Part II', *Economica*, XXVI, pp. 287–98.

256   *References*

Kaldor, N. and Mirrlees, J. A. [1962] 'A New Model of Economic Growth', *Review of Economic Studies*, XXIX, pp. 174–92.
Kaldor, N. [1966] 'Marginal Productivity and the Macro-Economic Theories of Distribution', *Review of Economic Studies*, XXXIII, pp. 309–19.
[1970] 'Some Fallacies in the Interpretation of Kaldor', *Review of Economic Studies*, XXXVII (1), pp. 1–7.
Katz, J. M. [1968a] 'The Sources of Manufacturing Growth in Australia and Argentina in the Period 1946–60', *Economic Record*, XLIV, pp. 377–81.
[1968b] ' "Verdoorn Effects", Returns to Scale, and the Elasticity of Factor Substitution', *Oxford Economic Papers*, XX, pp. 342–52.
Kemmeny, J. G., Morgenstern, O., and Thompson, G. L. [1956] 'A Generalization of the von Neumann Model of an Expanding Economy', *Econometrica*, XXIV, pp. 115–35.
Kennedy, C. [1964] 'Induced Bias in Innovation and the Theory of Distribution', *Economic Journal*, LXXIV, pp. 541–7.
Koopmans, T. C. [1965] 'On the Concept of Optimal Economic Growth', Pontificiae Academiae Scientiarvm, *Scripta Varia* (Amsterdam: North-Holland), pp. 225–87.
Kurz, Mordecai [1965] 'Optimal Paths of Accumulation under the Minimum Time Objective', *Econometrica*, XXXIII, pp. 42–66.
Laing, N. F. [1969a] 'Two Notes on Pasinetti's Theorem', *Economic Record*, XLV, pp. 373–85.
Lerner, Abba P. [1953] 'On the Marginal Product of Capital and the Marginal Efficiency of Investment', *Journal of Political Economy*, LXI, pp. 1–14.
Levhari, D. [1965] 'A Nonsubstitution Theorem and Switching of Techniques', *Quarterly Journal of Economics*, LXXIX, pp. 98–105.
Levhari, D. and Samuelson, P. A. [1966] 'The Nonswitching Theorem is False', *Quarterly Journal of Economics*, LXXX, pp. 518–19.
Lowe, A. [1954] 'The Classical Theory of Economic Growth', *Social Research*, XXI, pp. 127–58.
Lydall, H. F. [1969] 'On Measuring Technical Progress', *Australian Economic Papers*, VIII, pp. 1–12.
Meade, J. E. [1963] 'The Rate of Profit in a Growing Economy', *Economic Journal*, LXXIII, pp. 665–74.
Meade, J. E. and Hahn, F. H. [1965] 'The Rate of Profit in a Growing Economy', *Economic Journal*, LXXV, pp. 445–8.
Meade, J. E. [1966] 'The Outcome of the Pasinetti-Process: A Note', *Economic Journal*, LXXVI, pp. 161–5.
Miller, N. C. [1968] 'A General Equilibrium Theory of International Capital Flows', *Economic Journal*, LXXVIII, pp. 312–20.
Morishima, M. [1966] 'Refutation of the Nonswitching Theorem', *Quarterly Journal of Economics*, LXXX, pp. 520–5.
Nell, E. J. [1967a] 'Wicksell's Theory of Circulation', *Journal of Political Economy*, LXXV, pp. 386–94.
[1967b] 'Theories of Growth and Theories of Value', *Economic Development and Cultural Change*, XVI, pp. 15–26.
[1970] 'A Note on Cambridge Controversies in Capital Theory', *Journal of Economic Literature*, VIII, pp. 41–4.
Neumann, J. v. [1945–6] 'A Model of General Economic Equilibrium', *Review of Economic Studies*, XIII, pp. 1–9.
Ng, Y. K. [1970], 'Optimum Saving, Individual Decisions, and the Diminishing Marginal Productivity of Capital', *Economic Journal*, LXXX, pp. 749–52.
Nuti, D. M. [1969] 'The Degree of Monopoly in the Kaldor–Mirrlees Growth Model', *Review of Economic Studies*, XXXVI, pp. 257–60.

Nuti, D. M. [1970a] ' "Vulgar Economy" in the Theory of Income Distribution', *De Economist*, 4, pp. 363–9.

[1970b] 'Capitalism, Socialism and Steady Growth', *Economic Journal*, LXXX, pp. 32–57.

Pasinetti, L. L. [1962] 'Rate of Profit and Income Distribution in Relation to the Rate of Economic Growth', *Review of Economic Studies*, XXIX, pp. 267–79.

[1964] 'A Comment on Professor Meade's "Rate of Profit in a Growing Economy" ', *Economic Journal*, LXXIV, pp. 488–9.

[1965] 'A New Theoretical Approach to the Problems of Economic Growth', Pontificiae Academiae Scientiarvm, *Scripta Varia* (Amsterdam: North-Holland), pp. 571–696.

[1966a] 'Changes in the Rate of Profit and Switches of Techniques', *Quarterly Journal of Economics*, LXXX, pp. 503–17.

[1966b] 'The Rate of Profit in a Growing Economy: A Reply', *Economic Journal*, LXXVI, pp. 158–60.

[1966c] 'New Results in an Old Framework', *Review of Economic Studies*, XXXIII, pp. 303–6.

[1969] 'Switches of Technique and the "Rate of Return" in Capital Theory', *Economic Journal*, LXXIX, pp. 508–31.

[1970] 'Again on Capital Theory and Solow's "Rate of Return" ', *Economic Journal*, LXXX, pp. 428–31.

Pearce, I. F. [1962] 'The End of the Golden Age in Solovia: A Further Fable for Growthmen Hoping to be "One Up" on Oiko', *American Economic Review*, LII, pp. 1088–97.

Phelps, E. and Phelps, C. [1966] 'Factor-Price-Frontier Estimation of a "Vintage" Production Model of the Postwar United States Nonfarm Business Sector', *Review of Economics and Statistics*, XLVIII, pp. 251–65.

Phelps Brown, E. H. [1957] 'The Meaning of the Fitted Cobb–Douglas Production Function', *Quarterly Journal of Economics*, LXXI, pp. 546–60.

Pitchford, J. D. [1960] 'Growth and the Elasticity of Factor Substitution', *Economic Record*, XXXVI, pp. 491–504.

Quandt, R. E. [1961] 'Review of P. Sraffa, *Production of Commodities by Means of Commodities. Prelude to a Critique of Economic Theory*, 1960', *Journal of Political Economy*, LXIX, p. 500.

Ramsey, F. P. [1928] 'A Mathematical Theory of Saving', *Economic Journal*, XXXVIII, pp. 543–59.

Read, L. M. [1968] 'The Measure of Total Factor Productivity Appropriate to Wage-Price Guidelines', *Canadian Journal of Economics*, I, pp. 349–58.

Reder, M. W. [1961] 'Review of P. Sraffa, *Production of Commodities by Means of Commodities. Prelude to a Critique of Economic Theory*, 1960' *American Economic Review*, LI, pp. 688–95.

Riach, P. A. [1969] 'A Framework for Macro-Distribution Analysis', *Kyklos*, XXII, pp. 542–65.

[1971] 'Kalecki's "Degree of Monopoly" Reconsidered', *Australian Economic Papers*, X, pp. 50–60.

Robertson, D. H. [1949] 'Wage Grumbles', *Readings in the Theory of Income Distribution* (American Economic Association), pp. 221–36.

Robinson, Joan [1953–4] 'The Production Function and the Theory of Capital', *Review of Economic Studies*, XXI, pp. 81–106.

[1957] 'Economic Growth and Capital Accumulation – A Comment', *Economic Record*, XXXIII, pp. 103–8.

Robinson, Joan [1958] 'The Real Wicksell Effect', *Economic Journal*, LXVIII, pp. 600–5.

Robinson, Joan [1959] 'Accumulation and the Production Function', *Economic Journal*, LXIX, pp. 433–42.

[1961a] 'Equilibrium Growth Models', *American Economic Review*, LI, pp. 360–9.

[1961b] 'Prelude to a Critque of Economic Theory', *Oxford Economic Papers*, XIII, pp. 53–8.

[1962b] 'Comment on Solow *et al.*', *Review of Economic Studies*, XXIX, pp. 258–66.

[1964a] 'Factor Prices not Equalized', *Quarterly Journal of Economics*, LXXVIII, pp. 202–7.

[1964b] 'Solow on the Rate of Return', *Economic Journal*, LXXIV, pp. 410–17.

[1965a] 'Piero Sraffa and the Rate of Exploitation', *New Left Review*, pp. 28–34.

[1966] 'Comment on Samuelson and Modigliani', *Review of Economic Studies*, XXXIII, pp. 307–8.

Robinson, Joan and Naqvi, K. A. [1967] 'The Badly Behaved Production Function', *Quarterly Journal of Economics*, LXXXI, pp. 579–91.

Robinson, Joan [1969c] 'A Further Note', *Review of Economic Studies*, XXXVI, pp. 260–2.

[1969d] 'Review of A. Leijonhufvud, *On Keynesian Economics and the Economics of Keynes. A Study in Monetary Theory*, 1968', *Economic Journal*, LXXIX, pp. 581–3.

[1969e] 'The Theory of Value Reconsidered', *Australian Economic Papers*, VIII, pp. 13–19.

[1970a] 'Capital Theory Up to Date', *Canadian Journal of Economics*, III, pp. 309–17.

[1970b] 'Review of C. E. Ferguson, *The Neoclassical Theory of Production and Distribution*, 1969', *Economic Journal*, LXXX, pp. 336–9.

[1970c] 'Harrod after Twenty-one Years', *Economic Journal*, LXXX, pp. 731–7.

Rymes, T. K. [1968] 'Professor Read and the Measurement of Total Factor Productivity', *Canadian Journal of Economics*, I, pp. 359–67.

Salter, W. E. G. [1959] 'The Production Function and the Durability of Capital', *Economic Record*, XXXV, pp. 47–66.

[1962] 'Marginal Labour and Investment Coefficients of Australian Manufacturing Industry', *Economic Record*, XXXVIII, pp. 137–56.

[1965] 'Productivity Growth and Accumulation as Historical Processes', *Problems in Economic Development*, ed. by E. A. G. Robinson (London: Macmillan), pp. 266–91.

Samuelson, P. A. [1961] 'A New Theorem on Nonsubstitution', *Money Growth and Methodology*, published in honour of Johan Åkerman (Lund Social Science Studies, Vol. 28) (Lund: C. W. K. Gleerup), pp. 407–23.

[1962] 'Parable and Realism in Capital Theory: The Surrogate Production Function', *Review of Economic Studies*, XXIX, pp. 193–206.

[1964] 'A Brief Survey of Post-Keynesian Developments', *Keynes' General Theory. Reports of Three Decades*, ed. by R. L. Lekachman (London: Macmillan), pp. 331–47.

[1965] 'Review of J. E. Meade, *Efficiency, Equality and the Ownership of Property*, 1964', *Economic Journal*, LXXV, pp. 804–6.

[1966a] 'A Summing Up', *Quarterly Journal of Economics*, LXXX, pp. 568–83.

[1966b] 'Rejoinder: Agreements, Disagreements, Doubts, and the Case of Induced Harrod-neutral Technical Change', *Review of Economics and Statistics*, XLVIII, pp. 444–8.

Samuelson, P. A. and Modigliani, F. [1966a] 'The Pasinetti Paradox in Neoclassical and More General Models', *Review of Economic Studies*, XXXIII, pp. 269–301.

[1966b] 'Reply to Pasinetti and Robinson', *Review of Economic Studies*, XXXIII, pp. 321–30.

Sargent, J. R. [1968] 'Recent Growth Experience in the Economy of the United Kingdom', *Economic Journal*, LXXVIII, pp. 19–42.

Sato, K. [1966] 'The Neo-classical Theorem and Distribution of Income and Wealth', *Review of Economic Studies*, XXXIII, pp. 331–5.

Sen, A. K. [1963] 'Neo-Classical and Neo-Keynesian Theories of Distribution', *Economic Record*, XXXIX, pp. 53–64.

Shell, K. and Stiglitz, J. E. [1967] 'The Allocation of Investment in a Dynamic Economy', *Quarterly Journal of Economics*, LXXXI, pp. 592–609.

Shubik, Martin [1970] 'A Curmudgeon's Guide to Microeconomics', *Journal of Economic Literature*, VIII, pp. 405–34.

Smithies, A. [1962] 'Comment on Solow', *American Economic Review*, Papers and Proceedings, LII, pp. 91–2.

Solow, R. M. [1956a] 'The Production Function and the Theory of Capital', *Review of Economic Studies*, XXIII, pp. 101–8.

[1956b] 'A Contribution to the Theory of Economic Growth', *Quarterly Journal of Economics*, LXX, pp. 65–94.

[1957] 'Technical Change and the Aggregate Production Function', *Review of Economics and Statistics*, XXXIX, pp. 312–20.

[1960] 'Investment and Technical Progress', *Mathematical Methods in the Social Sciences 1959: Proceedings of the First Stanford Symposium*, ed. by K. J. Arrow, S. Karlin, and P. Suppes (Stanford: Stanford University Press), pp. 89–104.

[1961] 'Comment on Stigler' in National Bureau of Economic Research, Studies in Income and Wealth Series, *Output, Input and Productivity Measurement* (Princeton: Princeton University Press), pp. 64–7.

[1962a] 'Substitution and Fixed Proportions in the Theory of Capital', *Review of Economic Studies*, XXIX, pp. 207–18.

[1962b] 'Technical Progress, Capital Formation and Economic Growth', *American Economic Review*, Papers and Proceedings, LII, pp. 76–86.

[1963b] 'Heterogeneous Capital and Smooth Production Functions: An Experimental Study', *Econometrica*, XXXI, pp. 623–45.

Solow, R. M., Tobin, J., von Weizsäcker, C. C. and Yaari, M. [1966] 'Neoclassical Growth with Fixed Factor Proportions', *Review of Economic Studies*, XXXIII, pp. 79–115.

Solow, R. M. [1967] 'The Interest Rate and Transition between Techniques', *Socialism, Capitalism and Economic Growth, Essays presented to Maurice Dobb*, ed. by C. H. Feinstein (Cambridge: Cambridge University Press), pp. 30–9.

Solow, R. M. and Stiglitz, J. E. [1968] 'Output, Employment and Wages in the Short Run', *Quarterly Journal of Economics*, LXXXII, pp. 537–60.

Solow, R. M. [1968] 'Distribution in the Long and Short Run', *The Distribution of National Income*, ed. by Jean Marchal and Bernard Ducros (London: Macmillan), pp. 449–75.

[1970] 'On the Rate of Return: Reply to Pasinetti', *Economic Journal*, LXXX, pp.423–8.

Spaventa, L. [1968] 'Realism without Parables in Capital Theory', *Récherches récentes sur la fonction de Production*, Centre D'Etudes et de Récherches Universitaire de Namur, pp. 15–45.

[1970] 'Rate of Profit, Rate of Growth, and Capital Intensity in a Simple Production Model', *Oxford Economic Papers*, XXII, pp. 129–47.

Sraffa, P. [1925] 'Sulle relazioni fra costo e quantità prodotta', *Annali i Economica*, II, no. 1, pp. 277–328.

[1926] 'The Laws of Return under Competitive Conditions', *Economic Journal*, XXXVI, pp. 535–50.

[1962] 'Production of Commodities: A Comment', *Economic Journal*, LXXII, pp. 477–9.

Swan, T. W. [1956] 'Economic Growth and Capital Accumulation', *Economic Record*, XXXII, pp. 334–61.
  [1963] 'Wilfred Edward Graham Salter: 1929–1963', *Economic Record*, XXXIX, pp. 486–7.
Whitaker, J. K. [1966] 'Vintage Capital Models and Econometric Production Functions', *Review of Economic Studies*, XXXIII, pp. 1–18.
Worswick, G. D. N. [1959] 'Mrs. Robinson on Simple Accumulation. A Comment with Algebra', *Oxford Economic Papers*, XI, pp. 125–41.

UNPUBLISHED PAPERS, LETTERS, ETC.
Akyüz, Y. [1970] 'Capital Reversal and the Difference between Sraffa and Hicks Wage Profit Trade-off', East Anglia: unpublished paper.
Bliss, C. J. [1968b] 'Rates of Return in a Linear Model', Cambridge: unpublished paper.
Brown, Murray [1968] 'A Respecification of the Neoclassical Production Model in the Heterogeneous Capital Case', Discussion Paper No. 29, State University of New York at Buffalo.
Burmeister, E. and Dobell R. [1967] 'Steady-State Behavior of Neoclassical Models with Many Capital Goods', Discussion Paper No. 72, University of Pennsylvania.
Champernowne, D. G. [1966] 'Luigi Pasinetti's Note on "Changes in the Rate of Profit, etc." ' Cambridge: unpublished paper.
Fisher, F. M. [1970] 'Aggregate Production Functions and the Explanation of Wages: A Simulation Experiment', Working Paper 61, Department of Economics, M.I.T.
Laing, N. F. [1969b] 'Trade, Growth and Distribution. A Study in the Theory of the Long Run', Adelaide: unpublished monograph, 2nd edition.
Newbery, D. M. G. [1970] 'Vintage Models, Optimal Growth and the Importance of Specification', Paper presented to the Second World Congress of the Econometric Society, Cambridge.
Sampson, Gary [1969] 'Productivity Change in Australian Manufacturing Industry', Monash University: unpublished Ph.D. thesis.
Solow, R. M. [1969] Letter to author.
Stiglitz, J. E. [1966] 'Notes on the Switching of Techniques', Cambridge: unpublished paper.
  [1967] *Lectures on Economic Theory*, University of Canterbury, New Zealand.
  [1968] Letter to author.

Author Index

Subject Index

'accelerationists', 17
accountants, 23
accounting, national, 84, 204
accumulation of capital, 86, 110n, 112, 122, 123, 151, 162, 235; Champernowne's examination of, 32, 38–9; controlled by policy of firms and governments, 232; Golden Rule of, 10, 149, 240; and growth of productivity, 1, 47–51, 63–72, 83; Joan Robinson's model of, 5, 22, 25, 29, 96, 231–40; rate of, 232, 236, 238; Worswick's version of, 96–7
Accumulation of Capital (Robinson), 17
activities, 119n, 132; short-run level of, 202, 210, 211
aggregate supply curve, 104; *see also under* supply
aggregation, of heterogeneous capital goods, 6, 46, 51, 74, 92
analytical techniques, revolution in, 12
'animal spirits', 201, 209, 214, 232
'animal spirits' function, 236, 238–9
annuity method of calculation, 189
anti-Pasinetti (MSM) condition, 221–7
Argentina, productivity growth in, 87
Australia, 201n; productivity growth in, 48, 87
Austrian economists, 20, 92, 118, 123, 150

balancing ratio, 184
bargaining, collective, 169n, 201, 211
basic equations, 188
benefit–cost ratio, 152
butter, *see under* commodities

Cambridge, England, 1, 55, 89, 119, 120n, 221
Cambridge, Massachusetts, 1, 11, 89, 119, 120n, 221
capital, *see* accumulation of capital, circulating capital, deepening of capital, effective stock of capital, malleable capital, measurement of capital, organic composition of capital, real capital, revaluation of capital, social (aggregate) capital, *etc.*
capital gains, 85, 228, 230
capital goods, 18, 23–4, 47, 57, 87–9, 135, 137, 170; balanced stock of, 23, 192; durable (fixed assets), as joint products, 23, 186, 189; fossil, 48, 63, 114; heterogeneous, 2, 5, 6, 37, 46, 55, 74, 94, 144, 154, 155, 173, 175, 240, 243; model for heterogeneous, 10, 119, 120, 121, 131, 165, 167; separated from capital, 169–70; specificity of, 5, 6, 78; substitution of, one for another, 74; values of, 167, 168; vintages of, 64–6, 69–72, 73, 74, 81–2, 87, 96, 114–17, 233, 236, 244
capital intensity, 60, 78, 130, 135–6, 159
capital intensity uniqueness, 172
capital–labour ratio, 3, 4, 34, 46, 53, 65, 86, 87, 106, 136, 159, 172, 226–7, 241; physical, 135, 144
capital–labour substitution, 25, 55, 97, 138, 154; dynamic out-of-equilibrium process of, 144; elasticity of, 51–4, 75, 81–2; *ex ante* possibilities of, 6, 55, 64, 66, 69, 95, 114; in *ex post* situation, 6, 55, 64, 66, 69, 72, 76, 95, 114, 243; long-run implications of, 36, 77, 95–6
capital–output ratio, 3, 4, 9, 34, 65, 87, 113, 140, 141, 167, 209, 220–1, 222
capital product
  average, 35; curves for, 226
  marginal, 15–16, 53, 94, 111, 113, 114, 115, 116, 157; curves for, 226, 227; in one-commodity world, 37, 141–4; Pasinetti on, 45, 164, 168; and rate of profits, 35, 37, 38, 44–5, 87, 103,